T0271052

Survival

GLOBAL POLITICS AND STRATEGY

Volume 66 Number 5 | October–November 2024

'Meloni came to power with less political baggage than most far-right politicians in Europe. She did not feature prominently in the first wave of nationalist populism that swept Europe in 2014–18, nor has she shown the obsequious admiration for Putin expressed by her coalition partners.'

Riccardo Alcaro and Nathalie Tocci, The Janus Face of Italy's Far Right, p. 9.

'While there are options that could produce a viable European nuclear deterrent, they would require a degree of national flexibility and European financial support that is currently difficult to imagine. This reality check should give European nuclear hawks pause.'

Héloïse Fayet, Andrew Futter and Ulrich Kühn, Forum: Towards a European Nuclear Deterrent, p. 92.

'Social-media groupthink and insular academic communities have already narrowed the range of intellectual discourse … AI stands to exacerbate the trend, filtering out unconventional prose and content in languages and dialects that are not widely spoken.'

Michael Nevitt, Ersatz Intelligence, p. 236.

Survival

GLOBAL POLITICS AND STRATEGY

Volume 66 Number 5 | October–November 2024

Contents

Cover: Ludovic Marin/AFP via Getty Images

Survival GLOBAL POLITICS AND STRATEGY

Who will lead Europe?

On the cover
European Commission President Ursula von der Leyen, Italian Prime Minister Giorgia Meloni and French President Emmanuel Macron attend a summit on migration in Malta on 29 September 2023.

On the web
Visit www.iiss.org/ publications/survival for brief notices on new books on South Asia, Middle East and Economy.

***Survival* editors' blog**
For ideas and commentary from *Survival* editors and contributors, visit https://www.iiss. org/online-analysis/ survival-online.

Survival
GLOBAL POLITICS AND STRATEGY

The International Institute for Strategic Studies

2121 K Street, NW | Suite 600 | Washington DC 20037 | USA
Tel +1 202 659 1490   Fax +1 202 659 1499   E-mail survival@iiss.org   Web www.iiss.org

Arundel House | 6 Temple Place | London | WC2R 2PG | UK
Tel +44 (0)20 7379 7676   Fax +44 (0)20 7836 3108   E-mail iiss@iiss.org

14th Floor, GFH Tower | Bahrain Financial Harbour | Manama | Kingdom of Bahrain
Tel +973 1718 1155   Fax +973 1710 0155   E-mail iiss-middleeast@iiss.org

9 Raffles Place | #49-01 Republic Plaza | Singapore 048619
Tel +65 6499 0055   Fax +65 6499 0059   E-mail iiss-asia@iiss.org

Pariser Platz 6A | 10117 Berlin | Germany
Tel +49 30 311 99 300   E-mail iiss-europe@iiss.org

Survival Online www.tandfonline.com/survival and www.iiss.org/publications/survival

Aims and Scope *Survival* is one of the world's leading forums for analysis and debate of international and strategic affairs. Shaped by its editors to be both timely and forward thinking, the journal encourages writers to challenge conventional wisdom and bring fresh, often controversial, perspectives to bear on the strategic issues of the moment. With a diverse range of authors, *Survival* aims to be scholarly in depth while vivid, well written and policy-relevant in approach. Through commentary, analytical articles, case studies, forums, review essays, reviews and letters to the editor, the journal promotes lively, critical debate on issues of international politics and strategy.

Editor **Dana Allin**
Managing Editor **Jonathan Stevenson**
Associate Editor **Carolyn West**
Editorial Assistant **Conor Hodges**
Production and Cartography **Alessandra Beluffi, Ravi Gopar, Jade Panganiban, James Parker, Kelly Verity**

Contributing Editors

William Alberque	**Franz-Stefan Gady**	**Nigel Inkster**	**Benjamin Rhode**	**Robert Ward**
Aaron Connelly	**Bastian Giegerich**	**Jeffrey Mazo**	**Ben Schreer**	**Marcus Willett**
James Crabtree	**Nigel Gould-Davies**	**Fenella McGerty**	**Maria Shagina**	**Lanxin Xiang**
Chester A. Crocker	**Melissa K. Griffith**	**Irene Mia**	**Karen Smith**	
Bill Emmott	**Emile Hokayem**	**Meia Nouwens**	**Angela Stent**	

Published for the IISS by
Routledge Journals, an imprint of Taylor & Francis, an Informa business.

Copyright © 2024 The International Institute for Strategic Studies. All rights reserved. No part of this publication may be reproduced, stored, transmitted or disseminated, in any form, or by any means, without prior written permission from Taylor & Francis, to whom all requests to reproduce copyright material should be directed, in writing.

ISBN 978-1-032-80663-1 paperback / 978-1-003-49801-8 ebook

About the IISS The IISS, a registered charity with offices in Washington, London, Manama, Singapore and Berlin, is the world's leading authority on political–military conflict. It is the primary independent source of accurate, objective information on international strategic issues. Publications include *The Military Balance*, an annual reference work on each nation's defence capabilities; *Survival*, a bimonthly journal on international affairs; *Strategic Comments*, an online analysis of topical issues in international affairs; and the *Adelphi* series of books on issues of international security.

Director-General and Chief Executive
Bastian Giegerich

Executive Chairman
John Chipman

Chair of the Trustees
Bill Emmott

Chair of the Council
Chung Min Lee

Trustees
Caroline Atkinson
Neha Aviral
Hakeem Belo-Osagie
John O. Brennan
Chris Jones
Florence Parly
Kasper Rørsted
Mark Sedwill
Grace R. Skaugen
Matthew Symonds

IISS Advisory Council
Joanne de Asis
Caroline Atkinson
Linden P. Blue
Garvin Brown
Mark Carleton-Smith
Alejandro Santo Domingo
Thomas Enders
Michael Fullilove
Yoichi Funabashi
Alia Hatoug-Bouran
Eyal Hulata
Badr Jafar

Bilahari Kausikan
Thomas Lembong
Eric X. Li
Peter Maurer
Florence Parly
Charles Powell
Andrés Rozental
Mark Sedwill
Debra Soon
Heizo Takenaka
Marcus Wallenberg

SUBMISSIONS

To submit an article, authors are advised to follow these guidelines:

- *Survival* articles are around 4,000–10,000 words long including endnotes. A word count should be included with a draft.
- All text, including endnotes, should be double-spaced with wide margins.
- Any tables or artwork should be supplied in separate files, ideally not embedded in the document or linked to text around it.
- All *Survival* articles are expected to include endnote references. These should be complete and include first and last names of authors, titles of articles (even from newspapers), place of publication, publisher, exact publication dates, volume and issue number (if from a journal) and page numbers. Web sources should include complete URLs and DOIs if available.
- A summary of up to 150 words should be included with the article. The summary should state the main argument clearly and concisely, not simply say what the article is about.

- A short author's biography of one or two lines should also be included. This information will appear at the foot of the first page of the article.

Please note that *Survival* has a strict policy of listing multiple authors in alphabetical order.

Submissions should be made by email, in Microsoft Word format, to survival@iiss.org. Alternatively, hard copies may be sent to *Survival*, IISS–US, 2121 K Street NW, Suite 801, Washington, DC 20037, USA.

The editorial review process can take up to three months. *Survival's* acceptance rate for unsolicited manuscripts is less than 20%. *Survival* does not normally provide referees' comments in the event of rejection. Authors are permitted to submit simultaneously elsewhere so long as this is consistent with the policy of the other publication and the Editors of *Survival* are informed of the dual submission.

Readers are encouraged to comment on articles from the previous issue. Letters should be concise, no longer than 750 words and relate directly to the argument or points made in the original article.

Survival: Global Politics and Strategy (Print ISSN 0039-6338, Online ISSN 1468-2699) is published bimonthly for a total of 6 issues per year by Taylor & Francis Group, 4 Park Square, Milton Park, Abingdon, Oxon, OX14 4RN, UK. Periodicals postage paid (Permit no. 13095) at Brooklyn, NY 11256.

Airfreight and mailing in the USA by agent named World Container Inc., c/o BBT 150-15, 183rd Street, Jamaica, NY 11413, USA.

US Postmaster: Send address changes to Survival, World Container Inc., c/o BBT 150-15, 183rd Street, Jamaica, NY 11413, USA.

Subscription records are maintained at Taylor & Francis Group, 4 Park Square, Milton Park, Abingdon, OX14 4RN, UK.

Subscription information: For more information and subscription rates, please see tandfonline.com/pricing/journal/TSUR. Taylor & Francis journals are available in a range of different packages, designed to suit every library's needs and budget. This journal is available for institutional subscriptions with online-only or print & online options. This journal may also be available as part of our libraries, subject collections or archives. For more information on our sales packages, please visit librarianresources.taylorandfrancis.com.

For support with any institutional subscription, please visit help.tandonline.com or email our dedicated team at subscriptions@tandf.co.uk.

Subscriptions purchased at the personal rate are strictly for personal, non-commercial use only. The reselling of personal subscriptions is prohibited. Personal subscriptions must be purchased with a personal cheque, credit card or BAC/wire transfer. Proof of personal status may be requested.

Back issues: Please visit https://taylorandfrancis.com/journals/customer-services/ for more information on how to purchase back issues.

Ordering information: To subscribe to the journal, please contact T&F Customer Services, Informa UK Ltd, Sheepen Place, Colchester, Essex, CO3 3LP, UK. Tel: +44 (0) 20 8052 2030; email subscriptions@tandf.co.uk.

Taylor & Francis journals are priced in USD, GBP and EUR (as well as AUD and CAD for a limited number of journals). All subscriptions are charged depending on where the end customer is based. If you are unsure which rate applies to you, please contact Customer Services. All subscriptions are payable in advance and all rates include postage. We are required to charge applicable VAT/GST on all print and online combination subscriptions, in addition to our online-only journals. Subscriptions are entered on an annual basis, i.e., January to December. Payment may be made by sterling cheque, dollar cheque, euro cheque, international money order, National Giro or credit cards (Amex, Visa and Mastercard).

Disclaimer: The International Institute for Strategic Studies (IISS) and our publisher Informa UK Limited, trading as Taylor & Francis Group ('T&F'), make every effort to ensure the accuracy of all the information (the 'Content') contained in our publications. However, IISS and our publisher T&F, our agents and our licensors make no representations or warranties whatsoever as to the accuracy, completeness or suitability for any purpose of the Content. Any opinions and views expressed in this publication are the opinions and views of the authors, and are not the views of or endorsed by IISS or our publisher T&F. The accuracy of the Content should not be relied upon and should be independently verified with primary sources of information, and any reliance on the Content is at your own risk. IISS and our publisher T&F make no representations, warranties or guarantees, whether express or implied, that the Content is accurate, complete or up to date. IISS and our publisher T&F shall not be liable for any losses, actions, claims, proceedings, demands, costs, expenses, damages and other liabilities whatsoever or howsoever caused arising directly or indirectly in connection with, in relation to or arising out of the use of the Content. Full Terms & Conditions of access and use can be found at http://www.tandfonline.com/page/terms-and-conditions.

Informa UK Limited, trading as Taylor & Francis Group, grants authorisation for individuals to photocopy copyright material for private research use, on the sole basis that requests for such use are referred directly to the requestor's local Reproduction Rights Organization (RRO). The copyright fee is exclusive of any charge or fee levied. In order to contact your local RRO, please contact International Federation of Reproduction Rights Organizations (IFRRO), rue du Prince Royal, 87, B-1050 Brussels, Belgium; email ifrro@skynet.be; Copyright Clearance Center Inc., 222 Rosewood Drive, Danvers, MA 01923, USA; email info@copyright.com; or Copyright Licensing Agency, 90 Tottenham Court Road, London, W1P 0LP, UK; email cla@cla.co.uk. This authorisation does not extend to any other kind of copying, by any means, in any form, for any purpose other than private research use.

Submission information: See https://www.tandfonline.com/journals/tsur20

Advertising: See https://taylorandfrancis.com/contact/advertising/

Permissions: See help.tandfonline.com/Librarian/s/article/Permissions

All Taylor & Francis Group journals are printed on paper from renewable sources by accredited partners.

October–November 2024

MILITARY BALANCE+
THE ONLINE DATABASE

IISS

DATA AND ANALYSIS TOOLS

MILITARY BALANCE+, the online database from the IISS Defence and Military Analysis team, provides indispensable information for the private sector, governments, armed forces, academia, the media and more.

– **Perform your analysis on Military Balance+**
Utilising seven search engines and three data tools, you can ask complex questions of the data.

– **Save time and money**
It will take your researchers hours to do what the Military Balance+ can do in seconds.

– **Data you can have confidence in**
All data has gone through a rigorous verification process, meaning you can use it in your work without concern over its validity.

– **Original IISS insight**
Military Balance+ contains a searchable library of original IISS analysis, charts and graphics.

A WORLD OF DEFENCE DATA TO DRIVE YOUR STRATEGY

Deployments

Exercises

Forces

Equipment

Economics

Procurements

Analysis and graphics

🌐 173 countries

📊 Data tools

GSA Contract Holder
Contract # 47QTCA22D000H

www.iiss.org/militarybalanceplus

CONTACT

For an online demonstration, trial and subscription information:

Robert Hopgood
Sales Manager for Military Balance+

Direct: +44 (0)20 7395 9911
Mobile: +44 (0)7548 217 063
Email: robert.hopgood@iiss.org

The Janus Face of Italy's Far Right

Riccardo Alcaro and Nathalie Tocci

The rise of the far right in Europe and beyond has set off alarm bells among internationalist, liberal and pro-European Union forces, and rightly so, given the victories it has scored and the threat it represents to liberal democracy, multilateralism and European integration. Brexit was delivered by a campaign imbued with right-wing messages, including the mantra that the United Kingdom should 'take back control' from Brussels. A vision of Europe implicitly privileging a white, Christian population was also critical to the political fortunes of far-right parties in Eastern Europe, notably in Hungary and Poland. These parties attacked the supposedly elite-driven EU for promoting open borders, supranationalism and 'degenerate' progressive values – all while undermining the rule of law and media freedoms at home. Sympathy for Russian President Vladimir Putin, who has embraced social conservatism, authoritarianism and imperial aggression against Russia's neighbours, is unsurprisingly widespread across Europe's far right. So too is enthusiasm for Donald Trump, and the nativist and intolerant version of Republicanism that he embodies.

The election of Giorgia Meloni as prime minister of Italy in September 2022 appeared to be another victory for Europe's far right. Her party, Fratelli d'Italia (Brothers of Italy) – known for explicitly boasting about its

Riccardo Alcaro is Research Coordinator and Head of the Global Actors Programme at the Istituto Affari Internazionali (IAI) in Rome. **Nathalie Tocci** is the IAI's Director, a part-time professor at the European University Institute and a Europe's Futures fellow at the Institute for Human Sciences.

fascist roots – won a landslide in the election, forming a coalition with the far-right Lega (League party) and the centre-right Forza Italia (Let's Go Italy).[1] US President Joe Biden cited Italy during a speech later that month in which he warned about the potential consequences of the right's ascendancy for democracy.[2]

Such concerns soon dissipated, however, as Meloni – a self-declared admirer of Italy's wartime fascist dictator Benito Mussolini – defied expectations that she would lead a radical government.[3] She continued Italy's policy of supporting Ukraine against Russia, despite the presence in her government of notoriously pro-Kremlin politicians such as Matteo Salvini and Silvio Berlusconi, the heads of Lega and Forza Italia respectively. This stance, along with her adherence to Italy's post-war tradition of Atlanticism, won her praise from the While House, which held a bilateral summit with the Italian prime minister in July 2023.[4] Meloni also refrained from picking fights with Brussels, thus distinguishing her government from the 2018–19 coalition between the anti-establishment Five Star Movement and the eurosceptic Lega. On the contrary, she built a pragmatic relationship with European Commission President Ursula von der Leyen, notably focusing on the need to curb irregular migration to the EU. She even avoided unnecessary clashes with the Italian right's most beloved foe in Europe, French President Emmanuel Macron.

Italians have seemed to appreciate Meloni's approach, as seen by the results of the European elections in June 2024, when Fratelli d'Italia won 28.75% of votes, an improvement of more than 2.5 points on their result in the 2022 general election. Meanwhile, liberal-minded and pro-EU observers have begun to express the view that if Meloni can demonstrate that moderation can pay off electorally, other far-right parties could follow suit.[5] Meloni has appeared to prove that a nativist and socially conservative agenda can be compatible with a pro-Western foreign policy, thus lessening fears of a far-right takeover.

Meloni's moderation is, however, arguably more the result of circumstances than of a genuine change of heart. These circumstances include a strongly Atlanticist White House in the United States, Italy's need for EU cash and a lack of competition for leadership of the far right in the EU. All these conditions could change should, for example, other right-wing forces take power in a large EU state, Brussels insist on the tough reapplication of eurozone fiscal rules or an avowed eurosceptic like Trump be elected to the White House. Under circumstances like these, Meloni may find that her experiment in moderation is not politically expedient after all.

Moderation abroad

Meloni came to power with less political baggage than most far-right politicians in Europe. She did not feature prominently in the first wave of nationalist populism that swept Europe in 2014–18, nor has she shown the obsequious admiration for Putin expressed by her coalition partners. Even so, Meloni was aware that her neo-fascist past weighed heavily both in Europe and in a Democratic White House that had become suspicious of the European right and its ties to MAGA Republicanism. Therefore, when Meloni took office, her goal was to win credibility with Italy's allies, especially the US. International recognition would help Meloni to increase her domestic popularity and consequently her leadership over the Italian right.

Meloni has built her international reputation as a responsible leader mainly on her support for Ukraine. Her greatest contribution to the Ukrainian cause has been political in nature as she has expanded the coalition of forces backing Kyiv to encompass a major far-right party in Western Europe. That said, she has taken more tangible action as well. She has supported Kyiv's bid to join the EU, agreeing to the opening of accession talks in December 2023. Most importantly, in early 2024 she helped overcome Hungarian Prime Minister Viktor Orbán's opposition to a multiyear EU aid package to Ukraine worth €50 billion.[6] Italy has also continued to send military support to Ukraine and, like other G7 countries, signed a bilateral security pact with Kyiv.[7] Rome's support has included the transfer of SAMP/T air-defence systems that are crucial to the protection of Ukrainian skies.

This is not to say, however, that Meloni's government has been at the forefront of support for Ukraine. Italy's military assistance pales in comparison with that provided by other large European countries. Moreover, Meloni has remained staunch in her opposition to Ukraine's use of Western weapons to hit targets inside Russia, even as other Ukrainian partners have softened on this possibility (as evidenced by their lack of criticism of Ukraine's Kursk offensive in August 2024).[8] Ostensibly, Meloni's caution stems from fear of escalation, but a more important motive is pandering to public opinion, which is at best lukewarm towards Ukraine, and placating Meloni's coalition partners: Forza Italia, whose leader Berlusconi (who died in early 2023) personally befriended Putin, and Salvini's Lega.[9] It seems clear, in fact, that Meloni's electorate has backed her stance on Ukraine more because they see this as consistent with a transatlantic agenda and less out of genuine support for Kyiv or any appreciation of the threat posed by Russia.

Meloni's conduct on other foreign-policy problems, such as China, Israel–Palestine, the southern Mediterranean and Africa, has largely been in line with mainstream conservatism. Her government has skilfully (and quietly) withdrawn Italy's support for China's Belt and Road Initiative, endearing her to the US even more. She has done so while avoiding, for the time being at least, a backlash from Beijing, even making an official visit to China in July 2024.[10] On Israel–Palestine, she has placed Italy where it would have been under past centre-right governments, among Israel's supporters.[11]

Meloni's attention to her Atlanticist credentials appears to have been motivated in part to win US backing for her attempts to engage North and sub-Saharan African countries in partnerships on energy and migration under the so-called 'Mattei Plan' (named after the founder of Italian energy company Eni, Enrico Mattei).[12] While Biden's support did not go beyond a vague blessing, Meloni used this to bolster her reputation. She also used the migration card to rally EU support for her partnership plans. Most notably, von der Leyen joined in Meloni's visits to Tunisia in 2023 and Egypt in 2024, the main goal of which was to secure cooperation from countries of origin and transit to control maritime migration routes.[13]

Meloni's plans for cooperation with Africa are significant in two respects. Firstly, the emphasis – at least rhetorically – on equal partnerships and joint ownership places these plans entirely within the parameters of mainstream European policy.[14] More specifically, the special attention to migration has given Meloni much leeway to consolidate the EU's practice of externalising migration controls to origin and transit countries – as well as bolstering her standing among European centre-right leaders. Furthermore, her rhetorical emphasis on the relationship between migration and development, rather than focusing exclusively on security, has, at least temporarily, deprived centre-left forces of a frequent line of attack.[15] Unsurprisingly, migration has been a key policy area on which von der Leyen has sought a rapport with Meloni, another being the successful renegotiation of Rome's plans to spend the €190bn+ allocated to Italy under NextGenerationEU, the EU's €800bn post-pandemic recovery fund.[16]

Von der Leyen's interest in building ties with Meloni may have been motivated more by politics than by policy, however. The European Commission president likely foresaw that she might need Meloni's backing for her bid for a second presidential term, both because Meloni has a seat on the European Council and in anticipation of her strong showing in the European Parliament elections in June 2024. More broadly, von der Leyen likely hoped that Meloni would deliver the support of at least a portion of the European Conservatives and Reformists (ECR), the far-right grouping in the European Parliament that Meloni leads.[17] In the end, however, von der Leyen did not need Meloni's support for her reappointment, especially after she gained the support of the Greens. This was just as well for von der Leyen, considering that Meloni abstained from supporting her in the European Council while Fratelli d'Italia voted against her in the European Parliament. Nevertheless, the fact that von der Leyen contemplated and even took steps towards bringing Meloni's party into the European majority is further testament to the normalisation of certain far-right parties in EU politics that Meloni's presumed moderation has brought about.[18]

Ambitions and limits

Meloni took office at a time when, for the first time in decades, the EU was viewed not merely as the dispenser of rules and restrictions, but as a source of fiscal support. An abashedly eurosceptic stance, therefore, would not have served her well. Instead, she opted for a more conciliatory line with Brussels, so that it would take Italian fiscal needs into account while providing political momentum behind, and ideally financial resources towards, the Mattei Plan. Meloni also became leader of the EU's third-largest country having observed how far-right governments in Warsaw and Budapest had repeatedly clashed – to their own disadvantage – with the European Commission and other EU countries. By displaying moderation in foreign policy, Meloni sought to position herself as a reliable European leader among her peers with a view to eventually steering EU politics and policy to the right. The centre-right in the EU, she hoped, would eventually abandon its 'unnatural' alignment with other pro-EU forces from the political centre and left, and instead join the far right in support of a new vision of a purely intergovernmental, nationalistic and socially conservative EU.[19]

This grand ambition foundered just when it seemed within reach. When the European Parliament election in June 2024 saw an increase in support for the far right, especially in France and Germany, the Italian prime minister mistook her own domestic electoral strength for influence in the European Council and Parliament. Believing her own rhetoric at home, she made a gross miscalculation regarding the relative importance and dynamics of EU institutions, downplaying the lingering strength of pro-European forces within them. By overplaying her hand, Meloni was excluded from the process that led to the appointment of the three top jobs in the EU: European Commission president (filled by von der Leyen), European Council president (filled by António Costa, a socialist) and High Representative for Foreign Affairs and Security Policy (filled by Kaja Kallas, a liberal).[20] Meloni was left with little to show for her victory in the European election, with the most important posts in the European Commission allocated to other countries.

Even more relevant for Meloni is the foundering of her ambition to unite the European right under her leadership. A new formation has emerged to the right of Meloni's own ECR group in the European Parliament: the Patriots for Europe. Worryingly for the Italian premier, the Patriots include not only Orbán and her putative ally Salvini, but also Marine Le Pen's Rassemblement National (RN), the greatest threat to her ambition to lead the European right. Even though the RN failed to repeat its stellar performance in the European elections in the second round of France's National Assembly elections in July 2024, it remains on the ascendancy. For Meloni, playing the moderate carries fewer advantages than before, given she now has to contend with a formidable challenger for the role of Europe's most influential far-right leader, as well as with restless allies such as Salvini at home.

This, alongside the reapplication of eurozone fiscal rules on excessive deficits, which Italy has been running since the pandemic, and the gradual drying up of NextGenerationEU funds, sets Meloni on a more confrontational path with Brussels. This does not mean that Meloni will veer towards radical euroscepticsm by advocating that Italy leave the eurozone or the EU altogether. However, it does mean that Meloni's rather conciliatory EU line may be over, especially if elections in other EU countries confirm the shift to the right – something that is expected to happen in Austria and the Czech Republic when they hold elections later this year.

Disturbing signs at home

While Meloni's foreign policy has often reassured both liberal and conservative Atlanticists and EU supporters on both sides of the Atlantic,[21] the same cannot be said of her domestic policy. Italians have so far been spared Orbán-style authoritarianism and the kind of systematic assaults on the judiciary, press and opposition carried out by Prawo i Sprawiedliwość (PiS) governments in Poland before that party was voted out of office in 2023. Meloni's domestic agenda, however, still raises the spectre of culture wars, unrest over migration, threats to media freedom and the centralisation of power.

Italy's right wing has taken a cue from its American counterpart in seeking to attack the supposedly decadent 'woke' ideology of the left. Such attacks have taken the form, for example, of a directive by Interior Minister Matteo Piantedosi that blocked the registration of newborn children by same-sex couples.[22] While not uniformly applied by city councils (which are responsible for keeping records of newborn babies), the directive resulted in dozens of minors losing their legal connection to parents who were biologically unrelated and had not formally adopted them.[23] The governing majority has also regularly indulged in the rhetorical vilification of people identifying as transgender or non-binary, or presumed to be so. An example of this came during the Paris Olympics, when politicians such as Salvini and Meloni herself fed the public controversy over the decision of a female Italian boxer to withdraw almost immediately from a bout with an Algerian athlete who was rumoured to be transgender on the basis of having been previously disqualified by a Russian-controlled boxing association.[24] Very few (if any) members of the ruling coalition took the trouble to verify the validity of the rumour before amplifying it, though it was later shown to be false.[25]

In a similar fashion, several members of the ruling coalition have regularly condemned women who exercise their right to obtain an abortion. The government has adopted measures that allow hardline anti-abortion groups to access clinics where abortions are performed, ostensibly to make last-ditch attempts to dissuade women from terminating their pregnancies, including through guilt and stigmatisation.[26] Meanwhile, Italy, in its capacity as chair of the 2024 G7, raised the ire of its partners, particularly France, by insisting on having references to LGBTQ+ and abortion rights either expunged from or diluted in the G7's final communiqué released in June.[27]

The Italian right's fierce opposition to migrants – some members of the country's ruling coalition have embraced the concept of the 'great replacement' expounded by American white supremacists[28] – has resulted in policies that complicate the already difficult integration process of legal foreign-born residents and their children. When Forza Italia's new leader, Foreign Minister Antonio Tajani, suggested that immigrants' children who successfully complete the mandatory 16-year school cycle be given Italian citizenship, Salvini came out strongly against the proposal.[29] (Meloni remained silent, though she is known to dislike the idea.) Irregular migrants have no path towards regularisation, and asylum seekers have found it increasingly difficult to file their claims for protection in Italy.[30] The government has instead favoured the practice of keeping refugees in detention centres, one of which is being outsourced to Albania, with a view to ultimately deporting them.[31]

Meanwhile, the European Commission has publicly reprimanded Meloni's government over media freedom. Italy's coalition government has presided over the complete takeover of the top management of the state-funded broadcaster Rai, triggering 2,000 Rai journalists to strike for five non-consecutive days in protest against political interference in their reporting.[32]

Finally, the Meloni government has championed a constitutional reform that aims at considerably strengthening the powers of the executive – particularly the prime minister – at the expense of Italy's parliament and presidency, the latter serving as the guarantor of the constitution and the separation of powers enshrined within it.[33] Passing this reform will not be easy: lacking a two-thirds majority in parliament, Meloni's coalition would need to put the reform to a public referendum. Traditionally, Italians have proven resistant to broad-brush reforms of their post-war constitution. Still, Meloni's desire to steer the country in this direction has been clear.

Meloni's reputed moderation in foreign policy has sometimes served to provide cover from international criticism of troubling domestic measures, which are often explained away as necessary to satisfy Meloni's base. This lack of international criticism has also blunted the firepower of a divided domestic opposition. When the European Commission criticised the Italian government's infringements on media freedoms – a rare example of international scrutiny of domestic Italian policy – Meloni dismissed its report as having been influenced by Italy's leftist newspapers.[34]

Largely ignored by external observers, domestic developments in Italy reveal the similarities between Meloni's ideology and the hyper-conservative, nationalist and intolerant beliefs of MAGA Republicans in the US and their European epigones. Even if the Italian right has not yet unleashed the kind of democratic backsliding observable in Orbán's Hungary, Poland under the PiS or the US under Trump, the direction of travel is the same.

Prospects for a Trump comeback

Whether Meloni will continue to pursue a double act as a radical at home and a moderate abroad will also depend on who wins the US presidential election in November 2024. Were Kamala Harris to become the 47th president of the United States, a key factor constraining Meloni's radicalisation would remain in place. In fact, given the prominence of women's and LGBTQ+ rights in the Harris campaign, Meloni's hyper-conservative domestic agenda might become a problem for Italy's relationship with the United States under a Harris administration. Given the fragility of the Italian economy and its dependence on international markets, Meloni would still wish to avoid burning bridges across the Atlantic, all the more so if her relationship with Brussels were to become more confrontational. Under a Harris administration, Meloni's Janus face would probably remain in place.

A different calculus would apply, however, should Trump win the election. In this scenario, the most powerful constraint on Meloni would be removed, as a Trump White House would boost the legitimacy of the far right's civilisational framework. While Italy would remain part of the West, Meloni and others like her would probably be emboldened to throw off the straitjacket of liberal democracy and overtly champion their vision of a white, Christian, illiberal West, one made up of sovereign nations unbeholden to multilateral institutions, in which rights could be curtailed, media freedoms eroded and power increasingly centralised in the executive's hands.

On foreign policy, Meloni's approach would fit with Trump's preference for a West that engages with the rest of the world bilaterally and transactionally, rather than through the promotion of values and the strengthening of multilateral institutions. The ethos of the Mattei Plan would become more avowedly nationalistic: the Meloni government has found after two years in office that stemming migration through deals with countries of transit and origin is not as straightforward as originally foreseen, and thus the Mattei Plan is already morphing into an institutional machinery aimed at promoting Italian business interests in Africa. The transactionalism at its core fits well with Trump's approach to foreign policy, which Meloni's government would probably openly ascribe to.

Perhaps most significantly, a second Trump administration would likely end the kind of support that has been offered by the Biden administration to Ukraine, thus compelling European countries to revisit their own positions. In Italy, Salvini would try his best to pull Meloni to the right, not just on the domestic front but on foreign policy too. A volte-face by Meloni would not necessarily be abrupt: she would probably continue to embed her position within a shifting – or fracturing – European consensus in support of Kyiv. Still, given the nature of Meloni's coalition partners and the Italian public's lukewarm support for Kyiv, a Meloni government could be expected to buy into any Trump–Putin 'deal' over Ukraine. Meloni's support for Ukraine has always been driven more by Washington than by Kyiv; a change of heart in the former would thus probably be followed by Rome's abandonment of the latter.

This is not to say that Trump's return would be an unambiguous win for Italy or Meloni personally. In fact, it could spell deep trouble for Italy.

By the time the new US president takes office, the vast majority of NATO allies will be spending at least 2% of GDP on defence. Among the large European NATO countries, Italy will be alone in spending well below 2%.[35] Given Trump's obsession with defence spending in Europe and his arguably reduced grounds to lash out against his favourite foes – starting with Germany, which will have reached the 2% threshold by the end of 2024 – Rome could find itself in Trump's cross hairs, all the more so given Meloni's 'betrayal' over the last two years in befriending Biden.

Alongside defence, trade could represent another sore point in the Italy–US relationship. It is widely believed that a second Trump administration would trigger a transatlantic trade war as Trump would likely significantly raise US tariffs on European goods and the EU would probably retaliate.[36] Yet Italy is among the EU countries most exposed to international trade as its GDP is heavily dependent on exports. It would thus be disproportionally affected by souring trade ties across the Atlantic. While Meloni might hope to extract bilateral exemptions for Italian products, this would probably do more to further damage Rome's relationship with Brussels than to actually achieve meaningful gains from the Italy–US trade relationship.

* * *

Meloni's Janus face as a hyper-conservative at home and a moderate abroad has served her well during her first two years in office, but this is largely because of the political, economic and foreign-policy constraints in place when she took power. Some of these are being dismantled as Europe experiences a shift to the right and fiscal constraints return to the eurozone. The remaining limitations on Italy's foreign policy hinge mainly on the results of the US presidential election. Whereas a Harris administration might even tighten the screws on Meloni, the return of Donald Trump, while still posing significant problems for Italy, would likely heighten Meloni's instincts towards radicalisation. Whenever Meloni has faced a choice, as she did when determining Italy's position on the top jobs in Brussels, she has clearly preferred to look to the right. With Trump in the White House there would be little reason for her to do otherwise.

Notes

1   The Meloni-led coalition won more than 43% of the votes, with Fratelli d'Italia accounting for more than half of that (25.98%) and topping every other party.

2   Olivier Knox, 'Biden Expresses Gloom About Italian Election', *Washington Post*, 30 September 2022, https://www.washingtonpost.com/politics/2022/09/30/biden-expresses-gloom-about-italian-election/.

3   See Fareed Zakaria, 'On GPS: Meloni's Moment', CNN, 18 February 2023, https://edition.cnn.com/videos/tv/2024/02/18/gps-0218-melonis-moment.cnn.

4   See Peter Baker, 'Once Wary, Biden Welcomes Italy's Meloni to the White House', *New York Times*, 27 July 2023, https://www.nytimes.com/2023/07/27/us/politics/biden-italy-meloni-white-house.html.

5   See, for example, 'The Three Women Who Will Shape Europe', *The Economist*, 1 June 2024, https://www.economist.com/leaders/2024/05/30/the-three-women-who-will-shape-europe.

6   See Barbara Moens et al., 'How Giorgia Meloni and French Hospitality Got Orbán to OK Ukraine Aid', *Politico*, 12 February 2024, https://www.politico.eu/article/how-eu-leaders-pushed-hungary-orban-ukraine-aid-support-meloni-italy/.

7   'Agreement on Security Cooperation between Italy and Ukraine', 24 February 2024, https://www.governo.it/sites/governo.it/files/Accordo_Italia-Ucraina_20240224.pdf.

8   See 'Italy Says No to Using NATO Weapons for Russia Strikes', ANSA.it, 27 May 2024, https://www.ansa.it/english/news/politics/2024/05/27/italy-says-no-to-using-nato-weapons-for-russia-strikes_f46c8479-fba4-4826-9149-a86afb2c9199.html.

9   According to a recent poll, Forza Italia's electorate is the only one in which a slim majority (51%) still supports arms transfers to Ukraine. Fratelli d'Italia voters are equally split between those in favour (44%) and those against (43%), while Lega voters are strongly against (66%). Such opinions are reflected in the opposition: 48% of Democratic Party voters still support weapons transfers, while an overwhelming majority (78%) of the populist Five Star electorate is against. Instituto Demopolis, 'Gli orientamenti dell'opinione pubblica italiana dopo 2 anni di guerra tra Russia ed Ucraina', https://www.demopolis.it/?p=11459.

10 See Aurelio Insisa, 'Timing Is Everything: Italy Withdraws from the Belt and Road Initiative', *IAI Commentaries*, no. 23/67, December 2023, https://www.iai.it/sites/default/files/iaicom2367.pdf.

11 See Maria Luisa Fantappié, 'I Rapporti con il Medio Oriente e il Nord Africa', in Leo Goretti and Ferdinando Nelli Feroci (eds), *Il Governo Meloni alla Prova* (Rome: Istituto Affari Internazionali, 2023), pp. 38–46, https://www.iai.it/sites/default/files/9788893683128.pdf.

12 See Andrea Dessì and Akram Ezzamouri, 'Meloni's Visit to DC: Beware of Europe's Smokescreen on Tunisia', *IAI Commentaries*, no. 23/35, July 2023, https://www.iai.it/

it/pubblicazioni/melonis-visit-dc-beware-europes-smokescreen-tunisia.

13 See 'Meloni with VDL to Cairo for Tunisia-like Deal with Egypt', ANSA.it, 17 March 2024, https://www.ansa.it/english/news/2024/03/17/meloni-with-vdl-to-cairo-for-tunisia-like-deal-with-egypt_1fc693b6-af55-42a7-afc7-eca605d7dcff.html.

14 See Karim Mezran and Alissa Pavia, 'Giorgia Meloni's Foreign Policy and the Mattei Plan for Africa: Balancing Development and Migration Concerns', *IAI Commentaries*, no. 23/36, July 2023, https://www.iai.it/it/pubblicazioni/giorgia-melonis-foreign-policy-and-mattei-plan-africa.

15 See Nathalie Tocci, 'The EU's Fear of Migration Is Back – But a Squalid Deal with Tunisia Is No Way to Tackle It', *Guardian*, 2 August 2023, https://www.theguardian.com/commentisfree/2023/aug/02/eu-migration-deal-tunisia-europe-cash-regimes.

16 As of early August 2024, Italy had achieved only 232 spending targets out of 617 (37% of the total). It has been given €113.5bn from the EU in five instalments, with the EU expected to transfer the remaining €81bn in five more instalments. European Commission, 'Recovery and Resilience Scoreboard: Italy', https://ec.europa.eu/economy_finance/recovery-and-resilience-scoreboard/country_overview.html?lang=en.

17 See Simon Tisdall, 'Giorgia Meloni and Ursula von der Leyen, the Double Act that Is Steering the EU Ever Rightwards', *Guardian*, 4 May 2024, https://www.theguardian.com/commentisfree/2024/may/04/giorgia-meloni-ursula-von-der-leyen-double-act-steering-eu-rightwards.

18 See Barbara Moens and Hannah Roberts, 'Von der Leyen Tried to Make Friends with Meloni. It Backfired', *Politico*, 30 May 2024, https://www.politico.eu/article/ursula-von-der-leyen-giorgia-meloni-italy-eu-election-far-right/.

19 See Lucrezia Reichlin, 'Giorgia Meloni's Surprising Success', Project Syndicate, 29 March 2024, https://www.project-syndicate.org/commentary/giorgia-meloni-surprising-strength-and-impact-on-european-politics-by-lucrezia-reichlin-2024-03; and 'Meloni insiste sull'alleanza di destra in Europa, ma apre allo scenario alternativo: "Pronti a stare all'opposizione"', *La Repubblica*, 27 May 2024, https://www.repubblica.it/politica/2024/05/27/news/meloni_europee_opposizione_coalizione_ursula-423113681/.

20 See Hannah Roberts and Barbara Moens, 'Inside Meloni and von der Leyen's Messy Split', *Politico Europe*, 2 August 2024, https://www.politico.eu/article/giorgia-meloni-ursula-von-der-leyen-italian-prime-minister-european-commission-law-report-politics/.

21 See Ferdinando Nelli Feroci and Leo Goretti (eds), *Il governo Meloni alla prova, Rapporto sulla politica estera italiana. Edizione 2023* (Rome: Istituto Affari Internazionali, 2024), https://www.iai.it/it/pubblicazioni/il-governo-meloni-alla-prova.

22 See 'Ordine del governo, a Milano stop alla registrazione dei bimbi di Famiglie Arcobaleno', Rai News, 14 March 2023, https://www.rainews.it/articoli/2023/03/

ordine-del-governo-a-milano-stop-alla-registrazione-dei-bimbi-di-famiglie-arcobaleno-00ac41d3-e145-4d18-866d-d4bd1a90329c.html.

23 See Federica Olivo, 'No, non è vero che i diritti dei bimbi di coppie gay vengono tutelati a prescindere. Il fact checking che smentisce il governo', *Huffington Post*, 20 June 2023, https://www.huffingtonpost.it/politica/2023/06/20/news/no_non_e_vero_che_i_diritti_dei_bimbi_di_coppie_gay_vengono_tutelati_a_prescindere_il_fact_checking_che_smentisce_il_gover-12439886/.

24 See Kara Fox, 'Why Italian Boxer Angela Carini Apologized to Olympic Fight Winner Imane Khelif', CNN, 2 August 2024, https://edition.cnn.com/2024/08/02/sport/who-is-imane-khelif-olympic-boxer-intl/index.html.

25 See Leo Goretti, 'The Kremlin's and Far-right War on Gender at the Paris 2024 Olympics', *IAI Commentaries*, no. 24/52, August 2024, https://www.iai.it/it/pubblicazioni/kremlins-and-far-right-war-gender-paris-2024-olympics.

26 See Nicole Winfield, 'Abortion Returns to the Spotlight in Italy, 46 Years After It Was Legalized', AP News, 23 April 2024, https://apnews.com/article/italy-abortion-meloni-de7f4d2af81cf94ecf1d8cde5802fcec.

27 See 'Draft G7 Statement Makes No Mention of Abortion, Sparks LGBTQ Criticism', Reuters, 14 June 2024, https://www.reuters.com/world/draft-g7-statement-makes-no-mention-abortion-reiterates-past-commitments-2024-06-14/.

28 See Anchal Vohra, 'Italy Now Has Conspiracy Theory as National Policy', *Foreign Policy*, 8 May 2023, https://foreignpolicy.com/2023/05/08/italy-meloni-great-replacement-conspiracy-theory-immigration/.

29 See Claudio Bozza, 'Ius Scholae, chi è a favore e chi è contrario. La spinta di Forza Italia, l'asse con centrosinistra e cattolici (e il no di Lega e FdI)', *Corriere della Sera*, 22 August 2024, https://www.corriere.it/politica/24_agosto_22/ius-scholae-chi-e-a-favore-e-chi-e-contrario-la-spinta-di-forza-italia-l-asse-con-centrosinistra-e-cattolici-e-il-no-di-lega-e-fdi-acab8451-9cdb-457d-919a-d114a7e05xlk.shtml.

30 See Gabriel Echeverría and Claudia Finotelli, 'Much Ado About Nothing? Giorgia Meloni's Government and Immigration', *Contemporary Italian Politics*, vol. 16, no. 2, 20 March 2024, https://www.tandfonline.com/doi/abs/10.1080/23248823.2024.2330805.

31 See Hannah Roberts, 'Italy's Meloni Gets Tough on Migrants', *Politico Europe*, 18 September 2023, https://www.politico.eu/article/italy-prime-minister-giorgia-meloni-immigration-crackdown/; and Crispian Balmer, 'Explainer: How Does Italy's Migration Deal with Albania Work?', Reuters, 5 June 2024, https://www.reuters.com/world/europe/how-does-italys-migration-deal-with-albania-work-2024-06-05/.

32 See Amy Kazmin, 'Italian Journalists Strike in Dispute with Giorgia Meloni's Right-wing Government', *Financial Times*, 6 May 2024, https://www.ft.com/content/7fa1e71c-386d-45b6-b1ae-ec71bdace399.

33 See Michael Meyer-Resende and Nino Tsereteli, 'Meloni's Dangerous Constitutional Change in Italy', *Politico*

Europe, 21 December 2023, https://www. politico.eu/article/melonis-dangerous-constitutional-change-in-italy/.

34   Elena Giordano, 'Meloni Accuses Italian Newspapers of Manipulating Commission Report', *Politico*, 31 July 2024, https://www.politico. eu/article/giorgia-meloni-accuse-italy-newspaper-manipulate-eu-commission-report/.

35   In 2023, Italy spent 1.6% of GDP on defence (see Stockholm International Peace Research Institute, 'SIPRI Military Expenditure Database',

accessed on 27 August 2024, https:// milex.sipri.org/sipri), and it is unlikely to spend more than this in 2024 (see NATO Public Diplomacy Division, 'Defence Expenditure of NATO Countries (2014–2024)', https://www. nato.int/nato_static_fl2014/assets/ pdf/2024/6/pdf/240617-def-exp-2024-en.pdf).

36   See Andy Bounds, 'EU Prepares Two-step Trade Plan to Tackle Donald Trump', *Financial Times*, 29 July 2024, https://www.ft.com/content/9b1f982a-485c-4868-9a03-b7e58a6f5746.

Copyright © 2024 The International Institute for Strategic Studies

Europe's Leadership Void

Matthias Matthijs

As the geopolitical rivalry between the United States and China intensifies and the military conflict between Russia and Ukraine grinds on, Europe is struggling to shape world events. Its political elite is mostly bogged down by internal problems and finds it increasingly hard to agree on a common position or to speak with one voice. The return of war to its doorstep and the global rise of protectionism were always going to pose major challenges to the European project, which is fundamentally about peace and free markets. Europe's successful adaptation to a more volatile world – where interdependence is increasingly weaponised, and America's security guarantee is no longer implicitly reliable – will require greater cohesion and an enhanced ability to act together on the global stage.[1] For the European Union to unite around such a common vision, it will need to marshal the support of its most powerful national leaders and to achieve a dramatic overhaul of its current relationship of mutual mistrust with the United Kingdom.

On the face of it, there is reason for optimism. The elections for the European Parliament in June 2024 resulted in a broad, pro-EU centrist majority that paved the way for another successful five-year term for Ursula von der Leyen as president of the European Commission. The much-feared populist far-right surge failed once again to materialise.[2] National differences

Matthias Matthijs is Dean Acheson Chair and Associate Professor of International Political Economy at Johns Hopkins University's School of Advanced International Studies (SAIS) and Senior Fellow for Europe at the Council on Foreign Relations.

Survival | vol. 66 no. 5 | October–November 2024 | pp. 23–36   https://doi.org/10.1080/00396338.2024.2403213

and personal rivalries continue to make it difficult for the far right to organise into a coherent grouping that could upend business as usual in Brussels or Strasbourg. Almost miraculously, the 27 EU leaders managed to agree rather swiftly on their new leadership triumvirate.[3] With von der Leyen remaining at the helm of a new European Commission, former Portuguese prime minister António Costa installed as new president of the European Council, and former Estonian prime minister Kaja Kallas taking over as its new High Representative for Foreign Affairs and Security Policy, the EU seems to be in a strong position to complete the gradual geo-economic turn it began back in 2017.[4] That turn broke with the once sacred principles of free trade and fiscal orthodoxy, and charted a bold new course of EU budgetary solidarity and international economic competition.

Furthermore, since early July 2024, Europe's Big Three – France, Germany and the UK – are all led by progressive-centrist leaders with broadly pro-European leanings. British Prime Minister Keir Starmer's Labour Party wants a major reset in relations between the UK and the EU, including a new era in security and defence cooperation. French President Emmanuel Macron has another two-and-a-half years left in office and managed to fend off a challenge from Marine Le Pen's National Rally in snap elections in late June and early July. And though German Chancellor Olaf Scholz's 'traffic-light' coalition government may often quibble internally on matters of policy, it usually manages to agree in the end, and no one seriously doubts its pro-EU orientation. Finally, the sudden emergence of the pro-European Kamala Harris in the United States as a much tougher and promising challenger to Donald Trump than Joe Biden – with a real chance to win the US presidential election in November – has many EU leaders hopeful that a strong transatlantic relationship can endure.

Beneath the surface, however, things look more difficult. While the EU is in much better shape (indeed, almost unrecognisable) in 2024 from what it was a decade ago, the macroeconomic reforms and geo-economic innovations of the last five years remain largely incomplete. EU institutions alone cannot advance their implementation. National leadership is also needed. On that score, the outlook for the Big Three individually – let alone in coordination with one another – is uncertain at best.

The dire state of Britain's public finances, inherited from the Conservatives, and Labour's decision to accept the Conservatives' red lines about the UK's exit from the EU – including keeping out of the customs union and the single market – greatly limit Starmer's room for manoeuvre.[5] The gridlock resulting from France's recent election will inevitably weaken France's voice in Europe. This is deeply problematic as Macron, despite his many critics, is one of the few EU leaders with a coherent vision for Europe's future.[6] Scholz's unhappy government can only really agree on the desirability of avoiding early elections in the hope that the populist threat of the Alternative for Germany (AfD) on the extreme right and Sahra Wagenknecht on the far left will magically melt away in 2025. His coalition is also hobbled by the country's rigid and self-harming constitutional debt brake. Beyond the Big Three, leadership is unlikely to come from Italy, Poland or Spain, which also have their own shortcomings and constraining domestic issues.

Macron is one of the few leaders with a coherent vision

Finally, no matter who ends up in the White House in 2025, most EU capitals have not fully grasped that the era of unflinching American support for the Old Continent's security and prosperity is over, and that Europe needs to chart its own course – with the Americans if they can, without them if they must. The most likely course, once again, is for Europe to continue to kick the can down the road as the rules of the game are written elsewhere. There is an off-chance, however, that circumstances could compel the von der Leyen-led European Commission to rise to the occasion and jolt Europe out of its dysfunction with new and decisive institutional steps forward.

Under von der Leyen's authoritative leadership, the European Commission has emerged as the most decisive and capable actor in Europe – a far cry from the technocratic body that served to implement the decisions made by EU national leaders in the European Council. This ability to act was revealed by the commission's imaginative response to the COVID-19 pandemic in 2020 and through its comprehensive sanctions regime against Russia following its full-scale invasion of Ukraine in 2022. The rub is that only another major crisis is likely to create the conditions under which the commission could once again play that leading role.

Unfinished business

After a decade of crises – over the euro, refugees, democratic backsliding, Brexit, transatlantic bullying by Trump and Russian aggression – the EU got its act together during von der Leyen's first term as president of the European Commission. Jean-Claude Juncker had started Europe's gradual transition away from rigid rules towards more flexible tools, including the inward screening of foreign direct investment and a more supple interpretation of the EU's fiscal constraints. But during his term, between 2014 and 2019, the EU resisted the issuance of Eurobonds and pleaded for a 'pause' in new membership. It was not until von der Leyen's term that the EU would unify more boldly around fiscal solidarity and adopt a more genuine geo-economic – at times even geopolitical – mindset.[7]

During summer 2020, the EU set up the 'NextGenerationEU' economic-recovery fund in response to the COVID-19 pandemic: an €800 billion facility of grants and loans financed through jointly issued bonds that served as a de facto fiscal-transfer mechanism from richer to poorer member states.[8] In spring 2024, the EU adopted a reformed framework for its fiscal rules, allowing more budgetary leeway for structural reforms and greater public investment.[9] Between 2019 and 2024, the EU also created a whole series of geo-economic tools. Beyond its already existing framework for investment screening, under von der Leyen the European Commission added an International Procurement Instrument, a Foreign Subsidies Regulation and an Anti-Coercion Instrument. In response to Russia's full-scale invasion of Ukraine, the EU – in close coordination with the Biden administration – ratified more than ten rounds of biting sanctions, among other things cutting off Russian oil and gas and freezing of Moscow's official reserves. The profits from roughly $300bn in frozen Russian assets were eventually used to assist Ukraine's war effort.

While those actions have gone some way to address many of Europe's challenges, they remain unfinished, in need of greater imagination as well as stricter and more dynamic implementation. Firstly, on the macroeconomic front, the EU's reformed fiscal-rule framework did not move far enough away from the spirit of the old rules and continues to have a deflationary bias. It is hard for the EU and its member states to invest more aggressively in the energy transition or in security and defence if every year finance ministers must cut billions of euros from other programmes to do so. It also undermines popular support if extra spending on green energy or increased military capability comes at the expense of priorities like healthcare and education. Furthermore, the mandate of the European Central Bank remains too narrowly focused on price stability at a time when other central banks are also considering growth, employment and sustainability. And when it comes to the strategic use of the euro, while the United States occasionally uses the dollar and the Federal Reserve payments system to punish and coerce rogue actors, the Europeans generally abstain from such practices.[10]

Secondly, on the geo-economic front, many of the tools that the EU has created over the past five years are insusceptible to enforcement or leave implementation up to the member states. This is true for its framework on investment screening and anti-coercion instrument, where it is still up to the member state in question to make the ultimate call. Europe also continues to lack a joint and comprehensive answer to the protectionist challenge of the Inflation Reduction Act (IRA) – the ironic name for the Biden administration's major climate-investment legislation – in the United States and the mass government subsidies the Chinese have put into alternative energy, including the production of electric vehicles, solar panels and wind turbines. The same goes for economic competitors' investment in computer chips and artificial intelligence. While the EU set up the European Battery Alliance in 2017 and passed the European Chips Act in 2023, these still have not put Europe in a position to compete with the US or China. The EU's trade and industrial policy remains stuck in 1990s and 2000s thinking. Since the pandemic, the EU has softened its rules on state aid, but this has mostly benefited large member states like Germany and France, creating tensions with smaller member states.[11]

Thirdly, on the security and defence front, Europe's 'geopolitical' awakening has been painfully slow. The UK's 2016 vote to leave the EU did not help, as the UK and France had traditionally been the leaders in the military realm. Trump's presidency between 2017 and 2021, and his possible return in 2025, as well as the war in Ukraine, have jolted but not yet transformed Europe. The security guarantee by the United States through NATO can no longer be taken for granted. Both the EU and the United States have supported and financed Ukraine's heroic resistance to Russia's aggression, but it is clear that this cannot go on forever, and that Europe itself needs to construct a credible deterrent of its own. While the first von der Leyen Commission gave new momentum to EU enlargement by adding Georgia, Moldova and Ukraine to the existing list of prospective members, which encompassed the Western Balkans and Turkiye, their road remains extremely long and full of obstacles. While enlargement is 'the strongest instrument that the EU has to bring stability and foster reform in bordering countries', existing EU institutions are far from 'ready to accommodate a wider and more diverse membership', as Veronica Anghel and Erik Jones argued in these pages.[12]

Macroeconomic, geo-economic and geopolitical changes will not happen without a push from leading EU member states. And in the case of security and defence, it is hard to see how a credible European defence architecture can be arranged without the active involvement of the UK. The European Commission can take initiatives and make proposals, but member states – especially France and Germany – need to put their full weight behind them if they are going to be adopted. And, for better or worse, in a world of regional blocs in geopolitical competition, the UK will have to forge a much closer relationship with the EU if both are going to be geopolitically effective actors. But Europe's Big Three are hobbled by debilitating domestic politics.

Britain's encumbering departure

Starmer and the British Labour Party won an impressive victory in July 2024. He has promised to turn the page on the toxic relationship that had developed between the UK and the EU since the 2016 referendum in which the country voted to leave the EU. With a very large majority in the House of Commons, and the Conservative opposition much diminished and in disarray, Labour should be able to easily pass new legislation and play a much more constructive role in Europe. But Starmer exuded caution and lack of ambition towards the EU during the campaign, vowing to respect the Conservatives' red lines by staying out of the single market, the customs union and freedom-of-movement regime. In terms of the economy and public finances, Rachel

Reeves, the new Chancellor of the Exchequer, has pledged to stick to the Conservatives' spending plans, and may even bring back austerity.[13]

On security and defence, Foreign Secretary David Lammy had already put a new EU–UK Security Pact on the table during the Munich Security Conference in spring 2024, when Labour was still in opposition. But if the UK stays out of the single market, it will be hard for it to play a leading role in a new joint European military-industrial strategy or joint procurement of military hardware. Lammy's aspiration to follow 'progressive realism' in foreign affairs also masks the UK's instinctive reliance on the United States.[14] London is therefore likely to thwart any emerging European defence capability that could operate without substantial American involvement. While the Germans could welcome bilateral cooperation with the UK, the French may be weary of seeing the UK – and other non-EU NATO members like Turkiye and Norway – play prominent roles in a new European defence architecture, putting Berlin and Paris at odds once again and further paralysing EU decision-making.

In theory, a grand bargain should be possible. This would involve the EU's relaxation of its rigid 'in or out' approach to single-market membership for a bespoke deal that takes into account the UK's unique size and role in Europe's economy, in return for British participation and leadership in a European industrial-defence strategy. But that would require a break from the recent past and begin with a political declaration of intent from both sides that reinstitutionalises the relationship with regular meetings at the highest governmental levels. Starmer would need to abandon his innate caution, and the EU would need to abandon its technocratic predilections.[15] In practice, the EU's mistrust of UK politicians, built up over decades of British euroscepticism and crowned by Brexit, and its related fear of allowing 'cherry-picking' of benefits without the responsibility of EU membership, is likely to persist. Starmer's trepidation about being accused by the British tabloids and the Conservative opposition of reversing Brexit by stealth is likely to further inhibit him. The upshot is that what Britain can achieve over the next five years in European military and defence cooperation will probably be largely symbolic and continue to rely heavily on continued US involvement and leadership through NATO.

France's diminished voice

The one European leader who has never been shy of laying out grand visions for Europe is Macron. Early in his first term as French president, he dared the EU to embrace 'strategic autonomy' or 'EU sovereignty'. This made him Europe's most eloquent spokesman on how it could succeed on its own in a multipolar world. Even so, his attempts in 2022 to find diplomatic solutions with Russia after it had invaded Ukraine were treated with suspicion and often outright disbelief in Poland and the Baltics, as well as in other EU member states in Central and Eastern Europe. Berlin, keen to preserve the transatlantic relationship no matter who is in the White House, and several Eastern European capitals were sceptical of his preference, both during Trump's term and the first half of the Biden administration, to distance Europe from the United States. But Macron, in his famous 'mea culpa' speech in Bratislava in May 2023, promised to take the viewpoint and interests of the EU's eastern member states on board in any future vision of the EU.[16]

Macron, however, sabotaged his own presidency by calling snap national elections after the EU parliamentary elections in June 2024 saw the far-right National Rally top the polls in France, with more than double the votes of Macron's own Renew Europe coalition. The president hoped to rid France of its far-right populist fever once and for all. The stratagem did not prove disastrous, but did partially backfire. While the Republican Front – in which all democratic parties banded together in the second round of the vote against Marine Le Pen and her allies – denied the far right a governing majority, the vote resulted in three roughly equal and incompatible blocs in France's National Assembly. With the left-wing New Popular Front holding the most seats, Macron's centrist Ensemble coalition the next highest number, and Le Pen's National Front and its allies third-highest, it is hard to see a stable government emerging in the year ahead. New elections are possible as early as June 2025, but they could produce further gridlock or an outright victory for the far left or the far right.[17]

In these fraught political circumstances, it is doubtful that Macron and France can play their traditional leadership role in the EU. Furthermore, France's fiscal situation is now so dire that the country could see its debt-to-GDP ratio surpass 115% by 2029, when its budget deficit is still projected to be 4%. Over the next five years, it will need to find at least another €50bn in additional savings just to stay on that trajectory. And with three competing blocs in the National Assembly – two of which want to go in opposite budgetary directions – it is hard to imagine new French initiatives for Europe. There will be no new money to finance any of them, let alone a parliamentary majority to support them. EU leaders could of course agree, as they did during the pandemic summer of 2020, to initiate another round of jointly issued bonds, this time to finance common energy and defence projects. But this would be possible only with support from Berlin, and Scholz has already firmly ruled it out as he fights tooth-and-nail to complete his term in office.[18]

Germany's misguided loyalty

Scholz's term as chancellor of a nationally unprecedented German coalition government that included his own Social Democrats, the Greens and the pro-free-market Free Democrats started out quite promising in late 2021. The underlying bargain that kept his coalition together combined the green promise to fight climate change and invest in the country's energy transition, the liberal belief in low taxes and adoption of a digital economy, and the social-democratic desire to preserve Germany's welfare state. The Russian invasion of Ukraine in February 2022 took most policy elites in Berlin by surprise. They were now forced to let go of cheap Russian oil and gas by ending Germany's lucrative energy relationship with Russia through the Nord Stream pipelines and agreed to spend significant amounts of fresh money on military support to help Ukraine's war effort and get serious about their own defence.[19]

While this *Zeitenwende* – watershed moment, as Scholz characterised it in the Bundestag a few days after the invasion – seemed to ease the energy transition away from fossil fuels towards wind and solar, it put the digital transition the country so desperately needed on hold and increased pressure on the country's public finances. It also meant delaying Germany's nuclear phase-out, increasing imports of American liquefied natural gas and temporarily reopening coal plants. But the most important aspect of

Germany's policy shift was its one-off €100bn defence fund that would be spent over five years to revitalise and modernise the German military. While Paris welcomed Scholz's speech, the French would soon be disappointed that much of this new money would be used for American fighter jets rather than French armoured vehicles, while the bulk of the money would be invested in Germany's national-defence military industry rather than in joint EU initiatives.[20]

The war in Ukraine necessitated Germany's loss of cheap energy – a key ingredient of its industrial competitiveness – and it was forced to put the main burden of adjustment onto German society and industry as energy prices skyrocketed during winter 2022–23. It also meant that its key source of growth – exports to China – became even more important at a time of growing Western tensions with Beijing. Given German companies' significant exposure to the Chinese market, it is much harder for Berlin to de-risk from China than from Russia. Germany will therefore continue to resist tougher geo-economic measures at the EU level that will punish China for unfair business practices, human-rights violations or the intimidation of Germany's EU neighbours. At the same time, German Finance Minister Christian Lindner is finding it increasingly difficult to justify his Free Democratic Party's continued participation in Scholz's coalition, making him double down on the sanctity of the country's constitutional debt brake in his quest to rein in German public finances.[21]

Meanwhile, that coalition, which collectively received 52% of the vote during federal elections in September 2021, has barely garnered 30% support in opinion polls in 2024. Furthermore, the extreme-right AfD and the far-left Sahra Wagenknecht movement are now dominating the former East German states' regional politics in a way that makes it all but impossible to form stable governments there. There is pervasive fear in Berlin that far-right and far-left successes will percolate up to the national level and make the country increasingly ungovernable. Germans abhor political instability, so the smart money is on Scholz finishing out his term until new elections in September 2025. But given his embattled tenure, new German leadership initiatives at the EU level are unlikely to materialise in the next year. Much of the country's elite also remain unrealistically loyal to an American-led rules-based world of open trade and investment and minimal military conflict, which has not really existed since the 2010s and is unlikely to return any time soon.

Filling the void

There appear to be no alternative leaders from other European capital cities to fill the leadership void. Among the next three – Italy, Spain and Poland – Italy under Giorgia Meloni's far-right government remains economically weak and politically isolated. Her party, Brothers of Italy, does not belong to any of the EU's traditional political families, so it is not easy for her to put her stamp on EU decision-making in Brussels. The social-democrat Pedro Sánchez in Spain seems to have nine political lives and has defied the odds by staying in power. But with Madrid spending less than 1.3% of GDP on national defence – well below the 2% guideline for NATO members – Spain is not a serious player in security and defence. Sánchez's majority in Madrid is also fragile and subject to constant blackmail from regional separatist parties in Catalonia and the Basque region. Finally, it is true that Polish Prime Minister Donald Tusk, the centre-right former president of the European Council, managed to banish Jarosław Kaczyński's eurosceptic Prawo i Sprawiedliwość (PiS) to the opposition benches after eight years in government, and has emerged as a leading voice for closer European integration and stronger defence. But Tusk's room for manoeuvre in foreign policy is limited by President Andrzej Duda, who remains aligned with the politics of the previous PiS government, and, with Poland remaining outside of the eurozone, it can hardly be expected to lead big EU reforms on its own.

*   *   *

In the absence of national leaders able to initiate and sustain a decisive Europe-wide movement towards geo-economic resolve and geostrategic strength and coherence, that responsibility may fall to von der Leyen. She is without a doubt the most powerful European Commission president since Jacques Delors occupied the post from 1985 to 1995. During this auspicious period in European integration, the single market was completed, the single currency was launched and the 'big bang' decision to enlarge the EU to the east was taken. But Delors could achieve those major advances only with the support of three unusually powerful and pro-Europe Big Three leaders: Helmut Kohl in Berlin, François Mitterrand in Paris and, in London, leaving aside her refusal to enter the eurozone, Margaret Thatcher, who was an ardent proponent of a European single market, followed by John Major, who strongly supported enlargement.

The fact remains that over the last five years, von der Leyen has emerged as the most important player on the European scene. Her number is the one the White House is now inclined to call when it needs to consult Europe.[22] Christine Lagarde, the president of the European Central Bank, was asked during the IMF spring 2024 meetings in Washington whether the EU could see another 'Hamiltonian moment' in the future, as it did under von der Leyen's leadership during summer 2020 when she marshalled a strong response to the COVID-induced economic crisis. Lagarde responded that in Europe, more often than not, 'nécessité fait loi' – necessity makes law.[23] Von der Leyen would need explicit support from Germany and France, and the EU will need a much better relationship with the UK, if she is going to complete its geo-economic revolution and start a genuine geopolitical chapter.

In the absence of any new joint initiatives from Paris and Berlin, or a genuine reconciliation with London, only another crisis is likely to generate the conditions for the European Commission to fill the leadership vacuum left by Europe's most powerful states. Such a crisis is all but inevitable, and could come in the form of a second Trump presidential term in the United States, further military escalation in Eastern Europe by Russia, intensified commercial warfare by China, a new pandemic or another full-blown financial crisis. While the history of European integration is rife with crises, not all of them have led to positive change. Europe often does nothing or muddles through with small technocratic fixes. In the past, crises have only led to significant institutional innovations when national leaders have been able to coalesce and rally around a common project.

There is no iron law that states that a new blueprint of such a common project needs to come from national capitals. Today's European Commission is undoubtedly far more institutionally powerful and politically savvy than the one Delors led in the late 1980s and early 1990s. While today's EU counts 27 member states rather than the European Community's 12 – which makes consensus much more elusive, especially if unanimity is required – its major nation-states are also relatively diminished in both size and clout. Going it alone is no longer a realistic option for individual member states. Crises tend to focus minds and increase peer pressure to act. Von der Leyen has showed herself to be a highly capable operator in the past five years and someone who can seize a crisis and forge decisive interventions. When the next crisis comes, all eyes will be on her and the European Commission in Brussels to see if she can pull it off once more. Let's hope for Europe's sake that she can.

Notes

1   See Henry Farrell and Abraham Newman, 'Weaponized Interdependence', *International Security*, vol. 44, no. 1, Summer 2019, pp. 42–79; and Giovanna de Maio and Célia Belin, 'Europe's America Problem', *Foreign Affairs*, 23 August 2024, https://www.foreignaffairs.com/europe/europes-america-problem.

2   See Matthias Matthijs, 'Have European Voters Hamstrung the EU?', *Foreign Affairs*, 11 June 2024, https://www.foreignaffairs.com/europe/have-european-voters-hamstrung-eu-election.

3   See Barbara Moens et al., 'Von der Leyen, Costa and Kallas Bag EU Top Jobs', *Politico*, 27 June 2024, https://www.politico.eu/article/von-der-leyen-costa-and-kallas-bag-eu-top-jobs/.

4   See Matthias Matthijs and Sophie Meunier, 'Europe's Geoeconomic Revolution', *Foreign Affairs*, vol. 102, no. 5, September/October 2023, pp. 168–79.

5   See Dana H. Allin, 'Keir Starmer's Britain: Can the Centre Hold?', *Survival*, vol. 66, no. 4, August–September 2024, pp. 91–7.

6   See Catherine Fieschi, 'France's Political Crisis', *Survival*, vol. 66, no. 4, August–September 2024, pp. 115–26.

7   See Matthias Matthijs, 'The Right Way to Fix the EU', *Foreign Affairs*, vol. 99, no. 3, May/June 2020, pp. 160–70; and Matthijs and Meunier, 'Europe's Geoeconomic Revolution'.

8   See Directorate General for Communication, 'NextGenerationEU', 2020, https://next-generation-eu.europa.eu/recovery-and-resilience-facility_en.

9   See European Council, 'Economic Governance Review: Council Adopts Reform of Fiscal Rules', 29 April 2024, https://www.consilium.europa.eu/en/press/press-releases/2024/04/29/economic-governance-review-council-adopts-reform-of-fiscal-rules/.

10 See Paweł Tokarski, 'The Euro in a World of Dollar Dominance', Stiftung Wissenschaft und Politik, SWP Research Paper, 5 February 2024, https://www.swp-berlin.org/10.18449/2024RP02/.

11 See Jonathan Packroff, 'Smaller EU Countries Revolt Against State Aid Spree', Euractiv, 12 March 2024, https://www.euractiv.com/section/economy-jobs/news/smaller-eu-countries-revolt-against-state-aid-spree/.

12 Veronica Anghel and Erik Jones, 'The Geopolitics of EU Enlargement: From Club to Commons', *Survival*, vol. 66, no. 4, August–September 2024, pp. 101–14.

13 See Matthias Matthijs and Mark Blyth, 'Don't Bet on a British Revival', *Foreign Affairs*, 30 April 2024, https://www.foreignaffairs.com/united-kingdom/dont-bet-british-revival.

14 See David Lammy, 'The Case for Progressive Realism', *Foreign Affairs*, vol. 103, no. 3, May/June 2024, pp. 125–37. See also Anatol Lieven, 'Labour's Delusions About UK Foreign Policy', Quincy Institute for Responsible Statecraft, 17 July 2024, https://responsiblestatecraft.org/uk-foreign-policy/.

15 See, for example, Mujtaba Rahman, 'The EU's Approach to Britain and Brexit Needs Fixing', *Financial Times*, 11 August 2024, https://www.ft.com/content/d0f920a3-6c77-4f3a-baa2-701ab7151ff6.

16 See Emmanuel Macron, 'Closing Speech', GLOBSEC Summit, Bratislava, Slovakia, 31 May 2023, https://is.ambafrance.org/Slovakia-GLOBSEC-summit-in-Bratislava-Closing-speech-by-M-Emmanuel-Macron.

17 See Fieschi, 'France's Political Crisis'.

18 See Henry Foy, 'Why EU Leaders Reached a Stalemate on Joint Defence Bonds', *Financial Times*, 22 March 2024, https://www.ft.com/content/b73b8100-075b-471b-b2f8-f0d5d86c2196.

19 See Federal Government of Germany, 'Policy Statement by Olaf Scholz, Chancellor of the Federal Republic of Germany and Member of the German Bundestag', 27 February 2022, https://www.bundesregierung.de/breg-en/news/policy-statement-by-olaf-scholz-chancellor-of-the-federal-republic-of-germany-and-member-of-the-german-bundestag-27-february-2022-in-berlin-2008378.

20 See Max Bergmann and Sophia Besch, 'Why European Defense Still Depends on America', *Foreign Affairs*, 7 March 2023, https://www.foreignaffairs.com/ukraine/why-european-defense-still-depends-america.

21 See Sudha David-Wilp and Jacob Kirkegaard, 'Germany's Economic Reckoning', *Foreign Affairs*, 4 March 2024, https://www.foreignaffairs.com/germany/germanys-economic-reckoning.

22 See Suzanne Lynch, 'Why Ursula von der Leyen Matters to Biden', *Politico*, 10 March 2023, https://www.politico.com/news/2023/03/10/ursula-von-der-leyen-biden-00086591.

23 Council on Foreign Relations, 'A Conversation with Christine Lagarde', 17 April 2024, https://www.cfr.org/event/conversation-christine-lagarde-0.

Copyright © 2024 The International Institute for Strategic Studies

America's Election and Europe's Choices

Sarah Raine

Global interest in the outcome of the United States' forthcoming presidential election is a reminder that any decline in US global influence has been firmly relative. In the run-up to the November 2024 election, governments around the world will be acutely aware that the voting behaviour of Americans in states like Michigan and Wisconsin will shape their own futures and choices.

Those focused on upholding European defence and security have good reason to follow the US election closely. In President Joe Biden, Europeans were fortunate to find an American security partner – perhaps the last one – who was instinctively committed to the traditions of the transatlantic alliance and who instinctively understood the importance of European security. His imminent departure from office will come amid rising geopolitical tensions, Europe's worst war since 1945 and shifting priorities in Washington, which is increasingly focusing on the Indo-Pacific rather than Europe.

In July 2024, three events – the NATO summit in Washington DC, the European Political Community meeting in Oxfordshire and the vote in Brussels approving the European Union's senior leadership team for the next five years – signalled how Europeans are responding to transatlantic uncertainty and geopolitical insecurity. They demonstrated that Europeans are seeking to shore up the European pillar of NATO, improve defence

Sarah Raine is IISS Consulting Senior Fellow for Geopolitics and Strategy.

Survival | vol. 66 no. 5 | October–November 2024 | pp. 37–48   https://doi.org/10.1080/00396338.2024.2403214

relations between the United Kingdom and Europe, and support a greater focus on defence matters on the part of EU leaders.

Strengthening the European pillar of NATO

European leaders may fret over the reliability and durability of the United States' security commitment to Europe, but they have shown no serious inclination to develop alternatives to NATO. On the contrary, they have made efforts to develop the European pillar within NATO. According to NATO figures released in June 2024, based on constant 2015 pricing, European defence spending has risen by 73% since 2014.[1] European NATO members now account for 34% of NATO military spending, up from 26% in 2014. And whereas only two European NATO countries spent 2% or more of GDP on defence in 2014, and only nine did in 2023, by the end of 2024, 22 European NATO countries are likely to be at or above this threshold. Poland has increased its defence spending by 214% over the last ten years, and has now displaced Italy as the third-largest defence spender within the EU. In July it announced it would increase its defence budget by a further 10% in 2025.[2] Lithuania's budget has increased by 325% (albeit from near negligible levels).[3]

These facts are important for Europeans seeking to counter Republican claims that Europe will never 'step up' so long as the US continues to shoulder the main burden for its defence. After all, Americans making such arguments want to see a shift in the US role from 'provider of first resort to balance of last resort', arguing that it is reasonable to expect that the continent on which an attack would most likely take place would supply most of the readiness for such an eventuality, and that its collective resources ought to be more of a match to US capabilities.[4] As Max Bergmann put it in his *Foreign Affairs* article 'A More European NATO', the theory is that a stronger, less dependent Europe would give the US more rather than less reason to engage.[5]

There are other ways in which Europeans are slowly starting to make themselves into better partners. Five years after the collapse of the Intermediate-Range Nuclear Forces (INF) Treaty, the US and Germany announced at the NATO summit in July 2024 that from 2026, long-range US missiles would, for the first time since the Cold War, be deployed periodically in Germany. That same month, France, Germany, Italy and

Poland signed a memorandum of understanding on a European long-range-strike missile initiative, aimed at boosting European deterrence in the sub-strategic, non-nuclear domain.[6] This reflects broader European intent to ramp up long-range strike capabilities. For example, earlier this year the governments of Germany and Norway announced their investment in the initial development phase of a new supersonic long-range ship-based cruise missile.[7]

European voices within NATO's nuclear bodies have been helpfully strengthened by Sweden and Finland joining the NATO alliance. In June 2024, the Netherlands became the first European country to officially assign its F-35A stealth fighters to a nuclear-strike role, following the aircraft's October 2023 certification to carry the B61-12 thermonuclear bomb. The introduction of a fifth-generation nuclear-capable stealth fighter in Europe that is inter-operable with NATO is a significant enhancement to European and NATO military capabilities.

Germany's commitment permanently to station a German combat brigade in Lithuania faces domestic and logistical challenges, but sends an important signal of German investment in European security. This was further strengthened in June 2024 with the announcement by German Defence Minister Boris Pistorius of an order for 105 more *Leopard* 2A8 tanks to be delivered by 2027, some of which will be deployed to Lithuania to help bolster deterrence on NATO's eastern front.

A July 2024 implementation report on the EU's 2023 regulation on supporting ammunition production (ASAP) highlighted the 31 projects now under way that will substantially boost the EU's production capacity for artillery shells and missiles, and support the supply chains for these items.[8] Priorities include 'increasing the annual production capacity by more than 10 000 tons of powder, and by 4 300 tons of explosives', both of which are needed to ramp up the provision of 155 mm artillery ammunition to Ukraine.[9] Rheinmetall alone expects to produce 1.1 million artillery shells per year by 2027, aided by an ASAP grant.[10]

Of course, the European rearmament that is now belatedly under way is not without its problems. Ongoing deficits in European defence collaboration mean that increases in financing do not translate into comparable increases in capability. Despite a 2017 commitment to spend at least 35% of EU defence budgets on collaborative equipment purchases, only around 18% of EU defence budgets are spent in this way. Meanwhile, European armaments production, while increasing, lags behind the United States' own rising production, and is considerably off pace to meet what Ukrainian Defence Minister Rustem Umerov described in July 2024 as Ukraine's need for 200,000 shells per month.[11] In too many areas, European member states have exhausted their spare stocks of armaments, with SCALP EG/*Storm Shadow* missiles being one example.

There is also notably less agreement over the degree to which any strengthening of the European pillar within NATO should apply to NATO's ambitions in the Indo-Pacific. Indeed, one 'achievement' privately touted by French diplomats following July's NATO summit was France's success in blocking early ambitions for a separate NATO summit statement with the Alliance's four Indo-Pacific partners (Australia, Japan, New Zealand and South Korea). Encouragingly, in July the United Kingdom's new government quickly committed to the AUKUS partnership with Australia and the United States, and appeared to confirm Britain's deployment of a carrier strike group to the Indo-Pacific in 2025. However, hints in London's announcement of a Strategic Defence Review regarding the need to prioritise among theatres, and concerns over budgetary pressures – most obviously with relation to the *Tempest* fighter aircraft and the Global Combat Air Programme – mean that the UK's own 'tilt' towards the Pacific should stay on course but will merit careful tracking. Meanwhile, in early August, Germany and the Philippines agreed to work up a broad defence arrangement that will see the expansion of their bilateral training and exchange programme.

The focus on European capabilities within NATO is sparking some misguided concern across the Atlantic over the potentially divisive identification of 'pillars' within NATO, in particular should it implicitly help encourage European spending to be focused on the European defence industry. Indeed, US ambivalence to the European vision could be seen in July's summit statement, which contained scant reference to European or EU contributions to the support offered to Ukraine. Tensions are likely to grow over the degree to which increased EU funding aimed at supporting Europe's rearmament and the renewal of its defence-industrial base should be spent within the EU. According to EU Commission figures, between February 2022 and June 2023, 78% of weapons acquisitions by EU countries involved non-European manufacturers, with the United States accounting for 63% of EU countries' acquisitions.[12] These percentages will surely shrink in the years ahead, as Europeans invest more in their own defence industries (and as the US continues to prioritise its own defence-industrial interests). For the time being, however, the scale and pace of Europe's defence rearmament will continue to afford considerable market opportunities to non-European defence industries, such as South Korea's.[13]

Strengthening UK–Europe defence relations

The UK's new Labour government was clear in its campaign manifesto that it would look to 'reset' Britain's relations with the EU and its member states, including by seeking an 'ambitious new UK–EU security pact'.[14] Uncertainties over transatlantic relations are only serving to reinforce the desire to strengthen defence relations between the UK and the continent.

While it took former British prime minister Rishi Sunak 18 months to visit Berlin after taking office, it took new Prime Minister Keir Starmer just one week. To be fair, the previous Conservative government had been pushing to sign a bilateral defence agreement with Germany, but it took a visit by new UK Defence Secretary John Lesley to Berlin on 24 July 2024 to bring this 'joint defence declaration' to fruition. There are mutual ambitions to develop this declaration into a more formal Anglo-German bilateral treaty that promotes closer defence cooperation. Also in July, the EU and UK agreed that British Foreign Secretary David Lammy would attend October's meeting of the EU's Foreign Affairs Council. There has been revived impetus for a UK–France summit to further the Lancaster House treaties signed in 2010, including a renewed UK focus on sensitive nuclear cooperation as part of the TEUTATES agreement, which has seen the construction of a shared facility in France for testing the safety and reliability of nuclear-warhead designs.

Within two weeks of assuming office, the new British government had hosted 46 European leaders, including Ukrainian President Volodymyr Zelenskyy, at a meeting of the continent's newest strategic forum, the

European Political Community (EPC). This forum is the result of an initiative by French President Emmanuel Macron, who was championing greater European defence autonomy even before Russia's 2022 invasion of Ukraine. It was conceived as a gathering for Europe broadly defined, encompassing countries such as Iceland, Turkiye and Ukraine, but not Russia and Belarus. While the forum has not inspired the levels of devotion to which its initial advocates aspired, July's meeting at least served to showcase the new landscape in continental relations.

Of course, challenges lie ahead. The UK's vision for a 'reset' encompassing an EU-wide defence and security agreement will not be perfectly aligned with the EU's. There is a risk that the UK will see its defence cooperation with Europe as something it is 'giving' to the continent, in the expectation that it will receive something in exchange, such as a Trade and Cooperation Agreement (TCA) that has been reworked in ways that the EU might not be ready to consider. Meanwhile, a defence reset could be undermined by other areas of greater contention, such as ongoing deficits in the UK's implementation of the TCA, or irregular migration. The UK will push hard for its defence industry to have favourable access to the EU's developing Defence Industrial Strategy and its associated resources. Any obstacles that the EU may choose to erect here are likely to increase tensions given the contribution the UK is ready to make to mutually declared ambitions for enhancing continental defence capabilities.

Political considerations may also serve to undermine cooperative arrangements. Europe's leading governments are weak and poor. Even with a new government in France, there will be doubts over its longevity. It will be hard for partners to enthuse over major new European defence projects in the face of continuing credible prospects for a far-right president of France in 2027. Meanwhile, three problematic *Länder* elections in Germany in September will further expose the frailty of Germany's governing coalition. Through autumn, difficulties managing public finances will capture headlines in the UK as well as in many EU states.

Meanwhile, Europe continues to struggle with geopolitical problems beyond Ukraine. The Western Balkans remain a key cause for concern. Though still a candidate for EU membership, Serbia has failed to align with the EU on sanctions against Russia. In July, Serbia's president described his country's relations with Russia as 'very good' after a visit to Belgrade by Russian Deputy Foreign Minister Alexander Grushko.[15] Agreements following EU-brokered talks between Kosovo and Serbia are still not fully implemented. Secessionist behaviour by Republika Srpska President Milorad Dodik has been destablising Bosnia-Herzegovina. In December 2023, Dodik announced he would declare independence if Donald Trump were re-elected US president in 2024.[16] Efforts to advance a peace agreement between Armenia and Azerbaijan on the sidelines of July's EPC meeting were abandoned amid mutual recriminations.

A more engaged EU leadership

On 17 July, the EU Parliament approved the Union's senior leadership team for the next five-year term. Ursula von der Leyen was confirmed for a second term as European Commission president, alongside Vice President Kaja Kallas, who is also the High Representative of the European Union for Foreign Affairs and Security Policy (and the first holder of these offices to come from post-communist Europe), and European Council President António Costa. This is an unusually strong line-up.

Von der Leyen can be expected to continue to develop the European Commission's profile on economic security, as well as seeking a stronger EU role in the building of defence capabilities. She has promised to appoint a dedicated commissioner for defence and used her speech setting out her intended programme to call for a 'true European Defence Union'. She has been clear about the scale of the challenge and its urgency, arguing that the next five years 'will define our place in the world for the next 50'.[17] Under her leadership, the European Commission has committed to presenting a White Paper on the future of European defence within the first 100 days of its new term, while pushing forward a number of flagship European projects, including a European Air Shield and cyber defence. Still, the first defence commissioner will face limitations, including severe funding restrictions, at least until the EU's 2027–34 budgetary cycle.

Kallas has called on Europe to achieve a 'new, permanent state of defence readiness that will far outlast the war in Ukraine', and for the EU to dedicate more than the current 0.86% of its budget to defence.[18] Her time as Estonian prime minister was marked by strong support for Ukraine, including its path to EU and NATO membership. Costa, a Socialist and 'overseas citizen' of India, has declared himself to be 'focused on putting on track the Strategic Agenda' for 2024–29, as agreed by the June EU Council meeting. This includes a commitment to 'strengthening our security and defence' while 'urgently improv[ing] conditions for scaling up the European defence industry by creating a better integrated European defence market and by promoting joint procurement'.[19] His close relationship with von der Leyen, with whom he worked during Portugal's rotating presidency of the European Council in 2021, should help the EU leaders to coordinate their efforts, and thus to boost their collective influence. He will struggle not to be an improvement on his predecessor, Charles Michel, who was politically weak and had a problematic relationship with von der Leyen.

Interestingly, all three leaders are broadly aligned on adopting a more hawkish approach to China, which is arguably a first in the history of the EU. Von der Leyen invested considerable energy during her first term in strengthening the EU's trade-defence tools at a time when Europe's geo-economic influence was being undermined by Chinese over-capacity, as well as, more controversially, by the fallout from protectionist elements of the United States' Inflation Reduction Act. Given that China's Third Plenum in July 2024 failed to signal any major effort to combat Chinese over-capacity, these tools are likely to be even more important in von der Leyen's second term. Indeed, in July the EU announced provisional tariffs on imports of Chinese electric vehicles. Costa's own journey as Portuguese prime minister from welcoming Chinese investment in the wake of Europe's financial crisis to adopting a notably harder line should help him relate to other European countries still on this journey. It should also help the transatlantic dialogue on China, given the critical role that US lobbying played in changing Costa's own views. This should have demonstrated to US interlocutors that he is a reasonable partner willing to listen to rational argument. A Trump presidency, however, would potentially undermine this trend, risking some backtracking by European member states supported by a desire to distance themselves from Trump's populist 'America first' rhetoric.

As always, the EU's leadership can be undermined by its member states. Defence remains a national prerogative, and the pooling of resources will always be controversial. Meanwhile, although far-right political parties did not do as well in the 2024 EU elections as many feared, the increased presence of anti-establishment and populist parties in the EU Parliament from across the political spectrum will undoubtedly make legislating harder. Furthermore, Hungary's six-month presidency of the European Council, which began in July, means that little progress on key briefs is expected this year.

*　　　*　　　*

European perspectives on defence have generally become more clear-eyed. Ambitions have become more defined. But the question of how to measure progress is still sure to be contested. Timescales will continue to frustrate. Good intentions will fall short.

Germany's so-called *Zeitenwende* (turning point) is a case in point. It was announced in the days after Russia's invasion of Ukraine, when Chancellor Olaf Scholz genuinely feared that Europe's border with Russia might soon be Poland's, but Ukraine's success since then in holding back the Russians has created the illusion of a more permissive environment for the chancellery and its policy choices. While Germany will manage to spend 2% of GDP on defence this year, this is mainly thanks to the €100 billion special budget announced alongside the *Zeitenwende* that expires in 2027. The problem of what to do about the structural need for increased defence spending remains unsolved. Such medium-term uncertainty undermines the very investments by defence industries that governments are trying to encourage.

While public finances represent one key threat to progress on Europe's defence goals, public opinion represents another. Growing support for populist, nationalist parties on the far right and far left is spurring debate about the global order across Europe. For example, far-right actors are part of governing coalitions in Croatia, Finland, Italy, the Netherlands and Sweden. National elections in Austria this September are likely to continue this trend. A Trump presidency would likely further confuse continental debates on who is responsible for, and who is reacting to, threats to the rules-based order.

In the coming months, more announcements of new European defence ambitions, projects and even, occasionally, funding can be expected. But the risk remains that, in a contested fiscal environment characterised by waning public support for current defence priorities, defence spending is wrongly identified by European policymakers as an adjustable variable, with commitments that can be further extended and delayed. No European partner will be more acutely aware of this danger than Ukraine.

Notes

[1] Calculations based on data in Public Diplomacy Division, NATO, 'Defence Expenditure of NATO Countries (2014–2024)', press release, June 2024, p. 8, https://www.nato.int/nato_static_fl2014/assets/pdf/2024/6/pdf/240617-def-exp-2024-en.pdf.

[2] See 'Poland to Increase Defence Budget by About 10% in 2025, Says Minister', Reuters, 11 July 2024, https://www.reuters.com/world/europe/poland-increase-defence-budget-by-about-10-2025-says-minister-2024-07-11/.

[3] Public Diplomacy Division, NATO, 'Defence Expenditure of NATO Countries (2014–2024)', p. 10.

[4] Justin Logan and Joshua Shifrinson, 'A Post-American Europe', *Foreign Affairs*, 9 August 2024, https://www.foreignaffairs.com/europe/post-american-europe-justin-logan-joshua-shifrinson.

[5] Max Bergmann, 'A More European NATO', *Foreign Affairs*, 21 March 2024, https://www.foreignaffairs.com/europe/more-european-nato.

[6] See Steve Trimble, 'Four EU Governments Partner on Long-range Strike Missile', *Aviation Week*, 11 July 2024, https://aviationweek.com/defense-space/missile-defense-weapons/four-eu-governments-partner-long-range-strike-missile.

[7] Alex Luck, 'New 3SM "Tyrfing" Missile Receives German Development Funding', Naval News, 1 July 2024, https://www.navalnews.com/naval-news/2024/07/new-3sm-tyrfing-missile-receives-german-development-funding/.

[8] European Commission, 'Report from the Commission to the European Parliament and the Council on the Implementation of Regulation (EU) 2023/1525 of the European Parliament and of the Council of 20 July 2013 on Supporting Ammunition Production (ASAP)', 8 July 2024, https://www.parliament.bg/pub/ECD/6675871_EN_ACT_part1_v2.pdf.

[9] *Ibid.*, p. 14/16.

[10] Rheinmetall, 'Success in Brussels: Rheinmetall Receives Over €130 Million in EU-funds to Increase Production Capacities in the Artillery Sector', press

release, 26 March 2024, https://www.rheinmetall.com/en/media/news-watch/news/2024/03/2024-03-26-130-million-in-eu-funding-for-rheinmetall-to-expand-ammunition-production.

11 Anna Myroniuk and Valeria Yehoshyna, 'EU Shell-production Capacity, Supplies to Ukraine Fall Far Short of Promises', Radio Free Europe/Radio Liberty, 8 July 2024, https://www.rferl.org/a/ukraine-weapons-shells-european-union-eu-war-russia-investigation/33025300.html.

12 See Jean-Pierre Maulny, 'The Impact of the War in Ukraine on the European Defence Market', Institut de Relations Internationales et Stratégiques, September 2023, pp. 2, 15.

13 *Ibid.*, p. 15.

14 Labour Party, 'Change: Labour's Manifesto: Britain Reconnected', https://labour.org.uk/change/britain-reconnected/.

15 Quoted in 'Serbian–Russian Relations "Very Good," Vucic Says Following Deputy Foreign Minister's Visit', Radio Free Europe/Radio Liberty, 2 July 2024, https://www.rferl.org/a/serbia-russia-vucic-grusko-visit/33019047.html.

16 'Bosnian Serb Dodik Says He'll "Declare Independence" if Trump Retakes U.S. Presidency', Radio Free Europe/Radio Liberty, 3 December 2023, https://www.rferl.org/a/bosnia-dodik-declare-independence-trump/32712061.html.

17 European Commission, 'Statement at the European Parliament Plenary by President Ursula von der Leyen, Candidate for a Second Mandate 2024–2029', 18 July 2024, https://ec.europa.eu/commission/presscorner/detail/en/statement_24_3871.

18 Republic of Estonia Government, 'Address by Prime Minister Kaja Kallas in Paris', 3 May 2024, https://valitsus.ee/en/news/address-prime-minister-kaja-kallas-paris.

19 European Council, 'Strategic Agenda 2024–2029', https://www.consilium.europa.eu/media/4aldqfl2/2024_557_new-strategic-agenda.pdf.

Copyright © 2024 The International Institute for Strategic Studies

Putin's Ideological State

Vladimir Ryzhkov

Russian President Vladimir Putin is often seen and characterised as a venal thug – unprincipled, pragmatic, cynical and kleptocratic.[1] To deal with him effectively, however, it is important to understand that he has a genuine, if misguided, ideology. The Kremlin has not merely composed, disseminated and imposed an official ideology on Russian society as a means of controlling the masses and concealing the Putin regime's corruption. Ideology founded on grand ideas about Russia is central to Putin's ruling philosophy. He's a true believer.

The origin and expansion of Putin's ideology

By the end of the 1990s, a broad consensus had emerged among political elites in Moscow about the desirable future of Russia. Its key elements were stabilisation, restored order and a strengthened state. This called for centralising power, ending the acute confrontation between parties and branches of government, restricting regional autonomy, curbing pluralism and activism in civil society, and reviving Russia's foreign policy and military power, which included some political distancing from the West. While this mindset was to an extent a reaction to the chaos of the 1990s in implementing reforms and experimenting with liberal ideas, it also corresponded to a nostalgic ideal of Russia as a great world power.[2] When Putin was first elected president in 2000, the 'statesmen' and 'communists' challenging the Kremlin did

Vladimir Ryzhkov is a professor of history at Almaty Management University in Almaty, Kazakhstan, and a Russian opposition politician, having served as co-chair of the People's Freedom Party, a member of the Russian State Duma, First Deputy Chairman of the State Duma and leader of the parliamentary group Our Home–Russia.

Survival | vol. 66 no. 5 | October–November 2024 | pp. 49–54   https://doi.org/10.1080/00396338.2024.2403215

not have to be coerced to support the authoritarian, great-power course he had mapped.

Rhetorically rejecting the need to establish a state ideology, Putin immediately postulated its main provisions in the undeservedly half-forgotten programmatic article 'Russia at the Turn of the Millennium' published on 30 December 1999. One key aspect of the 'Russian idea' was patriotism, interpreted as 'a sense of pride in one's Fatherland, its history and accomplishments', thus implicitly a rejection of Boris Yeltsin's advocacy of a fundamental break between the Russian Federation and the Soviet era. Another was *derzhavnost*, roughly meaning enduring great-power status. The third component of the 'Russian idea' was *gosudarstvennichestvo*, or statehood, of a type directly opposed to liberal Western social models. Putin asserted the priority of state interests over freedom: 'For Russians, a strong state is not an anomaly, not something to be fought against, but, on the contrary, the source and guarantor of order, the initiator and the main driving force behind any change.' Finally, there was social solidarity, defined as the prevalence of collectivism over individualism and subsuming state paternalism.[3] In Putin's first strategically important presidential address, he enumerated major threats, adversaries and obstacles to his agenda, including independent parties and labour unions, free speech, regional and local authorities, big business and unnamed forces abroad.[4]

The big idea of Russia as a great power necessarily includes preserving and strengthening Russian influence in the post-Soviet space, as well as increasing Moscow's influence in world affairs. The radicalisation of these ideas in Putin's Munich speech in 2007, the claims of Russia's 'special interests' in the post-Soviet space announced by Dmitry Medvedev during his presidency, the Russian–Georgian war of 2008, the annexation of Crimea and infiltration of Ukraine in 2014, and the invasion of Ukraine in 2022 were responses to the growing independence of post-Soviet states and the intensification of US and Western strategic attention to the region.

On the domestic front, the expansion and rising political activism of the Russian middle class, public discontent with the slowdown in economic growth, unpopular pension reform, corruption, and increasing impatience with the government prompted Putin's conceptualisation of Russia's 'special path'. An emphasis on 'traditional values' and 'spiritual staples' since 2012 has recapitulated solidarist and corporatist ideas of the state and society as a single organism that cannot accommodate ideological, social, class, cultural, moral or political differences and debates. Political repression, punishment of 'foreign agents', and persecution of religious and sexual minorities, though certainly manifestations of an authoritarian government's intolerance for political opposition and an active civil society, are equally attempts to apply big ideas about unity and societal consolidation.

Latent and emerging totalitarianism

Since 2012, Putin's guiding ideology has largely unfolded as a complete and radical revision of the original project. While it posed Russia against its enemies by way of drastic distortions and oversimplifications, it offered a coherent political world view that harnessed images of an ideal Russia defined by its historical greatness, external and internal enemies, patriotism, solidarity and unique civilisation.

In this conception, Russia is a great global power with a global mission and a special model of development fundamentally different from the liberal Western one. With its glorious millennial history, today's Russia is not a new country but a continuation of a great and long-standing one. Its eternal enemies are the United States and the West because they seek its complete destruction. Russia is the real leader of the world majority, bravely opposing unreasonable and immoral Western claims to hegemony. Its internal enemies, who effectively serve its external ones, consist of all those who would undermine the organic harmony of the government and the people, including liberals, sexual and other minorities, non-governmental organisations (NGOs), political activists, and extremists and terrorists. The true Russian people are united in their patriotism and their traditional spiritual and moral values, purer and higher than those of the morally decayed West and safeguarded by the state and the Russian Orthodox Church. There is no place for the destructive transient cabinets, party squabbling, deceitful parliamentarism and sanctimonious 'human rights' of the West. Russia, then, is the centre and temple of a larger Russian world – in a word, a civilisation – extending far beyond the borders of the Russian Federation and in need of patronage and protection.

A canonical text of Putin's ideology or an authoritative collection of essays like Vladimir Lenin's *The State and Revolution* or Josef Stalin's *Short Course of the History of the All-Russian Communist Party (Bolsheviks)* has not yet been written. But there is little doubt that something along those lines will materialise. A course on scientific Putinism – analogous to Soviet 'scientific communism' – called 'Fundamentals of Russian Statehood' is already in preparation for mandatory use in all higher-educational institutions.[5] Putin's mature ideology can also be found in his historic speech of 18 March 2014 on the decision to annex Crimea and Sevastopol, which exalts the imperial past, laments the collapse of the Soviet Union, justifies claims to 'Russian lands' outside the Russian Federation, trumpets the threat from the 'fifth column' and casts the West as an existential threat.[6]

By 2012, Putin had eliminated the separation of powers, concentrated authority in his own hands and completely subordinated the party system to the Kremlin. Federalism and local self-governance were largely dismantled, a vertical power structure built, civil society significantly restricted and the political rights of citizens systematically violated. Between 2012 and 2023, the number of political prisoners in Russia increased exponentially. Elections were no longer free and fair, the opposition was often unable to take part in them, and voting results were falsified. The state began to systematically persecute not only the political opposition, NGOs, media and civil activists, but also religious groups, sexual minorities, and writers and artists. Laws on the defence of faith, morality and ethics appeared. Censorship was extended to art, literature, science and education. Official interpretations of history and politics were widely promoted and included in Putin's text of the updated constitution in 2020.

After the full-scale invasion of Ukraine in February 2022, the government closed the last few independent media outlets, established comprehensive censorship, mandated ideological history texts and purged liberal professors from universities. The state began to create mass youth movements along the lines of the Soviet model. LGBTQ+ individuals were declared 'extremist' and prosecuted. Many NGOs, authors and artists with views adverse to those of the state were criminalised as 'foreign agents'. On this evidence, Putin likely plans to devote the six-year presidential term he began in March of this year primarily to consolidating a totalitarian system. While its attributes probably will not be as extreme as those of the Soviet Union or Adolf Hitler's Germany, it will constitute a wholesale expansion of the state into the spheres of life and society that previously had not been subject to regulation, control and coercion. While there are departures from the Soviet model – in particular, Putin has replaced a ruling party with a presidential dictatorship and vertical state apparatus – that is the principal inspiration.[7]

It's important to understand what a stark and dramatic retrogression these developments represent. During the first decade of Putin's rule, he faced political, civil and cultural resistance. Russian society was modernising, becoming more complex and open. The urban middle class matured and expanded. Under Medvedev, civil society gained strength and demanded political liberalisation. In 2011–12, there were massive urban protests against Putin's return to power and the rigging of the Duma elections. He presented his radicalised ideology immediately after the 2012 election, and he had to work hard to enforce it.[8] External expansion and militarisation became an important part of his programme for doing so, culminating in the current war in Ukraine.

*   *   *

Putin has had a guiding ideology from his regime's earliest days. He consolidated power not merely to seize the country's wealth, but also to advance an ideal Russia and secure what he considered its rightful place in the world. From the outset, the project was authoritarian with totalitarian intentions that have been realised through progressive political radicalisation. For Putin, Russia's greatness is an end in itself and the highest attainment of the state and the Russian people. Security and geopolitics did not dictate his decisions on Crimea and Ukraine. The key driver was Putin's ideological premium on the preservation of great-power status.

Beyond that, a state of permanent war with a purportedly existential external enemy, as George Orwell argued, is the optimal political and psychological framework for mobilising an atomised population, justifying dictatorship and repression, and fostering an atmosphere of fear – in sum, for cultivating and perpetuating a totalitarian state. Putin's Russia will likely seek to continue war and confrontation. The Kremlin's main enemy is not Ukraine but the West. The weakening, retreat or, better yet, the collapse of the West is its goal. It is prudent to assume that Russia is preparing for a major, possibly world, war, and that at present peace agreements and workable compromises are infeasible.

Notes

1 See, for example, Vladimir Gelman, *Nedostoynoye Pravlenie. Politika v sovremennoy Rossii* ['Unworthy rule': politics in modern Russia] (St Petersburg: European University, 2019).

2 See Y. Levada, *Ot mneniy k ponimaniyu. Sotsiologicheskiye ocherki 1993–2000* [From opinions to understanding: sociological essays, 1993–2000], 2nd ed. (Moscow: Karpov E.V., 2011), pp. 212–45.

3 See Vladimir Putin, 'Russia at the Turn of the Millennium', in Andrei Melville and Tatiana Shakleina (eds), *Russian Foreign Policy in Transition: Concepts and Realities* (Budapest and New York: Central European University Press, 2005).

4 See President of Russia, 'Address to the Federal Assembly of the Russian Federation', 8 July 2000, http://www.kremlin.ru/events/president/transcripts/21480.

5 See Andrei Kolesnikov, 'Scientific Putinism: Shaping Official Ideology in Russia', Carnegie Politika, 21 November 2022, https://carnegieendowment.org/russia-eurasia/politika/2022/11/scientific-putinism-shaping-official-ideology-in-russia?lang=en.

6 President of Russia, 'Address by the President of the Russian Federation', 18 March 2014, http://kremlin.ru/events/president/news/20603. See also Vladimir Ryzhkov, *Dlinnaya Ten' SSSR. Ocherk istokov vneshnepoliticheskogo povedeniya sovremennoy Rossii* [The long shadow of the USSR: sketch of the origins of foreign policy behavior of modern Russia] (Riga: School of Civic Education, 2023), pp. 253–8.

7 See Ryzhkov, *Dlinnaya Ten' SSSR*.

8 *Ibid.*, pp. 240–61.

Copyright © 2024 The International Institute for Strategic Studies

The Significance of the Prisoner Exchange with Russia

Nigel Gould-Davies

On 1 August 2024, Russia and the West conducted a major prisoner exchange. Sixteen detainees in Russia were released to the West in return for eight Russian citizens, as well as two children who did not know they were Russian. This was significant for many reasons. The terms of the exchange, especially its novel features, reveal much about the dilemmas that Western governments face in managing 'prisoner diplomacy'. The recent exchange will also shape the conduct of future such deals.

The implications go further still. A prisoner exchange is a rare example of adversarial cooperation between Russia and the West. It thus casts light on other, more tacit forms of cooperation in the Russia–Ukraine war – notably, mutual restraint to prevent its disastrous escalation. The implicit lesson of this latest prisoner deal is that the West can loosen the restraints it has accepted, and support Ukraine more consistently, without undue fear of escalation.

Three features of the prisoner exchange were notable. Firstly, it was an exceptionally complex agreement, the largest and most multinational such exchange since the Cold War. Protracted negotiations took place among Western partners as well as with Russia – in particular, between the United States and Germany, which held Vadim Krasikov, the Russian intelligence officer, sentenced to life imprisonment for the 2019 murder of Chechen exile (and Georgian citizen) Zelimkhan Khangoshvili in Berlin.

Nigel Gould-Davies is IISS Senior Fellow for Russia and Eurasia.

Survival | vol. 66 no. 5 | October–November 2024 | pp. 55–63   https://doi.org/10.1080/00396338.2024.2403216

Secondly, Russia released twice as many people as the West did. This is a striking departure from the strict parity (or better) that Russia has typically insisted on in previous swaps with the West, as well as in tit-for-tat diplomatic expulsions. The only exceptions have been some recent exchanges of prisoners of war with Ukraine. The last major exchange, in 2010, was 10–4 in Russia's favour. In numerical terms, the West now got a far better deal.

Thirdly, seven of the 16 prisoners released from Russia were Russian activists without a second nationality. They were not being 'sent home' but rather forced into exile. Sentenced to punitive exemplary jail terms intended to deter others, these activists are now free to resume their work abroad.

Cold War precedents – and differences

During the Cold War, Soviet-bloc dissidents were occasionally traded for spies, but rarely on this scale. There are few precedents. In 1979, the Brezhnev regime exchanged four dissidents for two spies. More significant was the June 1985 exchange of 25 detainees, some of them dissidents, for four Soviet-bloc spies. This took place three months after Mikhail Gorbachev became general secretary. Further exchanges involving the prominent dissidents Yuri Orlov and Natan Sharansky occurred the following year.

This activity signalled Gorbachev's wish to thaw relations with the West and reform his country. It was a world apart from today. While there are partial precedents for the recent deal, it has novel features that make such agreements more difficult than in the past. The recent exchange occurred in conditions of increasingly acute conflict, not chronic systemic struggle. As a result, the question of whether either side 'won' from a voluntary agreement arises more insistently than before. There was performative satisfaction all round: US President Joe Biden and Russian President Vladimir Putin both greeted the planes that arrived with their respective human cargos. Some suggest that Putin prevailed, as he will have concluded that 'prisoner diplomacy' works and will use it again. With spurious arrests he can stack up human bargaining chips, then trade them for genuine criminals sentenced under the rule of law.

From this perspective, the case against such an exchange is the case against paying any kind of ransom for hostages: doing so merely incentivises taking new hostages. But there is an obvious flaw to the analogy with ransom paid to terrorists. The latter get money they can use to finance future operations. In a prisoner exchange, Russia gets only unmasked agents who are no longer operationally useful abroad – and, having spent time in prison, five years in Krasikov's case, are unlikely to have fresh and valuable insights to share with their colleagues. Payment in human kind cannot be invested in the future.

The real concern is more subtle. Putin has shown his intelligence officers that, even if they are sentenced indefinitely for heinous crimes, he will bring them home. When future Russian spies, murderers or saboteurs are detained, Putin will simply take new hostages to bargain for their release. It is a matter of 'when', not 'if': the consensus of the Western intelligence community is that Russia is planning more, and more aggressive, operations. If the culprits are caught, Russia will respond by rounding up new victims to trade. Indeed, it is already doing so pre-emptively. Not only were some Western detainees excluded from the latest deal, but two weeks after it happened, Ksenia Khavana, a US–Russian dual citizen, was sentenced to 12 years for making a $51 donation to Ukraine.[1] Ilya Yashin, one of the political prisoners freed in the deal, even said that it 'encourages Putin to take more hostages'.[2]

This dilemma has a pedigree. When British academic Gerald Brooke was released from Soviet captivity in 1969 in exchange for two US citizens spying for the Soviet Union in Britain, Alec Douglas-Home, the shadow foreign secretary, expressed his concern that

> this is an encouragement to the Russians to believe that they can always squeeze Her Majesty's Government in this way. The Foreign Secretary understands, does he not, that they are not in the least inhibited from starving a man until he is ill so as to play on the feelings and humanity of the British people? Their cold and brutish behaviour is part of the Russian make-up in this matter.[3]

This is a greater concern now. During the Cold War, nearly all exchanges were spies for spies or spies for dissidents. Soviet-bloc agents caught in the West ('illegals' under deep cover without diplomatic immunity) were traded for double agents caught at home (Soviet officials secretly working for a

Western country), or, less commonly, for imprisoned human-rights activists. As a result, nearly everyone exchanged in both directions was a citizen of a Soviet-bloc country. Since the West had no illegals in the Soviet Union, its spies operated under diplomatic cover and could only be expelled, not detained. Innocent Western citizens in the Soviet Union could be arrested on a pretext, of course. But tourism was limited and very few Westerners spent long periods in the Soviet Union. The Soviet authorities occasionally used them as bargaining chips, but it was rare.[4]

In the post-Cold War period, however, large numbers of Western citizens have visited Russia, and even resided there for many years. Some have ignored their governments' advice, since Russia's February 2022 invasion of Ukraine, to leave Russia. All are potential hostages. Those who nonetheless travel to, or continue to reside in, Russia are still the consular responsibility of embassies. Journalists want to be as close as possible to the story. Most, but not all, were withdrawn by their employers after the arrest of *Wall Street Journal* reporter Evan Gershkovich in March 2023 on espionage charges. Some Western citizens have settled in Russia. Living a quiet and blameless life is no guarantee of safety, yet the costs of uprooting oneself and moving back to the West, especially with a Russian family, may be considerable. Dual nationals – citizens with both a Russian and a Western passport, which the Soviet Union did not allow – may choose, for compelling personal reasons, to visit Russia.

Living a quiet life is no guarantee of safety

The problem of authoritarian states taking Western hostages is not confined to Russia, but it is most acute there.[5] If those who travel there despite the abundant risks are imprisoned as fodder for future exchanges, should their governments feel obliged to seek their release even at the price of returning Russian spies and assassins who have jeopardised Western security? There is little sign that Western governments have thought through this dilemma in a way that appropriately balances humanitarian concerns against strategic ones.

The dilemma is sharpened by another distinguishing feature of the recent prisoner exchange: it involved a convicted murderer. Soviet-bloc agents exchanged in prisoner swaps were guilty of espionage, not homi-cide.[6] Of course, espionage can itself result in death – actually and directly by exposing agents, or potentially and indirectly by making the country less secure – so this is arguably a distinction without a difference. But in practice, at least in the West, murderers and spies arouse different moral sentiments. As the German government acknowledged, it was Krasikov's killing of an exile in Berlin that made his release so difficult. It seems that the imminent execution of Rico Krieger, a German citizen, in Belarus was needed to secure a German decision that the US had long been pressing for. The fact that Belarus, unlike Russia, still has the death penalty enabled it to threaten the life of a foreign citizen, and Belarusian leader Alyaksandr Lukashenka to render a valuable service to Putin by pardoning him. But few will now wish to avail themselves of the visa-free entry that Belarus intro-duced for European citizens just two weeks earlier.

Moreover, it is no longer clear that those Russia releases in a prisoner exchange will be safe. Sergei Skripal, one of the prisoners released in the 2010 exchange, was a military-intelligence (GRU) officer convicted of treason. The Russian state had ample opportunity to kill him in captivity, yet it chose to release him. Eight years later he was nearly killed on British soil by GRU assassins using the military-grade nerve agent Novichok. Apparently, Putin's obsession with meting out retribution to those he considers traitors now extends even to prisoners whom he has voluntarily given up.

None of the prisoners whom Russia has just given up is a traitor in the obvious sense of having spied against their country. But it is no longer clear how expansively the Kremlin now defines the term 'traitor'. Three of the new exiles were colleagues of Alexei Navalny, the opposition leader who died suddenly, and was almost certainly killed, in an Arctic prison in February 2024. They cannot be confident that an insecure and vindictive Kremlin will not try to find them in due course. Not only have several exiled Russians died in suspicious circumstances over the past decade, but Russia is now known to be planning assassinations of European citizens. Earlier this year, an oper-ation against the CEO of Rheinmetall, a major German arms producer, was disrupted at a late stage.[7] Others are being planned. So will prisoner deals now stick? This is not a question that has had to be asked before.

Putin's *silovik* loyalty

The West should reflect, too, on what the exchange says about Putin's priorities. The terms he agreed show how important it is to him to secure the return of intelligence officers. His reportedly 'maniacal' obsession with bringing back Krasikov – whom the Kremlin confirmed had served alongside several current employees of the presidential security service – was key to the deal.[8] The only previous swap since Russia's full-scale invasion of Ukraine occurred in December 2022 and secured the return of Viktor Bout, a military-intelligence officer and notorious arms dealer. In the 2010 exchange, Putin – then prime minister and without formal responsibility for intelligence agencies – met the ten repatriated illegals within days of their arrival and sang spy-themed songs with them.[9]

Putin now appears to place such a high value on his spies that he is prepared to agree an unfavourable exchange – even though, once unmasked and expelled, they have no value as illegals. As a career KGB officer and former head of the FSB (the KGB's domestic successor), he appears to feel a strong personal loyalty to them and makes this known publicly. Although Putin has agreed some prisoner exchanges with Ukraine, the popular slogan 'we don't abandon our own', revived since Russia invaded Ukraine, in practice applies to the small number of spies in Western prisons rather than the hundreds of thousands of soldiers recklessly sacrificed on the battlefield.[10]

It may be, too, that such a commitment is not only a core part of Putin's identity but an expectation of the *siloviki* (security-service officials) whose presence across institutions is now greater than at any time in Russian history. In other words, fierce protective loyalty is part of the modus operandi of the regime – as important as the unremitting determination to hunt down 'traitors'. Since this is a high priority, it may also be a vulnerability. At the very least, it means that Russia does not hold all the cards in any future prisoner negotiation. Rather, such bargaining pits the regime's *silovik* solidarity against Western humanitarian impulses. When Western countries detain future spies, they will also have something to bargain with – and have now set a precedent for doing so effectively.

Wider implications

It is worth pondering the wider implications of the prisoner exchange for the West's overall Russia strategy, especially in assessing Putin's periodic hints of nuclear escalation. Prisoner exchanges and escalation management both involve cooperation between even the harshest adversaries. However opposed their ultimate goals, both sides share an interest in getting their people back alive and in preventing a mutually disastrous spiralling in the intensity or duration of conflict. Even amid the horrors of war, Ukraine and Russia have exchanged prisoners and are negotiating a further exchange; signed an agreement to allow limited grain shipments through the Black Sea, which lasted a year before Russia ended it; and held talks to try to end the war soon after it began.

Any agreement contains elements of cooperation and conflict: cooperation to agree an outcome that both sides prefer to the status quo; conflict over how much each side gains from it – the terms of trade, so to speak. Prisoner exchange and escalation management thus share a common logic as forms of adversary cooperation. In prisoner exchanges, the benefits are defined by the numbers and kinds of detainees that each side persuades the other to give up as the price of an agreement. In the more or less tacit communication of escalation management, the benefits are defined by the degree of restraint that each persuades the other to accept to keep the war limited. Each will seek to impose limits of permissible behaviour by shaping perceptions of the actions that would cross their 'red lines' and thereby jeopardise restraint.

The recent prisoner deal shows that, for all his ruthlessness, Putin can act rationally. He was willing to make concessions in order to achieve a goal he valued highly. Conversely, through firmness, patience and unity, Western negotiators induced concessions. In particular, they refused to release Krasikov in anything close to a one-for-one swap, as they had for Bout in 2022.

It is not clear, however, that the West has applied the same firmness, patience and unity in its escalation management. In one sense, this is understandable. There are no strategic consequences if the two sides cannot agree a prisoner exchange. But if they cannot tacitly agree on the terms of mutual restraint in the conduct of war, the outcome could be disastrous.

Caution is thus merited. Nevertheless, it may be argued that the West has too often allowed Russia to define the limits of escalation rather than doing so itself. By choosing not to take important steps that would materially help Ukraine, it could be accepting less favourable terms than necessary for keeping the conflict contained. Examples include limiting the provision of weapons systems to Ukraine; curtailing the range and targeting of some of the systems that it has provided; declining to impose a no-fly zone over Ukraine; and failing to provide safe passage for shipping through the Black Sea. There are few steps that Russia could take, and has chosen not to, that would escalate the war. Almost all the self-restraint has come from the West. It is Ukraine that pays the price for this complaisance.

*   *   *

The recent prisoner exchange shows that Russia can be persuaded to accept an agreement that is more favourable to the West. Putin was prepared to give up a great deal to get Krasikov back and acted rationally to achieve this. Since he values his regime's survival even more than he does Krasikov, the West can take a firmer, more proactive approach to defining the terms of mutual restraint. Putin is very unlikely to respond to a stronger Western policy in ways that would predictably threaten his own rule. The implicit lesson of the prisoner exchange is that the West can provide more uncompromising support for Ukraine without undue fear of escalation.

Notes

1   See Robert Tait, 'Russian Court Jails US–Russian Woman for 12 Years over $50 Charity Donation', *Guardian*, 15 August 2024, https://www.theguardian.com/world/article/2024/aug/15/russian-court-jails-us-russian-woman-for-12-years-over-50-charity-donation.

2   'Released Russians Say Swap Deal Was a "Difficult Dilemma"', DW, 2 August 2024, https://www.dw.com/en/released-russians-say-swap-deal-was-a-difficult-dilemma/live-69841168.

3   UK Parliament, 'Mr Gerald Brooke (Release)', Hansard HC Deb, vol. 787, cc2146–56, 24 July 1969, https://api.parliament.uk/historic-hansard/commons/1969/jul/24/mr-gerald-brooke-release.

4   For example, Walter Ciszek, a Jesuit priest, and Marvin Makinen, an

American student, were exchanged in 1963; Greville Wynne, a British businessman working for MI6, in 1964; Gerald Brooke, a British academic, in 1969; and US journalist Nicholas Daniloff in 1986. The first and most famous Cold War spy exchange was that involving CIA pilot Francis Gary Powers and Soviet intelligence officer Rudolf Abel in 1962. Powers was not, of course, a visitor: he was captured after his U2 spy plane was shot down in Soviet airspace.

5 China may emulate Russia. For example, soon after Meng Wanzhou, Huawei's Chief Financial Officer, was detained in Canada on fraud charges at the United States' request in 2018, China arrested two Canadian citizens, Michael Kovrig and Michael Spavor. In 2021, a swap deal allowed all three to return to their home countries.

6 Soviet agents carried out several 'wet deeds' (that is, killings), but they were not traded in exchanges.

7 See Katie Bo Lillis, Natasha Bertrand and Frederik Pleitgen, 'Exclusive: US and Germany Foiled Russian Plot to Assassinate CEO of Arms Manufacturer Sending Weapons to Ukraine', CNN, 11 July 2024, https://edition.cnn.com/2024/07/11/politics/us-germany-foiled-russian-assassination-plot/index.html.

8 See Shaun Walker and Deborah Cole, 'Kremlin Admits Vadim Krasikov Is a Russian State Assassin', *Guardian*, 2 August 2024, https://www.theguardian.com/world/article/2024/aug/02/kremlin-admits-vadim-krasikov-is-an-russian-state-assassin.

9 See Alexandra Odynova, 'Putin Sings with Deported Spies', *Moscow Times*, 25 July 2010, https://www.themoscowtimes.com/2010/07/25/putin-sings-with-deported-spies-a117.

10 See 'Zakharova on Prisoner Exchange: "We Don't Abandon Our Own"', *Federal Press*, 2 August 2024, https://fedpress.ru/news/77/policy/3330917.

Copyright © 2024 The International Institute for Strategic Studies

Noteworthy

Ukraine's Russian incursion

'Russia brought war to our land and should feel what it has done.'

> *Ukrainian President Volodymyr Zelenskyy gives his nightly address on 8 August 2024 without directly commenting on reports that Ukrainian forces had invaded Russian territory two days earlier.*[1]

'To be honest, we all have joy in our hearts.'

> *A Ukrainian soldier identified only as Oleksandr describes his participation in the assault on Russia.*[2]

'It is now becoming increasingly clear why the Kiev regime rejected our proposals for a peaceful settlement, as well as those from interested and neutral mediators.

It appears that the enemy, with the support from their Western backers, is executing their directives, and the West is using Ukrainians as proxies in this conflict. It seems the opponent is aiming to strengthen their negotiating position for the future. However, what kind of negotiations can we have with those who indiscriminately attack civilians and civilian infrastructure, or pose threats to nuclear power facilities? What is there to discuss with such parties?

[…]

The leaders of the Kiev regime are not only perpetrating crimes against the Russian people but are also, in effect, pursuing the destruction of their own citizens, the Ukrainian people, whom they evidently no longer view as their own. The casualties among the Ukrainian armed forces are rising sharply, including among their most effective units and divisions, which are being redeployed to our borders.

The adversary will undoubtedly face a strong response, and all the objectives we have set will certainly be achieved.'

> *Russian President Vladimir Putin speaks at a meeting of Russian security officials on 12 August.*[3]

'Unlike Russia, Ukraine does not need other people's property. Ukraine is not interested in taking the territory of the Kursk region, but we want to protect the lives of our people.'

> *Heorhii Tykhyi, spokesperson for Ukraine's foreign ministry, explains that Ukraine does not wish to occupy Russian territory but only to complicate Russia's military logistics.*[4]

'In the Kursk region, we clearly see how the military tool is objectively used to convince the Russian Federation to enter into a fair negotiation process. We have proven, effective means of coercion. In addition to economic and diplomatic ones … we need to inflict significant tactical defeats on Russia.'

> *Ukrainian presidential adviser Mykhailo Podolyak comments on 16 August on the purpose of Ukraine's incursion into Russia's Kursk region.*[5]

'The casual chit-chat of self-proclaimed intermediaries on the virtuous subject of peace has ceased. Even if they cannot say it out loud, everyone recognises the reality of the situation. They understand that there will be NO NEGOTIATIONS UNTIL THE ENEMY IS COMPLETELY AND UTTERLY DESTROYED!'

> *Dmitry Medvedev, deputy head of Russia's Security Council, posts to Telegram on 20 August about Ukraine's incursion into Kursk.*[6]

Survival | vol. 66 no. 5 | October–November 2024 | pp. 64–66   https://doi.org/10.1080/00396338.2024.2403217

Biden steps down

'It has been the greatest honor of my life to serve as your President. And while it has been my intention to seek reelection, I believe it is in the best interest of my party and the country for me to stand down and to focus solely on fulfilling my duties as President for the remainder of my term.'

US President Joe Biden withdraws his candidacy for president in a statement released on 21 July 2024.[7]

'We have 107 days until Election Day. Together, we will fight. And together, we will win.'

US Vice President Kamala Harris accepts Biden's endorsement as the Democrats' presidential candidate in a statement released on 21 July.[8]

Maduro holds on

'I am Nicolás Maduro Moros, re-elected president of the Bolivarian Republic of Venezuela … and I will defend our democracy, our law and our people!'

Nicolás Maduro claims victory in Venezuela's presidential election on 29 July 2024.[9]

'Our struggle continues and we won't rest until the will of the people of Venezuela is respected.'

Edmundo González Urrutia, Maduro's main rival in the election, alleges widespread electoral fraud.[10]

Netanyahu addresses Congress

'We meet today at a crossroads of history. Our world is in upheaval. In the Middle East, Iran's axis of terror confronts America, Israel and our Arab friends. This is not a clash of civilizations. It's a clash between barbarism and civilization. It's a clash between those who glorify death and those who sanctify life.

For the forces of civilization to triumph, America and Israel must stand together. Because when we stand together, something very simple happens. We win. They lose.

[…]

Now, here's my vision for the broader Middle East. It's also shaped in part by what we saw in the aftermath of World War II. After that war, America forged a security alliance in Europe to counter the growing Soviet threat. Likewise, America and Israel today can forge a security alliance in the Middle East to counter the growing Iranian threat.

[…]

The new alliance I envision would be a natural extension of the groundbreaking Abraham Accords … I have a name for this new alliance. I think we should call it: The Abraham Alliance.'

Israeli Prime Minister Benjamin Netanyahu addresses the US Congress on 24 July 2024.[11]

Middle East escalations

'We consider his revenge as our duty.'

Iranian Supreme Leader Ayatollah Ali Khamenei reacts to the killing of Hamas leader Ismail Haniyeh in Tehran on 31 July 2024.[12]

'Political assassinations and continued targeting of civilians in Gaza while talks continue leads us to ask: how can mediation succeed when one party assassinates the negotiator on [the] other side?'

Qatari Prime Minister Sheikh Mohammed bin Abdulrahman al-Thani expresses his dismay at Haniyeh's death.[13]

'Haniyeh's death makes the world a little better.'

Israeli Heritage Minister Amichay Eliyahu.[14]

'The IDF (Israel Defence Forces) announces that on July 13th, 2024, IDF fighter jets struck in the area of Khan Yunis, and following an intelligence assessment, it can be confirmed that [Hamas military leader] Mohammed Deif was eliminated in the strike.'

The Israeli military releases a statement on 1 August.[15]

'To the Israeli enemy: laugh a little now, but you will cry a lot as you don't know what red lines you have crossed.'

Hizbullah leader Hassan Nasrallah speaks on 1 August at the funeral of Fuad Shukr, an adviser killed in an Israeli airstrike on Beirut on 30 July.[16]

'Time is in our favour and the waiting period for this response could be long.'

Alimohammad Naini, spokesperson for Iran's Islamic Revolutionary Guard Corps, hints on 20 August at possible Iranian retaliation against Israel.[17]

'What happened today is not the end of the story. Hezbollah tried to attack the state of Israel with rockets and drones early in the morning. We instructed the IDF to carry out a powerful pre-emptive strike to remove the threat. The IDF destroyed thousands of short-range rockets, and the rockets were all intended to harm our citizens and our forces in the Galilee … We are hitting Hezbollah with surprising thrusts.'

Netanyahu speaks on 25 August after an attack on Israel by Hizbullah forces in Lebanon.[18]

Sources

1 Andrew E. Kramer, 'Ukraine's Push into Russia Is a Surprising Turn in the War', *New York Times*, 8 August 2024, https://www.nytimes.com/2024/08/08/world/europe/russia-border-ukraine.html.

2 *Ibid.*

3 President of Russia, 'Vladimir Putin Held a Meeting on Current Issues in Novo-Ogaryovo', 12 August 2024, http://en.kremlin.ru/events/president/news/74856.

4 Shaun Walker, 'Russian Authorities Scramble to Quell Ukraine's Week-long Kursk Incursion', *Guardian*, 13 August 2024, https://www.theguardian.com/world/article/2024/aug/13/russian-authorities-scramble-to-quell-ukraines-week-long-kursk-incursion.

5 Peter Beaumont, 'Ukraine Links Kursk Incursion to "Fair Talks" as Russia Closes In on Key City', *Guardian*, 16 August 2024, https://www.theguardian.com/world/article/2024/aug/16/ukraine-russia-offensive-talks.

6 'Russia's Medvedev Says There Will Be No Talks with Ukraine After Kursk Incursion', Reuters, 21 August 2024, https://www.reuters.com/world/europe/russias-medvedev-says-there-will-be-no-talks-with-ukraine-after-kursk-incursion-2024-08-21/.

7 'Read Biden's Letter Withdrawing From the Race', *New York Times*, 21 July 2024, https://www.nytimes.com/interactive/2024/07/21/us/biden-withdraw-letter.html.

8 Nik Popli, 'Read Kamala Harris' Statement on Biden Dropping Out', *TIME*, 21 July 2024, https://time.com/7001071/kamala-harris-reacts-biden-dropping-out/.

9 Patricia Torres and Tom Phillips, 'Venezuela Election: Maduro Declared Winner by Government-controlled Authority', *Guardian*, 29 July 2024, https://www.theguardian.com/world/article/2024/jul/29/venezuela-election-nicolas-maduro-edmundo-gonzalez-urrutia-results.

10 *Ibid.*

11 'We're Protecting You: Full Text of Netanyahu's Address to Congress', *Times of Israel*, 25 July 2024, https://www.timesofisrael.com/were-protecting-you-full-text-of-netanyahus-address-to-congress/.

12 Abby Sewell, 'Khamenei, Iran's Supreme Leader, Vows Revenge Against Israel over Killing of Hamas' Political Chief', *Washington Times*, 31 July 2024, https://www.washingtontimes.com/news/2024/jul/31/irans-khamenei-vows-revenge-against-israel-over-ki/.

13 Andrew England, Raya Jalabi and Najmeh Bozorgmehr, 'Iran Vows Revenge as It Accuses Israel of Killing Hamas Political Leader', *Financial Times*, 31 July 2024, https://www.ft.com/content/4a2e6014-7a53-4138-a04b-1aa0451114b0.

14 Helen Livingstone, 'Hamas Political Leader Ismail Haniyeh Killed in Iran: What We Know So Far', *Guardian*, 31 July 2024, https://www.theguardian.com/world/article/2024/jul/31/top-hamas-leader-ismail-haniyeh-killed-iran-explainer.

15 Nidal Al-Mughrabi and Maayan Lubell, 'Mohammed Deif: Hamas Military Leader and Oct 7 Mastermind Was Killed in Gaza Airstrike, Israel Says', Reuters, 1 August 2024, https://www.reuters.com/world/middle-east/death-hamas-military-leader-deif-july-confirmed-israel-says-2024-08-01/.

16 Raya Jalabi and Najmeh Bozorgmehr, 'Hizbollah Chief Says Beirut Killing Takes Battle with Israel to "New Phase"', *Financial Times*, 1 August 2024, https://www.ft.com/content/d2ee9acd-7c19-43d4-9b43-0726c14fc14d.

17 'Wait for Iran's Retaliation Against Israel "Could Be Long"', Revolutionary Guards Spokesperson Says', Reuters, 20 August 2024, https://www.reuters.com/world/middle-east/waiting-period-irans-retaliation-against-israel-could-be-long-revolutionary-2024-08-20/.

18 'Strikes on Hezbollah "Not the End of the Story", Says Netanyahu, Guardian News, 25 August 2024, https://www.youtube.com/watch?v=yZpjQ_xuo20.

Copyright © 2024 The International Institute for Strategic Studies

Forum: Towards a European Nuclear Deterrent

Héloïse Fayet, Andrew Futter and Ulrich Kühn

For decades, the primordial fear of European NATO allies has been that America would retreat from Europe and leave them threatened by a powerful foe in close proximity – first the Soviet Union, now Russia – and dependent on their own limited ability to organise security. Not only did Europeans dread losing America's military might, but some also felt that without its diplomatic heft to moderate internal European dynamics, the continent's erstwhile power struggles could return. America did not retreat for almost 80 years, and it still might not. But strategic and domestic circumstances could also force US policymakers to choose between engagement or disengagement, Europe or Asia.

Were the United States to opt for disengagement, Europeans would be caught unprepared amid the ongoing Russia–Ukraine war – the largest on the continent since the Second World War – and ill-equipped to face Russia alone. In the most extreme scenario, the power vacuum would allow ambitious leaders to claim the lead, while a cacophony of divergent national calls would undermine any sense of European unity. Some could go their own way and balance against Russia, including by nuclear means. Others could bandwagon with Moscow. The end of NATO and the European Union could be nigh.

Héloïse Fayet is a research fellow at the Security Studies Center and head of the deterrence and proliferation research programme at the Institut français des relations internationales (IFRI). **Andrew Futter** is Professor of International Politics at the University of Leicester. **Ulrich Kühn** is head of the arms-control and emerging-technologies programme at the Institute for Peace Research and Security Policy at the University of Hamburg, and a non-resident scholar at the Carnegie Endowment for International Peace.

Survival | vol. 66 no. 5 | October–November 2024 | pp. 67–98   https://doi.org/10.1080/00396338.2024.2403218

For purely self-interested reasons, of course, the US may never completely dissociate itself from European security. The Russia–Ukraine war,
now in its third year, could come to an end sooner rather than later, with
both sides having exhausted their military options. Given the current dyna-
mism in world affairs, making bold and specific predictions about when and
under what exact circumstances America might pivot away is a rash and
futile endeavour. What matters for European security is that, due mainly to
the rise of China, US imperial overstretch and rising populism in America,
chances are higher today than at most points in recent European history
that the continent will see some form of US pullback in the medium term.
Depending on the details, Europeans might then have to reassess the role of
nuclear weapons in European security.

The debate has already started, most prominently with French President
Emmanuel Macron's speeches on the European role of French nuclear forces
and German politicians' continued public musings about nuclear deterrence for Europe and Germany. If Donald Trump, who is openly disdainful
of NATO and admiring of Russian President Vladimir Putin, wins the US
presidential election, the issue could reach a head. Europe's major powers
– France, the United Kingdom and Germany – may be compelled to initiate
formal discussions on nuclear deterrence in a post-American Europe. These
anticipatory assessments of their national perceptions, policies and prefer-
ences, before the centrifugal forces of national self-interest gather, should
help identify similarities and differences in their respective positions and
facilitate a common European approach.

France's Tentative Overture for a European Nuclear Deterrent

In a January 2024 speech at the Swedish Defence University in Stockholm,
President Macron noted that 'French vital interests have a European dimension' and that French nuclear weapons therefore 'give a special responsibility
to France' in European defence.[1] This constituted a significant step forward

in French thinking on the role of French nuclear weapons in the defence of Europe. Yet the core message is not new. In the late 1950s, Charles de Gaulle had proposed a trilateral European nuclear project between France, Italy and West Germany, before Paris ultimately decided on a purely national deterrent.[2] A second proposed multilateral project, between France, the UK and the United States, to share nuclear arms or at least to manage nuclear military programmes together in the 1960s failed as well.[3] From the 1970s onward, however, French leaders have realised that France's vital interests were not limited solely to its national territories. As a consequence, the strategic and tactical weapons of the three branches of the French military were postured to defend not only France but also its neighbouring allies against a possible Soviet invasion. After the Cold War, this notion resurfaced when Jacques Chirac's government advanced the concept of 'concerted deterrence', though it generated little interest among European partners for which nuclear weapons had lost their importance.

More discreetly, Macron's statement highlighted French doubts about the credibility of US extended deterrence in Europe. This too has historical antecedents. The crux of the argument, put forward by French leaders during the Cold War and still valid today, is that vital US interests are not directly affected by what is happening in Europe. A US commitment to 'trade Boston for Berlin' seems dubious. Compared to America, France has much more to lose in a war in Europe. Europe's deep integration – particularly through the EU and the eurozone – makes it difficult to imagine a conflict scenario in which the vital security interests of, say, Germany, Poland or Sweden are affected while those of France are not. France would need to defend other European countries to protect itself.

While such a scenario seemed merely theoretical in the first two decades following the Cold War, the Russian invasion of Crimea in 2014 and the election of Trump in 2016 changed the picture. Fears spread in Paris that an increasingly insular America could one day be too preoccupied with Asia to protect Europe from a resurgent Russia. In his now famous speech in 2020 at the École de Guerre, Macron suggested a 'strategic dialogue to develop with our European partners, which are ready for it, on the role played by France's nuclear deterrence in our collective security'.[4] His offer gained new traction in February 2022, when Putin reminded everyone in Europe of the salience of nuclear weapons in geopolitics – something he had never forgotten.[5]

A dual threat to Europe

Being one of Europe's two nuclear powers, France had a special role to play in the deterrence dynamics that unfolded after Putin's invasion of Ukraine. Jean-Yves Le Drian, then the French minister of Europe and foreign affairs, responded to Putin's nuclear threats by highlighting the fact that NATO was also a nuclear alliance, thus implying that any use of nuclear weapons against a NATO country could be answered in kind.[6] More robust signalling from Paris followed. Even if not confirmed publicly by the Élysée, three out of the four French nuclear-armed submarines were sent on patrol during the early weeks of the war, reflecting a level of alert that France had not reached since the Cold War. Paris also maintained all planned nuclear exercises and missile tests, while a more risk-averse United States postponed two tests of its *Minuteman* III missile.

The second threat to the continent, also implicating France's special role, may come from a possible second Trump presidency. French leaders have three main worries and expect their European counterparts to share them.[7] Firstly, there is a high risk that Trump could withdraw from NATO, or at least significantly reduce US conventional forces in Europe, especially if he believes that Europeans are not spending enough on defence and therefore do not 'deserve' American protection. Secondly, he may also reduce the number of US nuclear weapons currently deployed in Europe, though not much evidence currently supports that prospect. Thirdly, and most importantly, a US president who loathes or dismisses many European countries is unlikely to risk American lives for Europe.

French reactions to Trump, both during his first term and in anticipation of a possible second, and to the war in Ukraine, focused on two tracks: reaching out to European partners and highlighting the credibility of the French deterrent. Macron's various statements and speeches about the continental extent of France's vital interests aimed to reassure nervous European allies. In the École de Guerre speech, Macron went so far as to invite France's European partners to 'be associated with the exercises of French deterrence forces', though only Italy took him up on this specific offer.[8]

A triad until the end of the Cold War, the French nuclear arsenal currently consists of roughly 290 strategic warheads. It is split between the Force océanique stratégique, which is composed of four missile submarines each equipped with 16 tubes for M51 ballistic missiles with an estimated range of up to 8,000 kilometres, and the Forces aériennes stratégiques, consisting of two squadrons of *Rafale* fighter aircraft equipped with supersonic air-launched cruise missiles. Both nuclear components are undergoing major modernisations, the *Rafale*s are being updated, and a third generation of missile submarines should be at sea in 2035. A fourth-generation air-to-surface nuclear missile – expected to be deployed in 2035 – will be hypersonic.[9]

The Russia–Ukraine war, the spectre of Trump and Macron's canvassing for a role for French nuclear forces in European security have triggered some interest in European capitals, perhaps most prominently in Berlin. Yet misunderstandings about Macron's 'nuclear offers' and significant domestic and international obstacles loom large.

Impediments

It's important to clarify what France's deterrent is not and what it cannot achieve, at least under current circumstances. To begin with, some French commentators have used the term 'extended deterrence' to describe Macron's proposals, thereby implicitly comparing them to US extended nuclear deterrence to Europe.[10] This comparison is misleading. French deterrence is based on the concept of 'strict sufficiency', whereby France's nuclear arsenal is calibrated to inflict 'unacceptable damage' on an adversary, with 'unacceptable' defined as incommensurate with any gain from attacking a middle power, as France sees itself.[11] A French arsenal capable of inflicting that level of damage on a superpower – such as Russia – able to threaten the whole of Europe would require France to significantly increase its number of warheads.

The principle of strict sufficiency also significantly limits France's ability to establish a nuclear sharing scheme for its European allies. Washington has an estimated 100 B61 gravity bombs deployed in Belgium, Germany, Italy, the Netherlands and Turkiye under NATO's nuclear-sharing arrangement.[12] France could not easily do the same because the air-launched component of its nuclear dyad consists currently of only one type of nuclear-equipped missile that France could not deploy abroad without degrading its own deterrent. Unless it developed another mission-specific weapon, a French nuclear-sharing arrangement would be infeasible. France is unlikely to develop such a weapon in the short to medium terms, as expanding the numbers, types or missions of French nuclear forces would be very costly. France's defence budget is already at record levels, with spending on the nuclear programme already estimated to constitute 13–20% of the total.[13] Thus, France's fiscal leeway is limited.

Another obstacle is domestic opposition. Despite its historical consistency, Macron's Stockholm speech and other iterations of his proposals during the EU parliamentary-election campaign triggered a massive populist backlash bordering on disinformation. Politicians from the far left (La France Insoumise) and the far right (Rassemblement national) attacked Macron for seeking to share French nuclear weapons and thus weaken France's nuclear doctrine. Any attempt to change France's customarily sceptical stance towards NATO and distancing from the Alliance, such as joining NATO's Nuclear Planning Group (NPG), could invite even more criticism. That said, some French elected politicians and defence analysts advocate such a move, which would allow France to become more involved in nuclear debates within NATO and promote an alternative view within the Alliance.[14]

Finally, expanded French deterrence commitments – vertically and horizontally – would negatively impact the global nuclear-disarmament architecture, jeopardising France's status as a 'responsible nuclear-weapons state'. France has cut its nuclear arsenal by half since the end of the Cold War – essentially by dismantling the land-based component of what was a nuclear triad – signed and ratified the Comprehensive Test-Ban Treaty and halted all production of weapons-grade plutonium and uranium. Deploying French nuclear weapons to other European countries could be seen as a violation of the spirit of the Treaty on the Non-Proliferation of Nuclear Weapons (NPT).

Ambitions, partners and possibilities

The fact remains that Macron's nuclear outreach stems from a genuine concern about the durability of US support for Europe and the continent's future security and independence. For Paris, Trump's arrival in the White House in 2016 was a pivotal moment for European strategic autonomy, of which it considered itself to be the strongest proponent and natural leader. Having now realised in the context of the Russia–Ukraine war that European countries cannot provide support for Ukraine comparable to that provided by the United States due to a lack of strategic unity and industrial-production capacity, French ambitions have become more modest. Accordingly, any French overtures stressing the European dimension of the French deterrent must come with a degree of humility to which Paris is not accustomed in foreign policy. France would also have to be sensitive to European partners' doubts about the political sustainability of any sharing arrangement. Even if Macron favoured opening up the French deterrent to the rest of Europe, it is unlikely that a far-right successor would maintain that course.[15]

Notwithstanding these constraints, energising France's strategic European partnerships seems essential for advancing the debate on European deterrence and defence. Three seem especially important.

The Franco-German *couple*, as it is known in Paris, is seen as the heart of Europe and European defence. Increasingly in recent years, the two countries have had their differences, including on defence issues. France apprehends the German plan for a Europe-wide missile-defence architecture, known as the European Sky Shield Initiative, as diminishing strategic stability. Competing national interests have slowed the French–German–Spanish effort to build a sixth-generation fighter aircraft – the Future Combat Air System (FCAS). Among other things, France needs the aircraft to be capable of carrying its next-generation nuclear-tipped cruise missile. While it has not been a German priority, Paris has welcomed Berlin's increased interest in nuclear deterrence, including Macron's proposals. At the same time, France has shown ambivalence about the possibility of Germany co-financing French nuclear weapons, which German Finance Minister Christian Lindner hinted at in an op-ed.[16] While French politicians and officials are inclined to 'make European countries pay' for expanded French deterrence, most recognise that this would pose a problem in terms of sovereignty in requiring France to make formal guarantees to Germany, cutting against the French practice of maintaining deterrence ambiguity.

The link between France and Poland, the third member of the so-called Weimar Triangle, is more promising. Building on long-standing French support for Poland's independence, France has appreciated Poland's substantial investments in defence in response to the Russia–Ukraine war, boosting several bilateral formats. From Warsaw's side, Polish President Andrzej Duda is one of few European leaders to publicly acknowledge a strong interest in a European nuclear deterrent along the lines suggested by Macron.[17]

France's most potent bilateral partnership may be the one with the UK, which ironically is now outside the EU. As the only other nuclear power in Europe, Britain is a natural partner for France in any exploration of how to strengthen European deterrence. The Chequers Declaration of 1995 recognised the interconnectedness of the two countries' vital interests, and the Lancaster House treaties on defence and security reinforced it in 2010. In addition, the TEUTATES Treaty provides a framework for bilateral scientific cooperation on nuclear issues and is considered of paramount political importance in Paris. Under the agreement, France and Britain share a sub-critical testing facility in France and regularly exchange data about nuclear safety and security. Other opportunities exist for better coordinating the two countries' deterrence missions – for example, by seconding British officers to French missile submarines and vice versa, or by arranging for British submarines to call at French ports. The British and French nuclear arsenals combined come to around 520 warheads, numerically equivalent to China's current deterrent force. This alone could send a stronger message to Russia. Sharing a pool of carriers and nuclear weapons in the spirit of the Multilateral Force (MLF) of the 1960s, sometimes discussed in expert circles, seems a step too far, however.[18] As the French–German FCAS project shows, questions of sovereignty, particularly when they involve nuclear issues, can greatly complicate even the best cooperative intentions.

Beyond bilateral and trilateral relationships, Paris should rethink its approach towards NATO. Instead of challenging the Alliance, whose appeal

Britain is a natural partner for France

is growing stronger with the addition of Finland and Sweden, it would make more sense for France to promote the establishment of a 'European nuclear pillar' within NATO. Such a course could preserve French decision-making autonomy while breaking with its tradition of voluntary exclusion from the NPG by requesting observer status and participating in NATO's conventional air-support missions, formerly known as SNOWCAT. Paris should also encourage foreign participation in its nuclear exercises. Foreign military personnel could fly in French aircraft, attend exercises from the Taverny command base, or visit the Île Longue nuclear base and the submarines anchored there; French officials arranged such visits during the Cold War to demonstrate French capabilities, and hosted a delegation of ambassadors from the North Atlantic Council there in 2023. While stockpiling French missiles and warheads abroad would be unrealistic, France could open a Strategic Air Force squadron to foreign European personnel, based either in France or abroad, training them in the manner employed for NATO's dual-capable aircraft missions.

The most obvious option for an efficient and credible French contribution to European deterrence and defence lies outside the nuclear field. Nuclear weapons are no magic wand, and nuclear weapons can deter only those threats affecting absolutely vital interests. Given the evolving threats from Russia, which in the coming years could range from disinformation and low-level attacks on critical infrastructure to limited conventional attacks in Eastern Europe accompanied by deep precision strikes, there is an urgent need for Paris to rethink its sceptical approach to conventional deterrence and US concepts such as 'integrated deterrence'.[19]

To overcome this inertia, Paris should work in two directions. Firstly, it should improve coordination between France's conventional and nuclear forces. Secondly, it should try to better articulate the role that France envisages for both French and other European conventional forces in the defence of Europe. The goal should be a clearer delineation of work between nuclear and non-nuclear European partners. In this regard, a positive development emerged from the sidelines of the NATO summit in Washington last July, when the defence ministers of France, Germany, Italy and Poland announced plans to jointly develop a European conventional long-range strike capability.[20] European partners should also undertake a critical examination of the escalation-management risks associated with such a project.

The clock is ticking

From a French perspective, the American political situation is a strategic wake-up call for Europe. Even if Kamala Harris is elected, it remains to be seen whether she will be as friendly to Europe as Joe Biden was. Even if she is, given the current instability of US politics, a new isolationist US president could test Europeans again as early as 2029. The Europeanisation of France's vital interests, stressed time and again by Macron, is necessary for strengthening European deterrence and defence, but it is not sufficient. France must be clearer and more concrete about what it can offer. Conversely, its partners should be more outspoken about their need for reassurance. Constructive results could be renewed arms-control diplomacy, especially with respect to non-nuclear strategic weapons, and with it the reinforcement of non-proliferation principles to check any nuclear temptations on the part of Poland, Sweden and potentially other European countries. Macron's successor might be less interested in keeping the door open to further cooperation. Europeans should therefore move quickly.

– Héloïse Fayet

The UK: Willing but Constrained

The invasion of Ukraine in February 2022 was a watershed moment for the British political and military establishment, and brought an end to a generation of relative peace and stability. While the 2014 seizure of Crimea and the 2018 Salisbury poisonings began to shift British perceptions of the Russian threat, the war marked a sea change in what that evolving threat might mean for British security. It propelled nuclear threats and nuclear deterrence back into politics, particularly since Britain has been singled out by various Kremlin and media spokespeople as a nuclear target. At the same time, the prospect of a victory for Trump in the November 2024 US presidential elections, growing isolationist sentiment in the US and pressing challenges for the country in other parts of the world have planted very real concerns that America could decouple its security from Europe's. While worries about Washington leaving NATO or reneging on the 1958 Mutual Defence Agreement (MDA) and the 1963 Polaris Sales Agreement (PSA) with the UK might seem far-fetched at present, it is dawning on British policymakers and analysts that the US security guarantee, and especially the nuclear commitment that has undergirded the security complex in Europe for 80 years, could be starting to waver.

These geopolitical dynamics add to a challenging domestic agenda for Keir Starmer, the first Labour prime minister since 2010. The Starmer government has stressed its unswerving commitment to retaining a British nuclear-weapons capability and to the NATO alliance. The future of British and European deterrence, however, is more uncertain than it has been for decades. The government is compelled to balance reviving economic productivity and fixing broken public services with the need to spend more on conventional forces, as well as financing a new fleet of missile submarines and building new nuclear warheads. In all but the most catastrophic future scenarios, America will remain the key partner for Britain on nuclear issues, but policy elites are increasingly speculating about whether other deterrence architectures for Europe might be needed.

Myriad challenges

In 2006, the Labour government led by Tony Blair began the process of replacing the fleet of missile submarines designed to carry Britain's nuclear weapons.[21] Every British prime minister since has supported the programme. Under the original plan, the first of the new *Dreadnought*-class submarines would have been deployed in the early 2020s, replacing the fleet of *Vanguard*-class boats that were designed in the 1980s. This timeline already involved extending the service lives of the submarines and their nuclear reactors beyond what had originally been intended. Under current plans, and assuming no further delays, the first submarine will be commissioned in the early 2030s.[22] This has put added pressure on an ageing fleet, as repair, overhaul and upgrading takes more and more time to complete, which might also be why several recent continuous-at-sea-deterrence submarine patrols have exceeded 200 days – more than double the normal patrol time.[23] The *Vanguard* class will have to continue operating for at least another decade, translating to a 40-year service life.

Other factors have exacerbated concerns about the age of the submarines and the pace of the replacement programme. Firstly, two successive tests of a *Trident* sea-launched ballistic missile (SLBM) – the most recent in January 2024 – failed.[24] Secondly, worries have increased about the robustness of the defence-scientific and industrial base, and the availability of personnel to fulfil the deterrence mission. Thirdly, designing and paying for a new nuclear warhead, known as *Astraea*, are major challenges. The previous Conservative government simply downplayed the significance of these factors. The fact remains that the overall programme appears to be in trouble.[25]

The modernisation of Britain's nuclear enterprise is occurring in a complex domestic context. The Conservative, Liberal Democrat and Reform parties all support retaining a national nuclear capability, and the Labour government has stressed its 'absolute' commitment to the nuclear deterrent.[26] But the new cabinet does contain prominent politicians who voted against the programme in 2016 – notably Deputy Prime Minister Angela Rayner and Foreign Secretary David Lammy, though Lammy has since lodged his strong support for it. Labour has also traditionally included many who support unilateral nuclear disarmament. While the decline of the Scottish National Party has eased pressure to remove British nuclear weapons from their base near Glasgow, nuclear-weapons policies may still face internal opposition going forward. The views of the general public appear mixed on the desirability of nuclear weapons. A poll conducted in 2024 found that 66% of Britons believe that no nation should possess nuclear weapons.[27] Some 83% thought it would be unacceptable for the UK to use nuclear weapons without being attacked first, while 55% said that if Britain were attacked with nuclear weapons, they would support using them in response. Support for the British nuclear programme historically hovers at around 50%.[28] And there continues to exist a vocal disarmament community in the country, though it is perhaps not as prominent as it was a generation ago.

Despite Brexit, the UK's relationship with Europe has continued to shape British politics. Most in the current Labour government supported remaining in the EU, and probably prefer a closer and more formal defence and security relationship with European partners. Yet the Brexit dispensation still looms large, and Starmer may be unwilling to be seen as reneging on previous commitments to British independence from Europe. This has little impact on NATO as it currently stands, but could influence the debate about extending Britain's nuclear umbrella to non-NATO Europe or a NATO without the United States. The perception of a recent nationalist lurch to the right in key European countries such as France and Germany has both sharpened and complicated the issues.

What US disengagement?

Political and military elites have begun to think through what a second Trump presidency might mean for Britain's security, the future role of the UK in European deterrence, and the British nuclear force.[29] British nuclear weapons are operationally independent, and only the prime minister can authorise their use. But the British deterrent remains dependent on the United States to a certain extent.[30] London leases the *Trident* SLBM from a common pool built and maintained by US company Lockheed Martin.[31] It does not have a sovereign ballistic-missile capability. It is also believed that the British warhead design utilises some US technology and information, and that the new *Astraea* will be developed 'in tandem' with the US W93 warhead. In addition, the two countries will likely cooperate on submarine design and stealth technology as well as on the Common Missile Compartment for the *Trident* missile. Disruption in the bilateral relationship would therefore have a significant knock-on effect on British deterrence, and by implication diminish Britain's ability to extend deterrence to Europe in a post-US NATO.

For London, the best consequence of a Trump victory would be continued pressure on NATO allies to increase their share of the financial burden of European defence with no substantive change in US support for the Alliance or in the US commitment to deterrence. European conventional forces and assets would then be beefed up to the benefit of all. A more worrying possibility, perhaps more likely, would be an attempt by Trump to make a deal with Putin to end hostilities in Ukraine that sidelines European partners.[32] He might accompany such an initiative with loose rhetoric to the effect that America's commitment to NATO's Article 5 is conditional on European allies 'paying their dues' or meeting certain demands, US support for NATO and European allies will be reduced, or the US will redeploy troops and other conventional military assets away from Europe or reduce preparedness by refraining from participating in NATO military exercises.

While the US commitment to Article 5, nuclear deterrence and maintaining US B61 bombs at air bases in Europe would remain, and presumably NATO allies in Europe would still be able to purchase the latest US non-nuclear military hardware, sandbagging Ukraine would be very destabilising. More disruptive still would be, say, an American decision to 'repatriate' the 100 or so B61 bombs stored in Europe. This disposition could form part of a bilateral arms-control deal between Washington and Moscow, or it could simply arise because they were needed elsewhere, especially if the United States faces major war in the Indo-Pacific. Britain does not currently have a separate sub-strategic platform that could substitute for the B61, the British WE177 free-fall nuclear bomb having been retired in 1997 and a replacement air-launched cruise missile having been cancelled.

An even bigger shift, still unlikely, would be for the United States to effectively leave NATO and remove all its nuclear (and conventional) forces from the Alliance's military-planning structures. Although Congress passed legislation in late 2023 barring a president from formally withdrawing the US from NATO without congressional approval, the president could challenge its constitutionality. There is, in any event, quite a bit a president could do short of formal withdrawal to limit US involvement in Europe's defence. Moreover, to cause major consternation, it may simply be enough for Trump to say that he would not feel bound by previous commitments.[33] Presumably, the MDA (which is subject to renewal every ten years) and other bilateral British–American security arrangements would remain in effect. London's nightmare scenario, and arguably by extension Europe's, would be a US decision to end both the MDA and the PSA, which would make it difficult for Britain to sustain a nuclear force. Again, this seems highly unlikely at present, but it is not inconceivable in the long run.

Relearning deterrence

For several decades after the Cold War, military threats posed by major powers almost disappeared from the academic, policy and public consciousness. After Russia illegally annexed Crimea and infiltrated eastern Ukraine, the UK's 2015 Strategic Defence and Security Review mentions deterrence and the 'resurgence' of the Russian threat.[34] Russia's war against Ukraine and the Kremlin's thinly veiled nuclear threats have fully restored nuclear deterrence to the British security discourse. Now, British experts and officials have to relearn the mindset of deterrence, escalation and crisis management, and strategic stability. Three major insights have emerged from the Russia–Ukraine war that would have a bearing on a weakened US security commitment to NATO or a post-US-led Alliance.

Firstly, nuclear weapons are back as tools of statecraft, and adversaries will attempt to use nuclear threats to coerce and shape British as well as NATO responses. Putin and those around him appear to see coercive value in issuing nuclear threats, and may even believe that these threats have prevented greater NATO involvement in the war.[35] It is almost certain that nuclear threats and rhetoric would accompany any future Russian aggression in Europe, with an eye to splitting European allies and blunting any response.

Secondly, British planners must contemplate how to deter and respond to limited Russian nuclear use. Speculation as to possible instances have included a Russian 'nuclear-demonstration shot' over an uninhabited area; a direct attack on Ukrainian forces, infrastructure or leadership; and a limited attack on NATO.[36] Tackling these contingencies is difficult enough in the current context, let alone in a future of diminished US engagement. The plausible role of forward-deployed US tactical nuclear weapons must be reconsidered. The most salient question is, if they are not available, what other non-nuclear capabilities might be needed. Most of Europe's credible retaliatory options – especially nuclear ones – rely on the United States.

Thirdly, the war has illuminated the centrality of modern, scalable and robust conventional forces. The ability to coordinate and supply Ukraine with large complements of weaponry and ammunition has significantly contributed to Moscow's inability to push significantly further into Ukraine.

And Ukraine's effective territorial defence has probably also sent a strong deterrent message to the Kremlin. The upshot is that conventional strength and a resilient industrial base are as important as nuclear weapons to deterring and, if necessary, defeating aggression on NATO's borders. Another lesson is that Britain's elites and public cannot ignore the possibility of fighting a major conventional war, with or without the United States.

To be sure, the credibility of nuclear forces' use will remain essential to any notion of deterrence. Britain is the only nuclear-armed state that relies on just one type of delivery platform and has a relatively small stockpile of SLBMs and warheads. Advances in Russian ballistic-missile defence technologies and undersea-warfare capabilities pose new concerns for London.[37] In 2021, Ben Wallace, then secretary of state for defence, noted that these may have factored into the British warhead-cap increase.[38] In the worst case, a post-US NATO – if indeed the rest of the Alliance could hold together – would be left reliant on combined British and French nuclear stockpiles. Strictly speaking, because French nuclear forces are not formally committed to NATO, Britain would be the sole nuclear guarantor of the Alliance. While French doctrine does have a European dimension, London would still be in a very uncomfortable position. It is difficult to imagine how the UK alone could credibly threaten nuclear retaliation against Russian conventional aggression on NATO's eastern flank given that it lacks a sub-strategic nuclear platform.

Britain's options

The spectre of a US withdrawal from Europe has driven a reassessment of British nuclear deterrence. One early result was the announcement in the 2021 Integrated Review that the total number of nuclear warheads that Britain might hold in its nuclear stockpile would be increased to 260. A decision was also taken to end transparency about how many warheads were deployed on each missile submarine when on patrol.[39] While making relatively little material difference to Britain's nuclear capability – the number was believed to be around 225 warheads in 2021[40] – the change did reverse several decades of nuclear reductions and increased transparency. Britain's current nuclear-deterrence plan is based on 'like-for-like' replacement. This means building four new missile subs, albeit with 12 rather than 16 missile tubes on each boat; continuing to lease up to 58 *Trident* SLBMs from the United States; building a new warhead to sit atop these missiles; and maintaining a policy of continuous-at-sea deterrence with a minimum of one submarine on patrol. This posture still appears designed to threaten 'unacceptable consequences' to an adversary. Britain does not have a no-first-use policy, but officials are careful not to talk in terms of battlefield or tactical nuclear employment.

One enhancement open to British planners would be to build one or more additional submarines beyond the four currently planned. This would theoretically make the continuous-at-sea deterrence mission easier to sustain and raise the possibility of having more than one submarine at sea at any given time. The additional submarine would be relatively cost-effective given the economies of scale and sunk costs. It could, however, potentially increase pressure on longer-term British submarine-building efforts – including for AUKUS, the trilateral Australian–British–US military arrangement – given the limited capacity of British dockyards.[41]

A more radical option to boost extended deterrence for Europe would involve alternative nuclear-delivery platforms.[42] Rather than simply expanding the existing force, the UK could add either an air-delivered weapon or a different submarine-delivered one.[43] The most obvious choice for an air leg would be to purchase the nuclear-capable variant of the US F-35A aircraft and apply to join the NATO nuclear-sharing mission, for which the United States provides the B61 nuclear warheads. The F-35A is a different aircraft from the non-nuclear-capable F-35B that the Royal Navy and the Royal Air Force already operate from aircraft carriers and the Royal Air Force Station in Marham. The former would have to be based on land, as British aircraft carriers are not equipped to launch them, and warheads would remain under US control.

A far harder challenge would be for the Atomic Weapons Establishment – Britain's nuclear lab – to develop its own air-launched warhead and possibly fit it onto a missile such as *Storm Shadow*. As for a different submarine-delivered nuclear platform, the Royal Navy currently operates conventional US *Tomahawk* cruise missiles from its *Astute*-class attack submarines, but the US Navy does not have a nuclear-capable version. Even if such a missile were made available, Washington could not provide a warhead without contravening the NPT unless the warhead was subject to a dual-key arrangement whereby it remained in US custody. To further complicate matters, several of these options assume a domestic political environment in which Washington would cooperate.

Most of these options would take many years to come to fruition, and at considerable cost. One way around the financial constraints might be through some sort of joint financing with European NATO partners. This is not a new idea, and it would entail ceding some decision-making power to other governments. Germany would seem to be the most obvious candidate for such an endeavour, and the new Labour government is keen to pursue a British–German defence treaty. Another option might be to revisit the MLF idea from the 1960s, whereby NATO would operate its own nuclear platforms and weapons based on British and French technology, though Paris would harbour understandable reservations. The final option is deepened nuclear cooperation between London and Paris, building on the Lancaster House treaties. While there may not be much political appetite for this now, a post-American NATO could compel integration between French and British nuclear forces. It could make sense to share development costs of certain platforms, especially missiles and warheads, and to conduct joint and integrated deterrence operations. Joint development may, however, prove too difficult as long as British nuclear forces are still reliant on the US for certain technologies, and as long as France remains outside NATO's NPG. Ultimately, however, any of the options discussed here would probably be preferable to horizontal nuclear proliferation in Europe.

Towards a Europe without US hegemony

Several decades of relative peace and the normalisation of Britain's annual defence budget at around 2% of GDP have shaped a perception that difficult decisions about national security could be postponed. This is no longer the case. Whoever wins the US election in November, the world is becoming more multipolar, and British officials have little choice but to account for it. There is a genuine risk of conventional war in Europe beyond Ukraine, and a serious possibility that the US commitment to European security could weaken or even collapse. Even if wholesale US disengagement from Europe does not occur, it is only prudent to plan for a world where primary US attention is focused elsewhere.

On nuclear weapons and deterrence, Britain and most European allies remain wedded to a twin policy of restraint and arms control. In fact, European publics have shown strong support for the Treaty on the Prohibition of Nuclear Weapons and disarmament. The mindset so reflected does not seem to match the short-term circumstances. The reality is that the next phase of European deterrence will probably have to involve building up rather than reducing conventional, and possibly nuclear, capabilities. Selling this politically in Britain and finding the resources to accomplish it will be stiff challenges, but meeting them may be necessary to keep the European continent at peace.

The UK's task is threefold. Firstly, it must ensure the credibility of its current nuclear deterrent in a more uncertain world and confront difficult choices about whether the current configuration remains sufficient. Secondly, it has to coordinate nuclear deterrence with a credible conventional deterrent, produced with European allies. Thirdly, the UK needs to assess how European security fits with other British global aspirations and commitments. Even in a post-US NATO, burden-sharing would still be key, as Britain is not capable of playing a role comparable to the one the United States has fulfilled for the past 80 years. Managed correctly, however, cultivating a more robust and sustainable integrated European role in deterrence should be possible.

– Andrew Futter

Germany's Nuclear Conservatism: Informed and Steady

Germany's strategic conservatism is rooted in its experience in three world wars. Germany started the first two when it sought to assert its nationalism and change its security environment, and failed with devastating consequences for its neighbours and itself. This record has made German leaders extremely cautious about initiating strategic change: in the twentieth century, whenever Germans led the way, disaster ensued. Germany endured a third world war, though a cold one, on both sides of the Iron Curtain, the border between East and West Germany amounting to its front line. Yet decades of US leadership and multilateral security arrangements via NATO – that is, *Westbindung* – brought West Germans peace and prosperity, and eventually the unexpected reward of reunification. Following America while coordinating security policies with European partners has massively paid off for Germans.

On nuclear weapons in particular, Germany is both conservative and dependent. It has pledged on multiple occasions not to acquire nuclear arms, the last time being in 1990, when the country reunified.[44] At the same time, Germany has long sought and received nuclear protection from the United States, US nuclear weapons having first been moved into what was then West Germany some 70 years ago.[45] Regardless of which parties or chancellors ruled in Berlin or Bonn, they all honoured and adhered to this arrangement. Today, an estimated 20 US warheads are still deployed at the Büchel Air Base. Relying on US extended nuclear deterrence is thus one of the oldest extant principles of German foreign and security policy. Another priority – arms-control and disarmament diplomacy – always ranked second to nuclear deterrence. For decades, German leaders have not had to question the third pillar of German strategic policy: abjuring a national nuclear arsenal.

Two shocks

Two major shocks in six years disturbed this state of affairs. The first was the unexpected election of Trump as US president in 2016. His constant questioning of NATO, his disdain for then-chancellor Angela Merkel, his affection for illiberal strongmen like Putin, his extortionate methods of pressuring allies into increased defence spending – these features of his official conduct rattled the German establishment. They did not, however, lead Berlin to change course on transatlantic matters. When the Trump administration declared its intention to withdraw about a third of its conventional forces from Germany in 2020, for instance, Berlin reacted with only mild distress.[46] Had German leaders really feared that America could retreat from Europe, the reaction would have been different. Merkel maintained faith that the US electorate would choose Joe Biden over Trump in 2020.

The second, even bigger, shock was Russia's full-scale attack on Ukraine in February 2022, upending the European peace and security order as established under the 1990 Charter of Paris and completely disrupting Berlin's often cosy relationship with Moscow. When German Chancellor Olaf Scholz appeared before the Bundestag and delivered an unscheduled government statement on 27 February 2022, his prime message to Germans was that Germany's post-Cold War comfort had ended: 'The twenty-fourth of February 2022 marks a watershed [*Zeitenwende*] in the history of our continent. With the attack on Ukraine, the Russian President Putin has started a war of aggression in cold blood ... We are living through a watershed era. And that means that the world afterwards will no longer be the same as the world before.'[47]

Fortunately, the two shocks were not synchronised. When Trump threatened Europe with abandonment, Putin's extra-territorial aggression moves were still limited to annexing Crimea – a fait accompli, however outrageous – and fomenting a lingering low-intensity conflict in eastern Ukraine. A massive land war, affecting the very security of Europe, was almost inconceivable at the time. When such a war materialised in Ukraine, and European leaders came to fully appreciate Russia's destructive potential, Trump was gone and Biden made sure that Washington stood by its European allies. Soon a third shock – Trump's re-election – could build on the first two, creating an all-too-well-synchronised danger to Europeans. From a German perspective, the scenario of war from the East and abandonment from the West echoes a historically catastrophic strategic situation. Europe's deteriorating security environment has stimulated several vexing and often confusing nuclear debates in Germany.[48]

What's real and what isn't
One of the most consequential of these debates involved a significant portion of policymakers who tried – ultimately without success – to end German participation in nuclear sharing. Germany continues to host US-made B61

nuclear gravity bombs. They are part of NATO's nuclear-sharing mission, under which German aircraft with German pilots would deliver the bombs once NATO decision-makers had decided on their use. Full authority over and custody of the weapons remains with the United States, though the German government has final say on the employment of German aircraft and crews. For several decades, the German Luftwaffe had designated an ageing fleet of *Tornado* aircraft for this mission, and they needed to be replaced for Germany to continue its nuclear-sharing role. Ending this arrangement had the support of several critical groups. The co-governing Social Democratic Party (SPD), rallying around the influential nuclear sceptic Rolf Mützenich, together with the Greens, then in opposition, made the issue a key topic in the run-up to the September 2021 general elections.[49] Almost every poll in the previous 20 years found a clear majority of Germans opposed to stationing US nuclear weapons on German territory.[50] In addition, the Free Democratic Party (FDP) – a former coalition partner of Merkel's – had pushed for the weapons' removal in 2010–11. When Scholz won a majority in those three parties, there was reason to believe that the new government could eventually end the practice.

Subsequent coalition negotiations in autumn 2021, however, reconfirmed Germany's conservative nuclear predilections. Berlin did not end Germany's participation in nuclear sharing and instead decided to replace the *Tornado* fleet with US-made F-35s. Discreetly pro-nuclear voices within all three parties and key external interventions – notably by NATO Secretary General Jens Stoltenberg – had secured the status quo.[51] In addition, a rapidly deteriorating security situation around Ukraine, where Russia was amassing troops, materially affected perceptions. Scholz also used the *Zeitenwende* speech to announce the purchase of the F-35s. While he apparently had not previously shared this decision with his own party, a majority of Germans suddenly favoured keeping US nuclear weapons in Germany.[52] While the domestic push in Germany to end nuclear sharing was real enough to draw in Stoltenberg, it failed because *Westbindung* and extended nuclear deterrence, which had worked for so long, trumped disarmament aspirations.

With Trump's election in 2016, another, more radical debate started in Germany, mainly among defence intellectuals, in which both US extended nuclear deterrence and the non-existence of a German nuclear arsenal were called into question, and the possibility of a robust European nuclear deterrent was mooted.[53] Macron's nuclear overtures reinvigorated it, and Russia's war against Ukraine increased its momentum and broadened its audience to include a range of politicians and officials. Both multilateral and unilateral options have been discussed.[54] Among the former, French nuclear forces could somehow replace the role that America had played for decades. Some proposed a 'Europeanised' French deterrent, with either the EU leadership or rotating European capitals having operational decision-making control over the weapons. Others urged the French to form a stronger European nuclear pillar within NATO, possibly with financial support from Germany and other European allies.[55] Among unilateral steps, fringe figures suggested that Germany could develop its own nuclear deterrent or purchase nuclear warheads from the United States.[56]

Berlin is not officially considering any of these options. Merkel stated in 2017 that there were 'no plans for nuclear armament in Europe involving the federal government'.[57] Likewise, Scholz and Defence Minister Boris Pistorius have voiced their opposition to such ideas on several occasions. 'I do not support this debate at all', Scholz told a German newspaper in early 2024. 'Germany decided a long time ago not to seek its own nuclear weapons. At the same time, however, we are part of NATO's nuclear deterrent. All those responsible in NATO would prefer it to stay that way and I warn expressly against negligently questioning American protection in quasi-anticipatory concern.'[58] Thus, Scholz's government is not questioning US nuclear guarantees, though it admits that Germany needs to invest more for its own defence and that of European allies, no matter who wins the next US election. A German nuclear deterrent is not, at this point, a plausible option: the German public is still staunchly opposed to it.[59] Yet the debate was a genuine political phenomenon. Germany would not be the first democracy in which once outlandish opinions about acquiring nuclear weapons migrated from the periphery to the centre of the political discourse, as South Korea demonstrates.[60]

Scholz and his coalition partners have not taken the bait, however, instead focusing on conventional deterrence and defence. Germany was the

United States' prime target for accusations of free-riding on defence matters well before Trump amplified them.[61] After 2014, when Russia took Crimea by force, however, Germany started to increase its military commitments to NATO. As part of its Enhanced Forward Presence (EFP), Berlin contributed up to 1,000 soldiers to its deterrence and reassurance mission in Eastern Europe and assumed command of the EFP contingent in Lithuania in 2017. Two years later, Berlin also took charge of NATO's multinational Very High Readiness Joint Task Force. But maintaining these costly commitments was possible only at 'the risk of an even further decline in the operational readiness of the systems for units without mission-equivalent obligations'.[62] Germany's armed forces were badly depleted.

Since Scholz's *Zeitenwende* speech, the German armed forces have received considerably more funding for personnel and new military equipment. But owing to the slow pace of modernisation, unclear long-term financing commitments and the SPD's internal critique of Scholz – often from the pacifist left wing of the party – some worry that *Zeitenwende* may lose steam.[63] Still, Germany's 2023 National Security Strategy, the first ever for the country, states that 'the Federal Government wants to further strengthen the European pillar of the transatlantic defence community. The more our European allies contribute militarily and politically to NATO, the more solid the transatlantic Alliance will be. Europe's ability to act on its own is increasingly a prerequisite for German and European security.'[64] To back up its EFP commitments to Lithuania, Berlin has set up a combat brigade in Germany, ready to deploy in a crisis.

More broadly, Berlin has identified the thinness of European air defences as a major concern. The German decision to purchase the US–Israeli *Arrow* 3 air-defence system aims to close a capability gap in defending against long-range missiles. In addition, the German-launched European Sky Shield Initiative aims to facilitate Europe's joint procurement of short-, medium- and long-range defence systems, including US-made *Patriots*.[65] At the sidelines of the 2024 NATO summit in Washington, Germany and the United States agreed to deploy new US conventional long-range missiles in Germany, previously banned for the United States and Russia under the now-defunct Intermediate-Range Nuclear Forces Treaty.[66] From Berlin's perspective, the deployment is an interim measure pending improvements in European capabilities. In turn, Berlin has curtailed its arms-control aspirations despite Foreign Minister Annalena Baerbock's admonition in 2022 that disarmament and arms control were complementary to deterrence and defence.[67] For the first time in decades, Germany is not pushing any arms-control initiative with respect to European security – perhaps the clearest indication that it is 'getting real' about European deterrence to prepare for a possible US pullback from Europe.

The Franco-German vector

Behind closed doors in Berlin, much of the discussion has revolved around the French nuclear deterrent and France's relationship to European and NATO defence. Like Merkel, Scholz has been cautious about responding to Macron's nuclear siren calls, to Paris's frustration. The differences are partly matters of style: Macron is dramatic and abrupt, Scholz reserved and deliberate. The French would still like to see a heightened sense of urgency on nuclear topics in Berlin, while the Germans want to pursue these topics slowly – perhaps not at all if Harris wins the US election.

German officials appear unconvinced that Paris can muster the political will to change long-standing biases and practices that cut against a generalised European nuclear deterrent. France's relationship with NATO has customarily been rocky, whereas Germany is steadfastly dedicated to the Alliance's existing structures. Some in Berlin also believe that France's nuclear doctrine of strict sufficiency is too restrained to credibly deter Russia and wonder whether France could really bring itself to reconsider it. Finally, there is a growing realisation among German policymakers and analysts that European nuclear deterrence is a critical issue not only for France and Germany, but also for the UK, especially given the possibility that French leadership itself could become pointedly disengaged from European security.[68]

Germany remains conservative on nuclear-deterrence issues, but its principles have become less rigid. In particular, arms-control diplomacy has been quietly buried for the time being. Whether German leaders will seek to revive it, perhaps in a European-only context, remains to be seen.

A significant US disengagement from European security would test the boundaries of German nuclear principles and make Berlin more receptive to alternative viewpoints than it has ever been.

– Ulrich Kühn

Comparing French, British and German perspectives on future European deterrence yields several insights. For one, neither French nor British nuclear forces, individually or in combination, could compensate for full US disengagement from Europe. Paris and London are fully aware of this fact. While there are options that could produce a viable European nuclear deterrent, they would require a degree of national flexibility and European financial support that is currently difficult to imagine. This reality check should give European nuclear hawks pause. Starting small, France and the UK could enhance their practical deterrence cooperation. In parallel, Germany and perhaps Poland could set up a four-way discussion platform. Meanwhile, below the nuclear level, a shared sense of the necessity for stronger conventional deterrence for the continent will continue to intensify. Better coordination between Berlin, London and Paris is urgently needed, and they need to net in other capitals. Arms control and disarmament remain shared European goals, but they have become increasingly remote. Given their international standing, the three countries have a responsibility to try to sustain the viability of those goals even under difficult circumstances.

Notes

1   'The Future of European Security – Speech by President Emmanuel Macron', Stockholm, 30 January 2024, Försvarshögskolan, YouTube.com, 30 January 2024, https://www.youtube.com/watch?v=9utMpXOnMmA.

2   See Georges-Henri Soutou, *L'Alliance incertaine: Les rapports politico-stratégiques franco-allemands, 1954–1996* [The uncertain alliance: Franco-German politico-strategic relations, 1954–1996] (Paris: Fayard, 1996).

3   See Céline Jurgensen, 'L'Europe, la France et la dissuasion nucléaire' [Europe, France, and nuclear deterrence], *Revue Défense Nationale*, no. 821, June 2019, pp. 56–68.

4   Élysée, 'Speech of the President of the Republic on the Defence and Deterrence Strategy', 7 February

2020, https://www.elysee.fr/en/emmanuel-macron/2020/02/07/speech-of-the-president-of-the-republic-on-the-defense-and-deterrence-strategy.

5   Shortly after Russia's full-scale invasion of Ukraine, Putin ominously warned Western countries that if they intervened in the conflict, they would 'face consequences greater than any [they had] faced in history', clearly alluding to nuclear weapons. See, for example, Catherine Philp and Tom Parfitt, 'Putin Threatens West with "Greatest Consequences in History" if It Interferes in Ukraine', *The Times*, 24 February 2022, https://www.thetimes.com/world/russia-ukraine-war/article/putin-threatens-west-with-greatest-consequences-in-history-if-it-interferes-in-ukraine-d8lthd2ov.

6   See Jérémy Bachelier et al., 'Strategic Signaling: A Lever for France in the Competition Between Powers?', IFRI *Focus stratégique*, no. 114, May 2023, https://www.ifri.org/en/publications/etudes-de-lifri/focus-strategique/strategic-signaling-lever-france-competition-between.

7   See, for instance, François Heisbourg, 'Planning for a Post-American Europe', *Survival*, vol. 66, no. 3, June–July 2024, pp. 7–20.

8   Élysée, 'Speech of the President, 7 February 2020'. In 2022, an Italian refuelling plane participated in one of the nuclear *Poker* exercises, which the French air force holds four times a year.

9   See Hans M. Kristensen, Matt Korda and Eliana Johns, 'French Nuclear Weapons, 2023', *Bulletin of the Atomic Scientists*, vol. 79, no. 4, 2023, pp. 272–81.

10 See, for example, Bastien Lachaud and Aurélien Saintoul, 'Emmanuel Macron a tort. La dissuasion nucléaire ne se partage pas' [Emmanuel Macron is wrong. Nuclear deterrence cannot be shared], La France Insoumise, 1 February 2024, https://lafranceinsoumise.fr/2024/02/01/emmanuel-macron-a-tort-la-dissuasion-nucleaire-ne-se-partage-pas/.

11 See Bruno Tertrais, 'La politique de dissuasion nucléaire française' [French nuclear-deterrence policy], Vie Publique, 27 July 2022, https://www.vie-publique.fr/parole-dexpert/285856-la-politique-de-dissuasion-nucleaire-francaise-defense-budget.

12 See Hans M. Kristensen et al., 'Nuclear Weapons Sharing, 2023', *Bulletin of the Atomic Scientists*, vol. 79, no. 6, 2023, pp. 393–406.

13 Pierre Haroche, 'La doctrine nucléaire de la France pourrait assumer plus directement sa mission européenne' [France's nuclear doctrine could take on its European mission more directly], *Le Monde*, 16 February 2024, https://www.lemonde.fr/idees/article/2024/02/16/pierre-haroche-specialiste-en-securite-la-doctrine-nucleaire-de-la-france-pourrait-assumer-plus-directement-sa-mission-europeenne_6216875_3232.html.

14 See Anne Genetet, 'Recommandations du rapport d'information en conclusion des travaux d'une mission d'information sur les enjeux, rôle et stratégie d'influence de la France dans l'OTAN' [Recommendations of the information report concluding the work of a fact-finding mission on the issues, role and strategy of France's influence in NATO], National Assembly, 22 May 2024, https://www.assemblee-nationale.fr/dyn/16/rapports/cion_def/l16b2651_rapport-information.

15 See '"Effet Trump": la dissuasion nucléaire française n'est pas suffisante pour l'Allemagne' [The 'Trump effect': the French nuclear deterrent is not enough for Germany], *Courrier International*, 15 February 2024, https://www.courrierinternational.com/article/europe-effet-trump-la-dissuasion-nucleaire-francaise-n-est-pas-suffisante-pour-l-allemagne.

16 See Christian Lindner, 'Europa muss an nuklearer Abschreckung festhalten' [Europe must maintain nuclear deterrence], *Frankfurter Allgemeine Zeitung*, 14 February 2024, https://www.faz.net/aktuell/politik/inland/christian-lindner-europa-muss-an-nuklearer-abschreckung-festhalten-19516582.html.

17 See President of the Republic of Poland, 'Wywiad Prezydenta RP dla francuskiego kanału telewizyjnego LCI' [Interview by the president of the Republic of Poland for the French television channel LCI], 26 February 2024, https://www.prezydent.pl/aktualnosci/wypowiedzi-prezydenta-rp/wywiady/wywiad-prezydenta-rp-francuski-kanal-telewizyjny-lci,81851.

18 See Alastair Buchan, 'The Multilateral Force: A Study in Alliance Politics', *International Affairs*, vol. 4, no. 13, October 1964, pp. 619–37.

19 See David Pappalardo, 'Does France Really Have a Problem with the Concept of Integrated Deterrence?', Réseau d'analyse stratégique, 30 January 2024, https://ras-nsa.ca/does-france-really-have-a-problem-with-the-concept-of-integrated-deterrence/.

20 See Lee Ferran, 'Let It Go (Long): France Joins Germany, Italy and Poland in New ELSA Long-range Missile Project', *Breaking Defense*, 12 July 2024, https://breakingdefense.com/2024/07/let-it-go-long-france-joins-germany-italy-and-poland-in-new-elsa-long-range-missile-project/.

21 See UK Government, 'The Future of the United Kingdom's Nuclear Deterrent', Cm6994, December 2006, https://assets.publishing.service.gov.uk/media/5a78ebe3e5274a277e690804/DefenceWhitePaper2006_Cm6994.pdf.

22 See Claire Mills, 'Replacing the UK's Strategic Nuclear Deterrent: Progress of the Dreadnought Class', House of Commons Library Research Briefing, 3 May 2023, p. 9, https://researchbriefings.files.parliament.uk/documents/CBP-8010/CBP-8010.pdf.

23 See Sebastien Roblin, 'A Royal Navy Nuclear Sub Just Spent 6 Months Underwater. That's Irresponsible', *Popular Mechanics*, 26 September 2023, https://www.popularmechanics.com/military/navy-ships/a45279628/royal-navy-nuclear-sub-completes-record-6-month-patrol/.

24 See William Alberque, 'The UK's Trident Launch Failure: A Cause for Concern?', IISS Online Analysis, 28 March 2024, https://www.iiss.org/online-analysis/online-analysis/2024/03/the-uks-trident-launch-failure-a-cause-for-concern/.

25 See Defence Nuclear Enterprise, 'Delivering the UK's Nuclear Deterrent as a National Endeavour', CP 1058, 25 March 2024, https://assets.publishing.service.gov.uk/media/6622702b49d7b8813ba7e576/Defence_Nuclear_Enterprise_Command_Paper_v6.pdf.

26 Labour Party, 'Change: Labour Party Manifesto 2024', p. 15, https://labour.

org.uk/wp-content/uploads/2024/06/
Labour-Party-manifesto-2024.pdf.

27 Milan Dinic, 'Part Five – The Nuclear
Dilemma: Britons on Weapons of
Mass Destruction', YouGov, 24 May
2024, https://yougov.co.uk/politics/
articles/49521-part-five-the-nuclear-
dilemma-britons-on-weapons-of-
mass-destruction.

28 The number is fairly fluid, and really
depends on how the question is
phrased. See Ben Clements, *British
Public Opinion on Foreign and
Defence Policy: 1945–2017* (London:
Routledge, 2018).

29 See, for example, Malcolm Chalmers,
'Bracing for 2025: The UK and
European Security Under a Trump
Presidency', RUSI Occasional Paper,
March 2024, https://static.rusi.org/
bracing-for-2025-security-under-
trump.pdf.

30 For an insightful assessment, see
Nuclear Information Service, 'US–
UK Mutual Defence Agreement: A
Nuclear Information Service Briefing',
July 2024, https://www.nuclearinfo.
org/wp-content/uploads/2024/07/
MDA-Briefing-digital.pdf.

31 UK *Trident* submarines are required
to regularly visit the US naval base at
King's Bay, Georgia, to return their
missiles to the US stockpile for maintenance and replace them with others.
For more on the UK's dependency
on the United States for its nuclear
capability, see Select Committee on
Defence, 'Annex B: UK's Trident
System Not Truly Independent', 7
March 2006, https://publications.
parliament.uk/pa/cm200506/cmselect/
cmdfence/986/986we13.htm; and Jake
Wallis Simons, 'How Washington

Owns the UK's Nukes', *Politico*, 30
April 2015, https://www.politico.eu/
article/uk-trident-nuclear-program/.

32 See Michael Hersh, 'Trump's Plan
for NATO Is Emerging', *Politico*,
2 July 2024, https://www.politico.
com/news/magazine/2024/07/02/
nato-second-trump-term-00164517.

33 See Zachary B. Wolf, 'Congress Acted
to Protect NATO. But It Might Not
Be Enough to Stop Trump', CNN, 13
February 2024, https://edition.cnn.
com/2024/02/13/politics/congress-
trump-nato-what-matters/index.html.

34 See UK Government, 'National
Security Strategy and the Strategic
Defence and Security Review 2015:
A Secure and Prosperous United
Kingdom', Cm 9161, November 2015,
https://assets.publishing.service.
gov.uk/media/5a74c796ed915d502
d6caefc/52309_Cm_9161_NSS_SD_
Review_web_only.pdf.

35 For a searching discussion, see
Lawrence Freedman, 'The Russo-
Ukrainian War and the Durability of
Deterrence', *Survival*, vol. 65, no. 6,
December 2023–January 2024, pp. 7–36.

36 See James Cameron, 'How to
Decode Putin's Nuclear Warnings',
Washington Post, 19 October 2022,
https://www.washingtonpost.
com/politics/2022/09/22/
russia-putin-nuclear-threat-nato/.

37 See Andrew Futter, 'UK Nuclear
Weapons in a Third Nuclear
Age', European Leadership
Network, 18 February 2022, https://
europeanleadershipnetwork.org/
commentary/uk-nuclear-weapons-in-
a-third-nuclear-age/.

38 See Helen Warrell and Sylvia Pfeifer,
'UK Nuclear Warhead Increase

Prompted by Russia's Missile Defence Capability', *Financial Times*, 21 March 2021, https://www.ft.com/content/a86e8ca8-365e-4774-b22c-fbdf12237935.

39 See UK Government, 'Global Britain in a Competitive Age: The Integrated Review of Security, Defence, Development and Foreign Policy', CP 403, March 2021, https://assets.publishing.service.gov.uk/media/60644e4bd3bf7f0c91eababd/Global_Britain_in_a_Competitive_Age-_the_Integrated_Review_of_Security__Defence__Development_and_Foreign_Policy.pdf.

40 Hans M. Kristensen and Matt Korda, 'United Kingdom Nuclear Weapons, 2021', *Bulletin of the Atomic Scientists*, vol. 77, no. 3, May 2021, pp. 153–8.

41 See Nick Childs, 'The AUKUS Anvil: Promise and Peril', *Survival*, vol. 65, no. 5, October–November 2023, pp. 7–24.

42 See Council on Geostrategy, 'How Could the UK Augment Its Nuclear Forces?', *Britain's World*, 28 March 2024, https://www.geostrategy.org.uk/britains-world/how-could-the-uk-augment-its-nuclear-forces/.

43 This option was examined and rejected in the 2013 Trident Alternatives Review. See UK Government, 'Trident Alternatives Review', 16 July 2013, https://assets.publishing.service.gov.uk/media/5a7c65b1e5274a7ee2567320/20130716_Trident_Alternatives_Study.pdf.

44 See UN, 'Treaty on the Final Settlement with Respect to Germany (with Agreed Minute)', 12 September 1990, https://treaties.un.org/doc/Publication/UNTS/Volume%201696/volume-1696-I-29226-English.pdf.

45 See National Security Archive, 'History of the Custody and Deployment of Nuclear Weapons (U), July 1945 through September 1977', February 1978, Electronic Briefing Book no. 20, p. 246, https://nsarchive2.gwu.edu/news/19991020/history-of-custody.pdf.

46 See Philip Oltermann, '"Regrettable": Germany Reacts to Trump Plan to Withdraw US Troops', *Guardian*, 6 June 2020, https://www.theguardian.com/world/2020/jun/06/regrettable-germany-reacts-to-trump-plan-to-withdraw-us-troops.

47 Federal Government of Germany, 'Policy Statement by Olaf Scholz, Chancellor of the Federal Republic of Germany and Member of the German Bundestag', 27 February 2022, https://www.bundesregierung.de/breg-en/news/policy-statement-by-olaf-scholz-chancellor-of-the-federal-republic-of-germany-and-member-of-the-german-bundestag-27-february-2022-in-berlin-2008378.

48 See Ulrich Kühn, Tristan A. Volpe and Bert Thompson, 'Tracking the German Nuclear Debate', Carnegie Endowment for International Peace, 5 March 2020, http://carnegieendowment.org/2017/09/07/tracking-german-nuclear-debate-pub-72884.

49 See Tobias Bunde, 'Nuclear Zeitenwende(n): Germany and NATO's Nuclear Posture', in Ulrich Kühn (ed.), *Germany and Nuclear Weapons in the 21st Century: Atomic Zeitenwende?* (Abingdon: Routledge, 2024), p. 87.

50 See Michal Onderco, 'German Public Opinion on Nuclear Weapons: Before and After Russia's Invasion of Ukraine', in Kühn, *Germany and*

Nuclear Weapons in the 21st Century,
pp. 136–54.

[51] See Bunde, 'Nuclear Zeitenwende(n)',
pp. 100–1.

[52] See Onderco, 'German Public Opinion
on Nuclear WWeapons', pp. 141–6.

[53] See Kjølv Egeland and Benoît
Pelopidas, 'European Nuclear
Weapons? Zombie Debates and
Nuclear Realities', *European Security,*
vol. 30, no. 2, 2021, pp. 237–58; and
Tristan A. Volpe and Ulrich Kühn,
'Germany's Nuclear Education: Why
a Few Elites Are Testing a Taboo',
Washington Quarterly, vol. 40, no. 3,
Winter 2017, pp. 7–27.

[54] For an overview, see Barbara Kunz
and Ulrich Kühn, 'German Musings
About a Franco-German or German
Bomb', in Kühn, *Germany and Nuclear
Weapons in the 21st Century,* pp. 112–35.

[55] See Lindner, 'Europa muss an nuklearer Abschreckung festhalten'.

[56] See Jochen Buchsteiner and Morten
Freidel, 'Die Angst vor der eigenen
Bombe' [The fear of one's own bomb],
Frankfurter Allgemeine Sonntagszeitung,
25 February 2024, https://www.
faz.net/aktuell/politik/inland/
deutschland-diskutiert-ueber-eigene-
nukleare-abschreckung-19540981.html.

[57] Quoted in Justin Huggler, 'Merkel
Forced to Deny Germany Planning
to Lead a European Nuclear
Superpower', *Telegraph,* 9 February
2017, http://www.telegraph.co.uk/
news/2017/02/09/merkel-forced-deny-
germany-planning-lead-european-
nuclear-superpower/.

[58] Quoted in 'Kanzler Scholz gegen
eigenen europäischen Atomschirm'
[Chancellor Scholz against own
European nuclear umbrella], *Der

Spiegel,* 16 February 2024, https://www.
spiegel.de/politik/deutschland/olaf-
scholz-gegen-einen-europaeischen-
atomschirm-a-b88c1513-c633-4e8d-
8882-87a2262f1dbc.

[59] See Onderco, 'German Public Opinion
on Nuclear Weapons'.

[60] See Toby Dalton, Karl Friedhoff and
Lami Kim, 'Thinking Nuclear: South
Korean Attitudes on Nuclear Weapons',
Chicago Council on Global Affairs, 21
February 2022, https://globalaffairs.
org/research/public-opinion-survey/
thinking-nuclear-south-korean-
attitudes-nuclear-weapons.

[61] See, for instance, Dustin Dehez, 'Yes,
Germany Is Free Riding on American
Security', *War on the Rocks,* 8 July 2015,
https://warontherocks.com/2015/07/
yes-germany-is-free-riding-on-
american-security/.

[62] Federal Ministry of Defence
of Germany, 'Bericht zur
Materiellen Einsatzbereitschaft der
Hauptwaffensysteme der Bundeswehr
2019' [Report on the operational
readiness of the Bundeswehr's
main weapon systems 2019], http://
www.verteidigungsministerium.
de/resource/blob/161576/80e0c3e58
6ef5fcef147304961048234/20191205-
download-bericht-zur-
materiellen-einsatzbereitschaft-
der-hauptwaffensysteme-der-
bundeswehr-2019-data.pdf.
Translation by Ulrich Kühn.

[63] See Jana Puglierin, 'Turning Point or
Turning Back: German Defence Policy
After *Zeitenwende*', European Council
on Foreign Relations, 19 March 2024,
https://ecfr.eu/article/turning-point-or-
turning-back-german-defence-policy-
after-zeitenwende/.

64   Federal Government of Germany,
     'Robust. Resilient. Sustainable.
     Integrated Security for Germany.
     National Security Strategy',
     June 2023, https://www.
     nationalesicherheitsstrategie.de/
     National-Security-Strategy-EN.pdf.
65   The first move produced technical crit-
     icism, as the *Arrow* 3 can only defend
     against a very limited spectrum of
     Russian missiles, and the second
     political friction, because Germany
     passed up French-made air-defence
     systems. See Lydia Wachs, 'Russian
     Missiles and the European Sky Shield
     Initiative', SWP Comment 2023 C/45, 3
     August 2023, https://www.swp-berlin.
     org/publikation/russian-missiles-and-
     the-european-sky-shield-initiative.
66   See Alexander Graef and Tim Thies,
     'Missiles on the Move: Why US Long-
     range Missiles in Germany Are Just

the Tip of the Iceberg', *Bulletin of the
Atomic Scientists*, 12 August 2024, https://
thebulletin.org/2024/08/missiles-on-the-
move-why-us-long-range-missiles-in-
germany-are-just-the-tip-of-the-iceberg/.
67   See Federal Government of Germany,
     '"Security for the Freedom of Our
     Lives": Speech by Federal Foreign
     Minister Annalena Baerbock at the
     Event to Launch the Development
     of a National Security Strategy',
     18 March 2022, https://www.
     auswaertiges-amt.de/en/newsroom/
     news/baerbock-national-security-
     strategy/2517790.
68   See Joschka Fischer, 'The Great
     Revision', Project Syndicate, 31
     March 2023, https://www.project-
     syndicate.org/commentary/
     russia-war-means-europe-
     transforming-and-global-order-
     realigning-by-joschka-fischer-2023-03.

Copyright © 2024 The International Institute for Strategic Studies

The War in Ukraine and Russia's Quest to Reshape the World Order

Jeffrey Mankoff

While Russia's desire to conquer territory and destroy Ukrainian identity is undeniable, Moscow is using the war in Ukraine primarily to advance its vision of a different international order. Russian President Vladimir Putin has stated that 'the Ukraine crisis is not a territorial conflict ... It is about the principles on which the new international order will be based.'[1] Leaders of major Western states tend to agree.[2] Given these stakes, understanding how Russia views the existing global order and envisions transforming it is strategically indispensable.

Moscow foresees a world fragmented into spheres of influence centred on a handful of 'civilisational states' embodying distinct political and historical cultures that are not necessarily compatible with liberalism and democracy. Russia is using its own sphere of influence in Eurasia as the incubator of an alternative set of norms and institutions that it seeks to socialise globally. This Russian programme appeals to other revisionist powers, notably China and Iran, which support Russia's war in Ukraine largely out of a desire to diminish US influence and consolidate their own regional spheres. Elements of it also appeal across the Global South, now a key arena for competition over the future world order.[3]

Jeffrey Mankoff is a Distinguished Research Fellow at National Defense University's Institute for National Strategic Studies and a Non-Resident Senior Associate at the Center for Strategic and International Studies (CSIS). He is the author of *Empires of Eurasia: How Imperial Legacies Shape International Security* (Yale University Press, 2022) and *Russian Foreign Policy: The Return of Great Power Politics* (Rowman & Littlefield, 2012). The views expressed in this article do not reflect the official policy or position of the National Defense University, the US Department of Defense or the US government.

Survival | vol. 66 no. 5 | October–November 2024 | pp. 99–126   https://doi.org/10.1080/00396338.2024.2403219

Driving Russia's long-standing critique of the liberal international order is its view that the world that emerged in 1991 did not take Russian interests into account and does not reflect Russian priorities.[4] By the mid-1990s, Russian officials were bristling against the expectation that Moscow should be incorporated into the '"civilized world" but as a second-rate power' – an approach they feared would degrade Russia's sovereignty and its inherited status as a great power.[5] As Putin noted in 2023, the United States and its partners believed that the new world 'would be built by those who declared themselves victors in the Cold War, in effect assuming that Russia was prepared to follow in someone else's wake'.[6] The influential scholar and Kremlin adviser Sergey Karaganov likewise characterised the post-1991 settlement as a 'Versailles peace in velvet gloves'.[7]

Putin has called for a more 'democratic world order without dividing lines and discrimination' from the beginning of his time as president in 2000.[8] Subsequent economic growth and political stabilisation reinforced Russian demands for more influence. Since the onset of the global economic crisis in 2007–08, Russian analysts have stressed the rise of new centres of economic and political power, along with a narrative of Western decline. Yet as a diminished power still angling for acceptance by the West, Russia has until recently been unable to articulate a credible alternative.

Putin's return to the Russian presidency in 2012 and the annexation of Crimea less than two years later cemented a rupture between Russia and the West that prompted the Kremlin to adopt a more openly revisionist posture. Observers remained divided, though, about the nature and extent of Russia's revisionist challenge.[9] Some portrayed Moscow as out-and-out revanchist. Others characterised its agenda as more limited and circumscribed, noting that Moscow valued some pillars of the existing system, including the United Nations Security Council, the then-existing arms-control framework and financial globalisation.[10] Some analysts questioned whether the 'revisionist' label even applied, suggesting Russia might instead be defending itself from an aggressive West, or acting as what Elias Götz and Camille-Renaud Merlen call an 'aggressive isolationist' power.[11]

With the full-scale invasion of Ukraine in February 2022, Russia embraced an aggressive form of revisionism. In the process, Russia has aligned itself with fellow revisionist powers such as Iran and North Korea, as well as – in a more qualified way – China, in an effort to overhaul the principles, rules and institutions underlying the putative international system.[12] Key to this effort is the belief that, as the influential Russian analyst Fyodor Lukyanov suggests, 'the era of universal organisations has passed, the trend is for more focused differentiation by regions and interests'.[13] Today, Russia values legacy institutions like the UN, but has become more outspoken in criticising them while calling for a 'future world order … built through mutual deterrence and dialogue between leading powers', abandoning 'the universalism of communism, liberalism, and other isms'.[14]

Russia is collaborating with other revisionist, expansionist states to promote regional spheres of influence. It has adapted the process of Eurasian integration to reduce its exposure to Western-centric institutions and socialise illiberal norms on issues such as information, cyber security and sexuality while supporting transnational illiberal networks to promote them.[15] Russian thinkers and analysts favour loose, non-exclusive and value-neutral bodies BRICS and the Shanghai Cooperation Organisation (SCO) as alternatives to Western multilateralism and models for a wider post-Western international order. These objectives, though far from realised, indicate the scale of Moscow's ambitions to undermine Western global leadership, consolidate regional supremacy in Eurasia, and reshape international norms and institutions.

Putin's return and Russia's revisionist pivot

For much of the period between Boris Yeltsin's second term (1996–99) as Russian president and Putin's return to power in 2012, Russia objected to the assertion that it had no choice but to join a Western-designed and -led international order as a subordinate actor. Moscow struggled, however, to articulate an alternative vision.[16] Instead, it sought to justify its actions within the order's normative frameworks, reproach the West for inconsistency, and secure the right to interpret these norms alongside the United States and its partners.[17] Western scholars and policymakers generally assumed that it would 'accept the global order's liberal characteristics' even if it sought to change 'the hierarchy that undergirds the system'.[18]

A more comprehensive alternative emerged after Putin's return to the Kremlin in May 2012 amid widespread protests in Russia that were blamed on Western interference. Driving Moscow's embrace of this vision was an ideological turn in Russian politics, with Putin cultivating the idea of Russia as a distinct civilisation alien to Western intellectual and political models. While not an all-encompassing intellectual system like Marxism–Leninism, this framework drew on traditional polemics about Russia's identity and role in the world.[19] It involved a renewed emphasis on Russian history and culture, including the centrality of the Orthodox Church and its version of 'traditional values', as well as historical continuity between the Russian Federation and its imperial and Soviet predecessors as justification for maintaining a sphere of influence beyond Russian borders.

Putin dropped all references to Russia's 'European choice'

While Yeltsin, Putin and Dmitry Medvedev, who served as president from 2008 to 2012, had at times recognised a Russian *Sonderweg* – that is, a 'special path' – they consistently described Russia as a European state. After 2012, however, Putin dropped all references to Russia's 'European choice' and deliberately played up 'Eurasia' as a distinct geographical and ideological pole.[20] This characterisation of Russia as a civilisation apart implied 'the total rejection of universalism, the great dream of Western writers', as well as a break from the prevailing discourse of the 1990s and 2000s that portrayed Russia as an aspiring member of the West.[21] It implied too that Russia had more in common with other self-proclaimed civilisational states like China, India or Iran than with the nation-states of Europe, whose sovereignty was, from Russia's perspective, compromised by their dependence on Washington.

The Kremlin's new ideological framework stressed the supremacy of the state and therefore defined the objectives of politics according to *raison d'état* rather than liberal principles. The elevation of the state marginalised alternative actors, including transnational corporations and non-governmental organisations. It also effectively elevated sovereignty as the key feature of order-forming states. Russian officials suggest that only states with the ability to make decisions independently of the United States are truly sovereign and worthy of participating in the elaboration of a new order.[22] Another key concept is justice.[23] Portraying the current world order as unjust enables Russia to align itself with some non-Western states that perceive Western power and influence as inequitable.

Despite these developments, the Kremlin professed to being interested in a modus vivendi with the West as long as it observed Moscow's red lines: not interfering in domestic politics, coordinating involvement in the former Soviet Union and allowing Russia to act as a rule-maker for global governance. Moscow presented its opposition to Western domination of global order in political rather than civilisational terms, and therefore as resolvable through normal political and diplomatic interaction.[24] While Moscow repeatedly vetoed US-led efforts in the UN Security Council that Washington hoped would bring an end to the Syrian civil war, it portrayed its military intervention in Syria as consistent with international law and the UN Charter insofar as Syrian President Bashar al-Assad's government had consented to Russian intervention. Russia hoped that its intervention would chasten the United States into re-embracing this state-centric version of international law while reinforcing an international norm prioritising strong states over efforts to spread democracy.[25] As late as autumn 2021, Russia's submission of draft security agreements to the US and NATO suggested a theoretical openness to resuming dialogue about the construction of a more consensual framework for European security – but only in the unlikely event that the US and NATO accepted Moscow's demands to roll back their strategic perimeter in Europe to where it lay in the mid-1990s, before the first round of NATO expansion.

With its 2022 invasion of Ukraine, Russia violated what G. John Ikenberry calls the 'holy trinity' of the liberal international order: not annexing another state's territory, not deliberately killing civilians and not threatening the use of nuclear weapons.[26] The war also accelerated the transition from a world based on a shared understanding of the international rules of the road to one defined by great-power competition.[27] Russian officials have celebrated these developments.[28] Since 2022, Russian think tanks and scholars have also focused on order as a topic of study. Their main point is that the era of Western hegemony – including not only post-Cold War Western pre-eminence but also 'systems and orders developed since the mid-17th century' – is over and that the ensuing instability is the result of a competition between incompatible visions of the future.[29]

Whereas earlier Russian analysis called for a new era of multipolarity, much of it now questions the very concept of polarity, noting that attributes of power are shifting and more widely distributed than in previous eras. The 2023 Valdai Discussion Club annual report speaks of moving beyond today's 'asynchronous multipolarity' towards a future based on a 'dynamic equilibrium' or 'pluralistic multipolarity' in which 'hierarchy will either not exist at all or will be extremely blurred, even where preconditions for maintaining it exist'.[30]

At the same time, the retreat from globalisation is placing renewed emphasis on regions as crucial factors in international affairs, highlighting the role of large civilisational states as drivers of regional integration – effectively, as builders of spheres of influence.[31] According to the Russian narrative, civilisational states and the regions they dominate each have their own historical and cultural identity, and do not share common values. The ascent of liberal principles after the Cold War stemmed from now-faded Western political, economic, military and cultural hegemony. Heterogeneity and the wide distribution of economic, political and military power mean that any future international order cannot be based on the diffusion or imposition of liberal principles.[32] And while Russian thinkers reject the idea of hierarchy at the global level, they maintain a hierarchical view of relations among states within a particular region, justifying the invasion of Ukraine through historical–cultural links and the claim to a sphere of influence in the former Soviet Union. They similarly emphasise the responsibility of regional stakeholders, rather than Western states or Western-backed multilateral organisations, for managing conflicts. Russia thus prefers working with neighbouring powers through informal mechanisms such as the Astana Process in Syria and the South Caucasus 3+3 to push for an illiberal peace while excluding Western influence.

A shifting approach to global governance

Russia's revisionism is evident in the evolution of its approach to the pillars of the post-Second World War order that it long prioritised, including the UN and the US–Russia arms-control regime. Both were products of Moscow's post-Second World War superpower status that the new Russian Federation sought to maintain to support its ongoing claim to global privilege. In the context of intensifying confrontation with the US, Russia's embrace of the UN and arms control has become more conditional owing to its perception that the West has weaponised them.

Moscow has long taken Washington to task for disregarding the authority of the UN, especially through its unilateral use of force and interference in other countries' internal affairs.[33] Putin noted at the 70th anniversary meeting of the UN General Assembly in 2015 that Russia believes such actions are 'illegitimate and contradict the Charter of the United Nations'.[34] Despite Russia's emphasis on the Security Council as the font of international legitimacy, Moscow has of course often acted without resort to the Security Council or adherence to UN norms in pursuit of its own interests, notably with its invasions of neighbouring Georgia and Ukraine. Moscow has justified these violations by pointing to what it claimed were analogous violations by Western powers, suggesting that the rules themselves were not wrong but that their implementation should be more consistent.[35] What Putin considered perhaps the most egregious example of Western powers doing an end-run around the Security Council was NATO's 2011 intervention in Libya. While then-president Medvedev had overruled his security chiefs to abstain on a resolution authorising 'all necessary measures' to protect civilians from Libyan ruler Muammar Gadhafi's vengeance, Putin later claimed that NATO had exceeded its mandate by becoming a party to the conflict and contributing to Gadhafi's ouster and murder.[36]

Russia has since grown more critical of the UN, even as its official statements have continued to refer to the UN as the cornerstone of a just world order. Seeking to dilute Western influence in the Security Council, Moscow has called for admitting new members while insisting that they maintain their 'own view of the world and the ability to be independent', which means they need not be aligned with the West.[37] It has a similar position with respect to reforming the International Monetary Fund and World Bank.[38]

Russia has lined up with China and other authoritarian states to push for the adoption of illiberal norms within other UN bodies, leading efforts to get the UN Human Rights Council (UNHRC) to recognise the protection of 'traditional values' as a pillar of the global human-rights regime. In 2017, Moscow supported a Chinese-sponsored UNHRC resolution pushing for a development-centric model of human rights and affirming the Chinese concept of a 'community of shared future' as a contribution to global governance.[39] Russia likewise voiced support at the UN for China's Global Development Initiative as a contribution to a 'truly equitable and multipolar world order'.[40]

Moscow nevertheless opposes the Security Council's ceding its role as the arbiter of international legitimacy to other bodies in which Western influence would be even stronger. In particular, Moscow contrasts the idea of legality rooted in decisions of the Security Council with the US notion of a broader rules-based order that privileges democracy and liberal values.[41] Russia's 2023 Foreign Policy Concept claims that 'the concept of a rules-based world order is fraught with the destruction of the international legal system and other dangerous consequences for humanity'.[42]

Russia's approach to the nuclear and other arms-control regimes that originated in the Cold War has similarly evolved. For much of the post-Soviet era, Moscow positioned itself as a proponent of the status quo and condemned US efforts to bypass or withdraw from agreements such as the 1972 Anti-Ballistic Missile (ABM) Treaty. It rejected US accusations that it was conducting missile tests violating the Intermediate-Range Nuclear Forces (INF) Treaty and called for a politically binding moratorium (which the US rejected) to replace the treaty when the US withdrew in 2019 over Russian violations.[43] While positioning itself as a responsible stakeholder within multilateral regimes and working with the United States to prevent Iran or North Korea from developing nuclear weapons, Russia criticised the United States' pursuit of unilateral sanctions and efforts to bypass the authority of the International Atomic Energy Agency.[44]

The war in Ukraine has shifted Russia's attitude towards the management of the nuclear balance with the United States and the broader non-proliferation agenda. A year into the war, Moscow announced it was suspending New START, its last bilateral arms-control treaty with the US. Moscow also stationed non-strategic nuclear weapons in Belarus, a move that mirrored US deployments in Europe but was at odds with Russia's long-standing position that such deployments represented a threat to the Nuclear Non-Proliferation Treaty. Moscow has now started to obstruct multilateral efforts to constrain the nuclear programmes of Iran and North Korea, vetoing a UN Security Council resolution to extend the work of an experts' group monitoring North Korea's nuclear programme.[45] Moscow also signed a defence pact with Pyongyang in June 2024, effectively accepting Kim Jong-un's regime as a legitimate partner and committing to assisting North Korea's military build-up. Furthermore, Russia has eroded the taboo on nuclear-weapons use by invoking that possibility against Ukraine or in response to foreign intervention in the conflict.[46] These steps suggest that Moscow is seeking to redefine the norms of nuclear governance on the basis of its status as a nuclear power rather than universal and inviolable standards.[47]

Eurasia and Russian dreams of empire

Russia's enduring pursuit of Eurasian integration has been both cause and consequence of the liberal international order's dilution. Throughout the post-Soviet era, Moscow has sought to build multilateral institutions throughout the former Soviet Union to consolidate its influence over neighbouring states and – especially since Putin's return to the Kremlin in 2012 – to lay the foundation of an alternative world order. This Eurasian order is based on different norms and principles. Above all, it is an imperial order, with Russia as a regional hegemon maintaining a hierarchical relationship over its smaller neighbours while implicitly threatening their sovereignty and territorial integrity. In theory, Russia's Eurasian order both insulates its participants against outside pressure and provides a platform for the implementation of alternative norms and institutions globally. Sergey Karaganov characterises this Russo-centric Eurasia as the hub of a new 'fairer and freer world of multipolarity and multiplicity of civilizations and cultures'.[48]

For much of the post-Soviet period, where Eurasia fit into Russian foreign policy was contested. Pro-Western liberals in the Yeltsin era wanted to jettison responsibility for the former Soviet region in favour of rapid integration with the West, but a strand of Russian thought persisted that promoted a different means for Russia to regain its global influence.[49]

For instance, Yevgeny Primakov, who served as Yeltsin's second foreign minister and challenged Putin for the presidency in 1999, argued that post-Soviet Eurasia was Russia's natural zone of influence and that Moscow should seek to limit Western penetration of the area. Under Medvedev, the Kremlin envisioned Eurasian integration that would develop 'harmonious, mutually reinforcing, and mutually advantageous cooperation with other countries, international economic groupings, and the European Union'.[50] In 2011, Putin described what he now called the Eurasian Union as 'a powerful supranational association capable of becoming one of the poles in the modern world and serving as an efficient bridge between Europe and the dynamic Asia- Pacific region'.[51] Putin portrayed the Eurasian Union as analogous to the European Union in its composition and designed to maintain bloc-to-bloc relations with it.

Above all, Moscow has envisioned Eurasian integration as a tool for preventing the loss of its smaller neighbours to the siren song of Euro-Atlantic integration. Moscow denigrated the EU's Eastern Partnership while pressuring states like Ukraine and Armenia to shelve their ambitions for Euro-Atlantic integration and join the Eurasian Economic Union (EAEU) instead. These competing integration processes were instrumental to the deterioration of relations between Moscow and the West and helped trigger the war in Ukraine.[52] Owing to the political, legal and economic incompatibility of Euro-Atlantic and Eurasian integration, Moscow recognised that states like Georgia and Ukraine that chose deeper integration with the EU and NATO would be more or less permanently excluded from the sphere of influence it sought to maintain in Eurasia. Starting with the 2008 invasion of Georgia, Moscow demonstrated that it was willing to use force to prevent former Soviet republics from leaving that sphere. In February 2022, the Kremlin gambled on an all-out invasion after Ukrainian President Volodymyr Zelenskyy began rooting out Russian influence and recommitting Kyiv to its Western course.

Moscow has more recently used Eurasian integration to institutionalise the civilisational divide between the West and the rest, reinforcing the claim that liberal norms and institutions are a product of the West's historical experience and therefore hold limited relevance for non-Western states. It is also a way for Russia to forge links with other Eurasian powers – China above all – for building new multilateral frameworks that embody non-liberal principles: a leaked Kremlin strategy document described the Sino-Russian Greater Eurasia Partnership as Russia's 'flagship foreign policy project'.[53] While the functional scope of these mechanisms remains limited, they are strategically important insofar as they challenge the Western monopoly on global governance and standards. Their geographic contiguity also creates opportunities. For example, it facilitates the establishment of transit routes linking Russia with other Eurasian powers and thereby insulating trade from outside sanctions.[54]

With war ongoing in Ukraine and the liberal international order under challenge, Russia is rendering its Eurasian order more openly imperial. Officials and analysts are making the historical and strategic case for Russia's territorial expansion.[55] After its 2008 invasion of Georgia, Russia supported the 'independence' of the breakaway regions of Abkhazia and South Ossetia, pointing to Western recognition of Kosovo as a precedent.[56] Russia has now de facto annexed Crimea and four partially occupied *oblasts* of eastern Ukraine. Since helping Belarusian President Alyaksandr Lukashenka quell protests against his rule in 2019, Russia has established a comprehensive protectorate over Belarus, which leaked Kremlin documents suggest Moscow aims to annex by 2030.[57]

Russia is rendering its Eurasian order more imperial

The war in Ukraine has further broadened the pretext for airing imperial ambitions.[58] Since February 2022, Russia has expanded its territorial threats against other post-Soviet states. Moscow has hinted it could now annex South Ossetia and Abkhazia, allowing it to build a new naval base on Abkhazia's Black Sea coast.[59] It has also floated the possibility of seizing Transnistria from Moldova, which would require further territorial conquests in Ukraine.[60]

Russia casts the alternative norms and values it is promoting as reflecting Eurasia's distinct historical development. Rhetoric about 'traditional values' and the harmful impact of LGBTQ+ propaganda has accompanied the promotion of Russian-backed institutions like the EAEU.[61] Russia-aligned parties have deployed such language in elections in several states.[62]

Activists have called for the EAEU to regulate the import of items 'that harm physical and psychological health' or 'moral and social development' of their children.[63] By instrumentalising anti-LGBTQ+ sentiment, Russia has curried favour with Eurasian and African governments, among others, which at times have rejected recognition of LGBTQ+ rights as a condition of participation in multilateral institutions.[64]

Russia and the new 'axis of revisionists'

As Russia has become increasingly severed from the West and Western-led multilateral institutions, it has made common cause with other revisionist states – particularly China, Iran and North Korea. While these states remain competitors for investment in energy markets and in their shared Eurasian neighbourhood, their mutual interest in bypassing sanctions and reducing Western influence has produced closer ties. All four states see the US-led order as constraining their power and ambitions.[65] The alignment among Moscow, Beijing, Tehran and Pyongyang is not an alliance, though it does have a military dimension, most visible in the assistance China, Iran and North Korea are providing for the Russian war effort in Ukraine. Nor are all four states equally committed to upending the global status quo; China, in particular, benefits from the post-1991 international order, leading many in Beijing to see Russian revanchism as excessive.[66]

Nevertheless, Russia's war in Ukraine has strengthened Moscow's bonds with these powers and enhanced the revisionist potential of their cooperation. Prior to Russia's invasion of Ukraine, the entente among Russia, China and Iran was largely performative.[67] Since then, Beijing, Tehran and Pyongyang have all made substantive contributions to the Russian war effort. Owing to Western sanctions and Russia's limited defence-industrial base, Iran has emerged as Russia's principal supplier of military drones and has set up training and technical assistance on drone production inside Russia.[68] North Korea has become Russia's largest supplier of artillery ammunition and ballistic missiles, among other military kit.[69] In return, Russia provides Iran and North Korea with hard currency and diplomatic support, impeding Western-led efforts to contain their nuclear programmes and supporting their ambitions for regional power projection.

Beijing's position is more complex. Regarding the Russia–Ukraine war, Chinese President Xi Jinping has stated that China is 'not at the origin, nor a party to it, nor a participant'.[70] Beijing is wary of actions that could subject it to US or European secondary sanctions. China has adopted a posture of 'pro-Russian neutrality' and refrained from providing lethal military assistance to Russia.[71] While echoing Russia's narrative about Western responsibility for the war, China has still taken advantage of Russia's isolation to advance its own commercial and strategic interests at Russia's expense.[72] Even so, Chinese companies have provided a lifeline for the Russian economy by boosting purchases of Russian hydrocarbons. They also provide Moscow with a wide range of dual-use goods including semiconductors, drone technology, nitrocellulose and machine tools for Russia's defence industry, and are moving towards joint development of new military systems.[73]

Politically, the three countries have aligned with Russia's revisionist campaign.[74] The SCO's admission of Iran as a full member in 2023, in particular, energised the organisation's function as a front against liberal norms and a bulwark of regime security.[75] Weeks before the invasion of Ukraine, Putin and Xi signed a joint declaration emphasising their shared commitment to a 'democratic' and 'multipolar' world order.[76] An updated May 2024 joint statement calls for 'a more just and stable multipolar world order'.[77] Similar language has arisen from meetings between Russian and Iranian officials. During Putin's visit to Tehran in summer 2022, the two countries agreed to craft a new strategic-partnership agreement in response to 'the unilateral actions of the West'.[78] In the past few years, the four states have converged around a normative critique of democracy coupled with an appeal to civilisational greatness to legitimate aggressive regional policies.[79] They have shared techniques for hobbling press freedom, enhancing surveillance and targeting foreign support for civil society.[80] Their respective strategic-communications campaigns involve mutual support for aggression against neighbouring states.[81]

To bypass legacy frameworks, Russia, China and, increasingly, Iran are developing a mosaic of institutions outside the framework of the liberal international order, including the SCO and BRICS. For lessons on weathering sanctions, Russia also has looked to Iran and North Korea, which have provided concrete instructions for obscuring beneficial ownership and using third parties to source foreign exchange.[82] Russia and China now commonly route transactions through their respective domestic payment systems, while Iran agreed in 2023 to link to Russia's Mir system.[83] A growing volume of trade is settled in national currencies. In the first half of 2023, around 75% of Sino-Russian trade and 25% of Russia's trade with third parties occurred in yuan.[84]

The contest for the 'world majority'

While Russia, Iran and China's rejection of democracy and embrace of civilisational rhetoric is in part a response to concerns about regime vulnerability, it is also an ideological tool they use to compete for influence within the international system.[85] Russian analysts pose what they refer to as the 'world majority' (*mirovoe bol'shinstvo*) against a privileged 'golden billion' (*zolotoy millyard*) residing primarily in the West. Russian officials and commentators locate this world majority in states that 'have no binding relationships with the United States and the organizations it patronizes' and that have resisted the 'sanctions tsunami' devised by the West since the invasion of Ukraine.[86] These states broadly constitute the Global South. Russia sees these states as potential partners in the 'joint creation of cooperation infrastructure … and an alternative system of international public goods' not controlled by the West.[87]

Moscow recognises that these states are 'companions' (*soratniki*) rather than allies, and that arguments for bandwagoning against the US-led international order have to be couched in terms of international balance and fairness.[88] Russia nevertheless has several advantages across the Global South, including ties with ruling elites dating to the Soviet era, a history of support for anti-colonial movements that helped obscure Russia's own history as a colonial empire, and a shared scepticism of the West's moral claims, now especially in light of American and European support for Israel's invasion of Gaza.[89] These assets have been notably useful in Sub-Saharan Africa, where Moscow has leveraged its anti-colonial legacy, preference for strong states and indifference to democratic principles to reinforce campaigns by military juntas in several states, most recently Niger, to drive out Western influence.

Prominent Russian commentators note that 'the vanguard of the world majority is the BRICS' and to an extent the SCO owing to 'their potential for making rules, setting standards, conducting policies, and creating institutions alternative to Western ones'.[90] These institutions are examples of what Russia's 2023 Foreign Policy Concept describes as 'multi-format partnerships to solve common problems' amid a 'crisis of the world order'.[91] Such bodies champion a regime-centric model of security, eschew the adoption of binding commitments and emphasise the norm of non-intervention and states' right to choose their own form of government. They also embody the kind of loose, issue-specific forms of cooperation that Russia has long promoted under the concept of 'network diplomacy' (*setovaya diplomatiya*), in contrast to the closed blocs with binding rules that make up much of the US-led international order.[92] While members of the SCO and BRICS are not all necessarily illiberal or anti-Western, they tend to be at least agnostic about liberal norms and to espouse a hard version of state sovereignty that rejects unsolicited interference in states' internal affairs.

Russia has long envisioned the SCO as the nucleus of a non-Western political order.[93] The SCO encourages the adoption of illiberal forms of cooperation, visible for instance in its commitment to fighting the 'three evils' of extremism, separatism and terrorism.[94] Through its engagement in Middle Eastern conflicts, the SCO has reinforced a preference for regional mechanisms rather than Western states or international organisations for conflict resolution.[95] The SCO has also adopted Russia's paradigm on ensuring information security, according to which states have the right to control flows of information on their territory.[96] Beijing's promotion of trade, transit, energy and supply-chain cooperation has been crucial to attracting new SCO members, but the group's expansion and diversification into new areas is reinforcing Moscow's ambition to turn the organisation into a rival platform for global governance.[97]

BRICS is more central than the SCO to advancing Russia's global ambitions. In Putin's thinking, Eurasia is an arena for Russian power and an incubator of alternative norms and institutions, and BRICS a complementary means for Russia to expand its global influence outside the West.[98] BRICS constitutes a model for the kind of loose cooperation free of binding political conditions that Moscow prizes. BRICS members are 'sovereignty hawks' who reject interference in their domestic affairs and aspire to greater autonomy.[99] They also are underrepresented in legacy international institutions and receptive to Russian calls for a more just global order. This convergence of views has made BRICS a key tool of Russia's strategy for resisting Western pressure over the war in Ukraine and for pressing Moscow's broader revisionist agenda. The BRICS states refused to impose sanctions on Russia over its invasion of Ukraine despite varying degrees of internal criticism of Russian actions, regarding Western calls to punish and isolate Russia as hypocritical, especially measured against Western policy on Gaza.[100]

According to a report prepared for Putin by three leading Russian policy analysts, BRICS 'is essentially a prototype for an organization of the new world order'.[101] Russia values BRICS as an open architecture that can coordinate the efforts of non-Western states on a functional basis without imposing binding commitments or the requirement of consensus. The Greater Eurasia Partnership, centred on Sino-Russian cooperation but open to other states and multilateral groupings, has a similar design.

International order after the Russia–Ukraine war

Russia's efforts to consolidate new norms and institutions have already transformed the international order in ways that will be hard to undo. Europe has undergone what German Chancellor Olaf Scholz termed a *Zeitenwende* or change of eras. Sanctions and counter-sanctions have reoriented trade flows and supply chains. Europe's success in weaning itself off Russian hydrocarbons is a major shift, girding European resolve to support Ukraine and accelerating the decoupling of a more Atlanticist Europe and a Russo-centric Eurasia. The EU is committed to Ukraine's and Georgia's membership, and NATO has remained open to it. With the impending expiration of New START, the US–Russia arms-control regime is moribund.

The deepening rift between Russia and the West has accelerated Russia's alignment with the other 'axis' states. Military and economic support has made China, Iran and North Korea into an 'arsenal of autocracy'.[102] They are supporting Moscow not because they are committed to the idea that Russians and Ukrainians are 'one people', as Putin asserts, but because they too favour a world that is less Western-centric, with more scope for regional powers to maintain spheres of influence. The war in Ukraine allows them to gauge Western responses to aggression while straining Western defence-industrial capacity. It stands to reason that Russian success in Ukraine could prompt kindred campaigns by China, Iran or North Korea.[103]

The war in Ukraine has also revealed that outright revisionist states are not alone in seeing the current international order as problematic. The disinclination of Brazil, India, Saudi Arabia, the United Arab Emirates and others to help isolate Russia reflects the resonance of Russia's critique of the liberal order as too Western-centric and too ideological. Such states do not see the Russia–Ukraine war as their fight and resent being told to take sides. While most UN members voted to condemn Russia's invasion and called for Russian forces to withdraw, their reluctance to impose penalties suggests that they share, at least in part, Russia's claim that the West seeks to weaponise the international order to maintain its own dominance.

The West's efforts to invoke the moral virtue of decolonisation to rally the Global South's opposition to Russia's aggrandisement in Ukraine have failed in part because Moscow has successfully portrayed the US, the EU and NATO as heirs to the West's colonial legacy, intent on imposing their 'decadent' way of life on others. Observers in the Global South also note that Western concern for white, Christian Ukrainians is not matched by comparable empathy for inhabitants of Gaza, Darfur and other crisis zones outside Europe. And Moscow has scored rhetorical points by contrasting Western policy in Ukraine and Gaza, embracing the Palestinian narrative portraying Israel and its Western backers as echoing Western imperialism.

Although Russia's turn against the liberal international order has been a gradual process, the invasion of Ukraine was a turning point. While the war's outcome remains uncertain, it is safe to say that it will not result in Russia's reintegration with the liberal international order. Moscow appears convinced that the West is using the war to construct an anti-Russian alliance to weaken it and deny it a role as a global decision-maker. This outlook is not unique to Putin and will endure even when he leaves power.[104]

*   *   *

Russia's invasion of Ukraine is not the sole driver of global fragmentation. The return of protectionism and industrial policy, including competition over access to dual-use technologies and paralysis at the World Trade Organization, are unravelling post-1991 globalisation. The consensus around liberalism and democracy that prevailed during the 'third wave' of democratisation is vulnerable as well. Ideological dissolution is occurring not only between the West and the rest, but also within Western countries – including the United States – that have seen surges of illiberalism. Amid this multicausal erosion, Russia remains a pivotal actor, and its vision of global order has matured over the course of three decades. Through its war in Ukraine, Moscow is conducting the most comprehensive revisionist campaign the world has seen since the end of the Cold War at a time when key pillars of the post-1991 dispensation already appear unstable. Accordingly, the outcome of that war is likely to be the most important determinant of the world order yet to emerge.

Notes

[1] President of Russia, 'Zasedaniye diskussionnogo kluba «Valday»' [Meeting of the Valdai Discussion Club], 5 October 2023, http://kremlin.ru/events/president/news/72444.

[2] See White House, 'Remarks by President Biden Before the 78th Session of the United Nations General Assembly', 19 September 2023, https://www.whitehouse.gov/briefing-room/speeches-remarks/2023/09/19/remarks-by-president-biden-before-the-78th-session-of-the-united-nations-general-assembly-new-york-ny/. See also Nigel Gould-Davies, 'Belarus, Russia, Ukraine: Three Lessons for a Post-war Order', *Survival*, vol. 64, no. 5, October–November 2022, pp. 39–46.

[3] See G. John Ikenberry, 'Three Worlds: The West, East and South and the Competition to Shape Global Order', *International Affairs*, vol. 100, no. 1, January 2024, pp. 121–38.

[4] See Nadezhda K. Arbatova and Alexander A. Dynkin, 'World Order After Ukraine', *Survival*, vol. 58, no. 1, February–March 2016, pp. 71–90; and Roger E. Kanet, 'Russia and Global Governance: The Challenge to the Existing Liberal Order', *International Politics*, vol. 55, no. 3, March 2018, pp. 177–88.

[5] Yevgeny Primakov, *Russian Crossroads: Toward the New Millennium*, trans. Felix Rosenthal (New Haven, CT: Yale University Press, 2005), p. 125.

[6] President of Russia, 'Meeting of the Valdai Discussion Club'.

[7] Quoted in Evgeniy Shestakov, 'Sergey Karaganov: Amerikanskaya politika natselena na smenu rezhima v Rossii' [Sergey Karaganov: American policy

is aimed at regime change in Russia], *Rossiyskaya Gazeta*, 23 April 2014, https://rg.ru/2014/04/23/karaganov-site.html.

8   See President of Russia, 'Vystupleniye pered deputatami Velikogo gosudarst-vennogo khurala Mongolii' [Speech to the deputies of the State Great Khural of Mongolia], 14 November 2000, http://kremlin.ru/events/president/transcripts/21133.

9   See Andrej Krickovic, 'Revisionism Revisited: Developing a Typology for Classifying Russia and Other Revisionist Powers', *International Politics*, vol. 59, no. 3, June 2021, pp. 616–39.

10 See Anne L. Clunan, 'Russia and the Liberal World Order', *Ethics & International Affairs*, vol. 32, no. 1, Spring 2018, pp. 45–59; Andrew Radin and Clint Reach, *Russian Views of the International Order* (Santa Monica, CA: RAND Corporation, 2017); and Tatiana Romanova, 'Russia's Neorevisionist Challenge to the Liberal International Order', *International Spectator*, vol. 53, no. 1, January 2018, pp. 76–91.

11 Elias Götz and Camille-Renaud Merlen, 'Russia and the Question of World Order', *European Politics and Society*, vol. 20, no. 2, November 2018, pp. 133–53. See also Richard Sakwa, *Russia Against the Rest: The Post-Cold War Crisis of World Order* (Cambridge: Cambridge University Press, 2017), pp. 105–35.

12 See Andrea Kendall-Taylor and Richard Fontaine, 'The Axis of Upheaval: How America's Adversaries Are Uniting to Overturn the Global Order', *Foreign Affairs*, vol. 103, no. 3, May/June 2024, pp. 50–63.

13 Fyodor Lukyanov, 'ShOS protiv blokovogo myshleniya' [The SCO is against bloc thinking], *Rossiya v globa'noy politike*, 6 July 2023, https://www.globalaffairs.ru/articles/shos-protiv-blokovogo-myshleniya.

14 Sergei A. Karaganov and Dmitry V. Suslov, 'A New World Order: A View from Russia', *Russia in Global Affairs*, 4 October 2018, https://eng.globalaffairs.ru/articles/a-new-world-order-a-view-from-russia/.

15 See Alexander Cooley and Daniel Nexon, *Exit from Hegemony: The Unraveling of the American Global Order* (Oxford: Oxford University Press, 2020), pp. 148–58.

16 See Andrew C. Kuchins and Igor Zevelev, 'Russia's Contested National Identity and Foreign Policy', in Henry R. Nau and Deepa M. Ollapally (eds), *Worldviews of Aspiring Powers: Domestic Foreign Policy Debates in China, India, Iran, Japan, and Russia* (Oxford: Oxford University Press, 2012), pp. 181–209.

17 See Romanova, 'Russia's Neorevisionist Challenge to the Liberal International Order'.

18 Oliver Stuenkel, *Post-Western World: How Emerging Powers Are Remaking Global Order* (Cambridge: Polity, 2016), p. 193.

19 See Maria Snegovaya, Michael Kimmage and Jade McGlynn, 'The Ideology of Putinism: Is It Sustainable?', Center for Strategic and International Studies, September 2023, https://csis-website-prod.s3.amazonaws.com/s3fs-public/2023-09/230927_Snegovaya_Ideology_Putinism.pdf.

20 See Alexey Arbatov, 'Krusheniye miroporyadka? Kuda povernet Rossiya' [The collapse of the world

order? Where will Russia turn], *Rossiya v global'noy politike*, no. 4, July/ August 2014, https://globalaffairs.ru/ articles/krushenie-miroporyadka/.

21 Christopher Coker, *The Rise of the Civilizational State* (Cambridge: Polity, 2019), p. 167.

22 See Vladislav Inozemtsev, 'Russia's "Real Sovereignty" in Foreign Policy Is Just a Means of Consolidating Its "Domestic Sovereign Powers"', MEMRI Daily Brief No. 334, 1 November 2021, https://www.memri. org/reports/russias-real-sovereignty-foreign-policy-just-means-consoli dating-its-domestic-sovereign.

23 See Timofei Bordachev, *Europe, Russia and the Liberal World Order: International Relations after the Cold War* (Abingdon: Routledge, 2022), pp. 73–82; and Mikhail Suslov, '"A More Just World Order" in the Regime Ideology of Putinism', in Ninna Mörner (ed.), *A World Order in Transformation? A Comparative Study of Consequences of the War and Reactions to These Changes in the Region* (Stockholm: CBEES, 2024), pp. 15–22.

24 See Rachel S. Salzman, *Russia, BRICS, and the Disruption of Global Order* (Washington DC: Georgetown University Press, 2020), p. 52.

25 See Dmitri Trenin, *What Is Russia Up to in the Middle East?* (Cambridge: Polity Press, 2018), pp. 47–8.

26 Ikenberry, 'Three Worlds', p. 124.

27 See Trine Flockhart and Elena A. Korosteleva, 'War in Ukraine: Putin and the Multi-order World', *Contemporary Security Policy*, vol. 43, no. 3, June 2022, pp. 466–81.

28 See, for example, 'Lavrov: novyy mirovoy poryadok ne budet podchinen odnomu gegemonu' [Lavrov: new world order will not be subordinated to one hegemon], *International Affairs*, 6 November 2023, https://interaffairs.ru/news/ show/43103.

29 Oleg Barabanov et al., 'Vremya vzroslet', ili Opravdanie anarkhii' [Time to grow up, or a justification for anarchy], Valdai Discussion Club, September 2019, https:// ru.valdaiclub.com/a/reports/vremya-vzroslet-ezhegodnyy-doklad/. See also Dmitriy Evstafiev, 'Shagnut' za porog global'nogo mira' [Step over the threshold of the global world], *Rossiya v global'noi politike*, March/April 2023, https://globalaffairs.ru/articles/ shagnut-za-porog-globalnogo-mira/.

30 Oleg Barabanov et al., 'Attestat zre-losti, ili Poryadok, kakogo eshche ne bylo' [Maturity certificate, or the order that never was], Valdai Discussion Club Report, October 2023, https:// ru.valdaiclub.com/files/45987/.

31 See Amitav Acharya, 'The Emerging Regional Architecture of World Politics', *World Politics*, vol. 59, no. 4, July 2007, pp. 629–52.

32 See Oleg Barabanov et al., 'Mir bez sverkhderzhav' [A world without superpowers], Annual Report of the Valdai Discussion Club, October 2022, https://ru.valdaiclub.com/files/43157/.

33 See Russian Ministry of Foreign Affairs, 'Vystupleniye i otvety na voprosy Ministra inostran-nykh del Rossiyskoy Federatsii S.V.Lavrova na mezhdunarodnom forume «Primakovskiye chteniya» v rezhime videokonferentsii' [Speech and answers to questions by the Minister of Foreign Affairs of the Russian Federation S.V. Lavrov at

the International Forum 'Primakov Readings' via videoconference], 9 June 2021, https://www.mid.ru/ru/foreign_policy/news/1752157/.

34 See President of Russia, '70-ya sessiya General'noy Assamblei OON' [70th session of the UN General Assembly], 28 September 2015, http://www.kremlin.ru/events/president/news/50385/videos.

35 See John Reid, 'Putin, Pretext, and the Dark Side of the "Responsibility to Protect"', *War on the Rocks*, 27 May 2022, https://warontherocks.com/2022/05/putin-pretext-and-the-dark-side-of-the-responsibility-to-protect/.

36 See, for instance, Julia Ioffe, 'What Putin Really Wants', *Atlantic*, January/February 2018, https://www.theatlantic.com/magazine/archive/2018/01/putins-game/546548/.

37 Sergey Lavrov, 'Mir na pereput'ye i sistema mezhdunarodnykh otnosheniy v budushchem' [The world at a crossroads and the system of international relations in the future], *Rossia v global'noy politike*, September/October 2019, https://globalaffairs.ru/articles/mir-na-perepute-i-sistema-mezhdunarodnyh-otnoshenij-v-budushhem/.

38 See President of Russia, 'Vneocherednoy sammit «Gruppy dvadtsati»' [Extraordinary G20 summit], 22 November 2023, https://www.kremlin.ru/d/72790.

39 See 'Full Text of Xi Jinping Keynote Speech at the United Nations Office in Geneva', CGTN America, 18 January 2017, https://america.cgtn.com/2017/01/18/full-text-of-xi-jinping-keynote-speech-at-the-united-nations-office-in-geneva; and UN Human Rights Council, 'The Contribution of Development to the Enjoyment of All Human Rights', 35th session, 23 June 2017, https://www.right-docs.org/doc/a-hrc-res-35-21.

40 Government of the Russian Federation, 'Vystupleniye Alekseya Overchuka na vstreche vysokogo urovnya po Global'noy initsiative v oblasti razvitiya Sammita po tselyam ustoychivogo razvitiya, prokhodyashchego pod egidoy Genassamblei OON' [Speech by Alexey Overchuk at the high-level meeting on the Global Development Initiative of the Sustainable Development Goals Summit, held under the auspices of the UN General Assembly], 20 September 2023, http://government.ru/news/49547/.

41 See Ministry of Foreign Affairs of the Russian Federation, 'Vystupleniye Ministra inostrannykh del Rossiyskoy Federatsii S.V.Lavrova na zasedanii SB OON po teme «Podderzhaniye mezhdunarodnogo mira i bezopasnosti: sodeystviye realizatsii printsipov i tseley Ustava OON cherez effektivnuyu mnogostoronnost': podderzhaniye mira i bezopasnosti Ukrainy»' [Speech by the Minister of Foreign Affairs of the Russian Federation S.V. Lavrov at the UN Security Council meeting on the topic 'Maintenance of International Peace and Security: Promoting the Implementation of the Principles and Purposes of the UN Charter Through Effective Multilateralism: Maintaining Peace and Security in Ukraine'], 20 September 2023, https://www.mid.ru/ru/press_service/minister_speeches/1905317/.

42 Ministry of Foreign Affairs of the Russian Federation, 'The Concept of the Foreign Policy of the Russian Federation', 31 March 2023, https://mid.ru/en/foreign_policy/fundamental_documents/1860586/.

43 See Ministry of Foreign Affairs of the Russian Federation, 'Statement by Vladimir Putin on Additional Steps to De-escalate the Situation in Europe After the Termination of the Intermediate-Range Nuclear Forces Treaty (INF Treaty)', 26 October 2020, https://mid.ru/en/foreign_policy/international_safety/1445386/.

44 See Nicole Grajewski, 'Russia and the Global Nuclear Order', CNA, March 2024, https://www.cna.org/reports/2024/03/Russia-and-the-Global-Nuclear-Order.pdf.

45 See Michelle Ye Hee Lee and Min Joo Kim, 'Russian Veto Ends U.N. Panel Monitoring North Korea Sanctions', *Washington Post*, 29 March 2024, https://www.washingtonpost.com/world/2024/03/29/russia-veto-brings-end-un-panel-monitoring-north-korea-sanctions/.

46 Sergey Karaganov, 'Tyazhkoye, no neobkhodimoye resheniye Primeneniye yadernogo oruzhiya mozhet uberech' chelovechestvo ot global'noy katastrofy' [A difficult but necessary decision: the use of nuclear weapons can save humanity from a global catastrophe', *Rossiya v global'noy politike*, 13 June 2023, https://globalaffairs.ru/articles/tyazhkoe-no-neobhodimoe-reshenie/.

47 See Grajewski, 'Russia and the Global Nuclear Order', p. 22.

48 Serge Schmemann, 'Why Russia Believes It Cannot Lose the War in Ukraine', *New York Times*, 3 August 2022, https://www.nytimes.com/2022/07/19/opinion/russia-ukraine-karaganov-interview.html.

49 See K.F. Zatulin and A.M. Migranyan, 'SNG: nachalo ili konets istorii. K smene vekh' [CIS: The beginning or the end of history. Towards a change of milestones], *Nezavisimaya Gazeta*, 26 March 1997, https://zatulin.ru/sng-nachalo-ili-konec-istorii-k-smene-vex/.

50 President of Russia, 'Deklaratsiya o formirovanii Yedinogo ekonomicheskogo prostranstva Respubliki Belarus', Respubliki Kazakhstan, i Rossiyskoy Federatsii' [Declaration on the formation of the common economic space of the Republic of Belarus, the Republic of Kazakhstan, and the Russian Federation], 9 December 2010, http://www.kremlin.ru/supplement/802.

51 Vladimir Putin, 'Novyy integratsionnyy proekt dlya evrazii – buduschee kotoroe rozhdaetsya segodnya' [A New Integration Project for Eurasia – the future that is being born today], *Cyberleninka*, 3 October 2011, https://cyberleninka.ru/article/n/novyy-integratsionnyy-proekt-dlya-evrazii-buduschee-kotoroe-rozhdaetsya-segodnya.

52 See Samuel Charap and Mikhail Troitskiy, 'Russia, the West, and the Integration Dilemma', *Survival*, vol. 55, no. 6, December 2013–January 2014, pp. 49–62.

53 'Postanovlenie zasedaniya Kollegii MID Rossii' [Resolution of the Collegium of the Ministry of Foreign Affairs of Russia], *Washington Post* archive, 11 April 2023, https://www.washingtonpost.com/

documents/e7843591-08c7-4dab-98e1-d6faad68e048.pdf. On the Greater Eurasia Partnership, see David Lewis, 'Geopolitical Imaginaries in Russian Foreign Policy: The Evolution of "Greater Eurasia"', *Europe–Asia Studies*, vol. 70, no. 10, November 2018, pp. 1,612–37.

54 See Jonathan Tirone and Golnar Motevalli, 'Russia and Iran Are Building a Trade Route that Defies Sanctions', Bloomberg, 21 December 2022, https://www.bloomberg.com/graphics/2022-russia-iran-trade-corridor/.

55 See Aleksey Rybin, 'Medvedev zayavil, chto strategicheskie granitsy stran mogut byt' shire geo-graficheskikh' [Medvedev announced that strategic borders could be broader than geographic ones], *Rossiyskaya Gazeta*, 4 March 2024, https://rg.ru/2024/03/04/medvedev-zaiavil-chto-strategicheskie-granicy-stran-mogut-byt-shire-geograficheskih.html.

56 See Valur Ingimundarson, 'The "Kosovo Precedent": Russia's Justification of Military Interventions and Territorial Revisions in Georgia and Ukraine', LSE Ideas, Strategic Update, July 2022, https://www.lse.ac.uk/ideas/Assets/Documents/updates/2022-SU-Valur-RussKosovo.pdf.

57 See Michael Weiss and Holger Roonemaa, 'Revealed: Leaked Document Shows How Russia Plans to Take Over Belarus', Yahoo! News, 20 February 2023, https://news.yahoo.com/russia-belarus-strategy-document-230035184.html.

58 See Alexander Dugin, 'Moment Imperii. Chto skryvayetsya za terminom "Gosudarstvo-Tsivilizatsiya"' [The moment of empire: what is hidden behind the term 'state-civilisation'], RIA Novosti, 6 October 2023, https://ria.ru/20231006/imperiya-1900924123.html.

59 See 'Gundarov rasskazal, chem tsenen novyy punkt bazirovaniya flota v Ochamchire' [Gundarov explained the value of the new naval base in Ochamchire], *Moskovskiy komsomolets*, 5 October 2023, https://www.mk.ru/ politics/2023/10/05/gundarovrasskazal-chem cenen-novyy-punktbazirovaniya-flota-v-ochamchire.html.

60 See Andrew Gardner, 'Russia to Annex Transnistria?', *Politico*, 19 March 2024, https://www.politico.eu/article/russia-to-annex-transnistria/.

61 See Nona Shakhnazarian, 'Yevraziyskaya sem'ya protiv yev-ropeyskoy tsennostey' [The Eurasian family against European values], PONARS Eurasia, October 2017, https://www.ponarseurasia.org/wp-content/uploads/attachments/Pepm488_rus_Shahnazarian_Oct2017.pdf.

62 Amnesty International, 'Menee ravnye: LGBTI-pravozashchitniki v Armenii, Belarusi, Kazakhstane, i Kyrgyzstane' [Less equal: LGBTQ-rights activists in Armenia, Belarus, Kazakhstan, and Kyrgyzstan], May 2021, https://www.amnesty.org/en/wp-content/uploads/2021/05/EUR0475742017RUSSIAN.pdf.

63 'Spasti detey ot psikhozov: kak stranam YEAES zakryt' rynok ot zhutkikh igrushek?' [Save children from psychosis: how can the EAEU countries close the market to creepy toys?], Sputnik Belarus, 18 September 2023, https://sputnik.by/20230918/spasti-detey-ot-psikhozov-kak-

stranam-eaes-zakryt-rynok-ot-
zhutkikh-igrushek-1079533007.html.

64 See Thomas O'Reilly, 'Uganda Pivots
    to Russia amid World Bank LGBT
    Boycott', *European Conservative*, 13
    August 2023, https://european
    conservative.com/articles/news/
    uganda-pivots-to-russia-amid-world-
    bank-lgbt-boycott/.

65 See generally Daniel Byman and Seth G.
    Jones, 'Legion of Doom? China, Russia,
    Iran and North Korea', *Survival*, vol.
    66, no. 4, August–September 2024, pp.
    29–50; and 'How China, Russia, and Iran
    Are Forging Closer Ties', *The Economist*,
    18 March 2024, https://www.economist.
    com/finance-and-economics/2024/03/18/
    how-china-russia-and-iran-are-forging-
    closer-ties.

66 See Pavel K. Baev, 'China Evaluates
    Partnership with Russia', *Eurasia Daily
    Monitor*, vol. 21, no. 69, 6 May 2024,
    https://jamestown.org/program/china-
    evaluates-partnership-with-russia/.

67 See Nicole Grajewski, 'An Illusory
    Entente: The Myth of a Russia–China–
    Iran "Axis"', *Asian Affairs*, vol. 53, no.
    1, February 2022, pp. 164–83.

68 See Dalton Bennet and Mary
    Ilyushina, 'Inside the Russian Effort to
    Build 6,000 Attack Drones with Iran's
    Help', *Washington Post*, 17 August
    2023, https://www.washingtonpost.
    com/investigations/2023/08/17/
    russia-iran-drone-shahed-alabuga/.

69 See Aamher Madhani, 'US Says North
    Korea Delivered 1,000 Containers
    of Equipment and Munitions to
    Russia for Ukraine War', Associated
    Press, 13 October 2023, https://
    apnews.com/article/north-korea-
    russia-us-munitions-ukraine-war-
    7091eaba254b680888a9b1ec8a68135f.

70 Quoted in Roger Cohen, 'Xi Bristles
    at Criticism of China over the War in
    Ukraine', *New York Times*, 6 May 2024,
    https://www.nytimes.com/2024/05/06/
    world/europe/xi-macron-europe-
    trade-war.html.

71 See US Department of State, 'People's
    Republic of China Efforts to Amplify
    the Kremlin's Voice on Ukraine',
    2 May 2022, https://www.state.
    gov/disarming-disinformation/
    prc-efforts-to-amplify-the-kremlins-
    voice-on-ukraine/.

72 See Sheena Chestnut Greitens,
    'China's Response to War in Ukraine',
    Asian Survey, vol. 62, nos 5–6, October
    2022, pp. 751–81.

73 See Nathaniel Sher, 'Behind the
    Scenes: China's Increasing Role
    in Russia's Defense Industry',
    Carnegie Politika, 6 May 2024,
    https://carnegieendowment.org/
    russia-eurasia/politika/2024/05/
    behind-the-scenes-chinas-increasing-
    role-in-russias-defense-industry.

74 See Lucas Winter, Jemima Baar and
    Jason Warner, 'The Axis Off-kilter: Why
    an Iran–Russia–China "Axis" Is Shakier
    than Meets the Eye', *War on the Rocks*,
    19 April 2024, https://warontherocks.
    com/2024/04/the-axis-off-kilter-why-an-
    iran-russia-china-axis-is-shakier-than-
    meets-the-eye/.

75 See Nicole Grajewski, 'Iran and the
    SCO: The Quest for Legitimacy and
    Regime Preservation', *Middle East Policy*,
    vol. 30, no. 2, May 2023, pp. 38–61.

76 President of Russia, 'Sovmestnoye
    zayavleniye Rossiyskoy Federatsii i
    Kitayskoy Narodnoy Respubliki o
    mezhdunarodnykh otnosheniyakh,
    vstupayushchikh v novuyu epokhu,
    i global'nom ustoychivom razvitii'

[Joint statement of the Russian Federation and the People's Republic of China on international relations entering a new era and global sustainable development], 4 February 2022, http://kremlin.ru/supplement/5770.

77   President of Russia, 'Sovmestnoye zayavleniye Rossiyskoy Federatsii i Kitayskoy Narodnoy Respubliki ob uglublenii otnosheniy vseob'yemlyushchego partnerstva i strategicheskogo vzaimodeystviya, vstupayushchikh v novuyu epokhu, v kontekste 75-letiya ustanovleniya diplomaticheskikh otnosheniy mezhdu dvumya stranami' [Joint statement of the Russian Federation and the People's Republic of China on deepening comprehensive partnership and strategic interaction relations entering a new era, in the context of the 75th anniversary of the establishment of diplomatic relations between the two countries], 16 May 2024, http://kremlin.ru/supplement/6132.

78   Sergey Strokan, 'Rossiya i Iran dogovoryatsya o mnogom' [Russia and Iran will agree on many things], *Kommersant*, 2 April 2024, https://www.kommersant.ru/doc/6612635.

79   See Anne Appelbaum, 'The New Propaganda War', *Atlantic*, 6 May 2024, https://www.theatlantic.com/magazine/archive/2024/06/china-russia-republican-party-relations/678271/.

80   See Stephen G.F. Hall and Thomas Ambrosio, 'Authoritarian Learning: A Conceptual Overview', *East European Politics*, vol. 33, no. 2, May 2017, pp. 143–61.

81   See Hal Brands, 'The New Autocratic Alliances: They Don't Look Like America's – But They're Still Dangerous', *Foreign Affairs*, 29 March 2024, https://www.foreignaffairs.com/united-states/new-autocratic-alliances.

82   See Tom Keatinge, 'Developing Bad Habits: What Russia Might Learn from Iran's Sanctions Evasion', Royal United Services Institute, Occasional Paper, 2023, https://static.rusi.org/developing-bad-habits-what-russia-might-learn-from-irans-sanctions-evasion.pdf; and International Institute for Strategic Studies, 'Russia and Sanctions Evasion', *Strategic Comments*, vol. 28, no. 15, July 2022, https://www.iiss.org/publications/strategic-comments/2022/russia-and-sanctions-evasion/.

83   See Maziar Motamedi, 'What's Behind Iran and Russia's Efforts to Link Banking Systems?', Al-Jazeera, 8 February 2023, https://www.aljazeera.com/news/2023/2/8/whats-behind-iran-and-russias-efforts-to-link-banking-systems.

84   See 'Minekonomiki raskrylo stepen' «yuanizatsii» torgovli Rossii bez ucheta Kitaya Chetvert' oborota s tret'imi stranami obsluzhivayetsya v kitayskoy valyute' [The Ministry of Economy has revealed the extent of the 'yuanisation' of Russia's trade without taking China into account: a quarter of turnover with third countries is processed in Chinese currency], *RBK*, 28 September 2023, https://www.rbc.ru/economics/28/09/2023/651465e49a79473740bd3834.

85   See Amitav Acharya, 'The Myth of the "Civilizational State": Rising Powers and the Cultural Challenge to World Order', *Ethics & International Affairs*, vol. 34, no. 2, July 2020, pp. 139–56.

86 Angela Stent, 'Russia, the West and the "World Majority"', *Russia Matters*, 25 January 2024, https://www.russiamatters.org/analysis/russia-west-and-world-majority; and Ivan Timofeev, 'Russia's Path to the "World Majority"', Valdai Discussion Club, 5 April 2023, https://valdaiclub.com/a/highlights/russia-s-path-to-the-world-majority/.

87 Sergey A. Karaganov, Alexander M. Kramarenko and Dmitry V. Trenin, 'Russia's Policy Towards World Majority', Ministry of Foreign Affairs of the Russian Federation, 2023, https://www.mid.ru/upload/medialibrary/c98/cjmfdf73760bmeoy99zqllj51zzllrvs/Russia%E2%80%99s%20Policy.pdf.

88 See Sergey Karaganov, 'Rossiya zakonchila svoye yevropeyskoye puteshestviye' [Russia has completed its European journey], Russian Council, 27 December 2023, https://russiancouncil.ru/analytics-and-comments/comments/rossiya-zakonchila-svoe-evropeyskoe-puteshestvie/.

89 See Stent, 'Russia, the West and the "World Majority"'.

90 Karaganov, Kramarenko and Trenin, 'Russia's Policy Towards World Majority'.

91 See Ministry of Foreign Affairs of the Russian Federation, 'The Concept of the Foreign Policy of the Russian Federation'.

92 Elena Grebenkina, 'Sovremennaya diplomatiya na puti k setevoy strukture mira' [Modern diplomacy on the way to a network structure of the world], *International Affairs*, no. 4, 2017, https://interaffairs.ru/jauthor/material/1839.

93 See Stephen Aris, 'Russia–China Relations Through the Lens of the SCO', IFRI, September 2008, https://www.ifri.org/sites/default/files/atoms/files/Ifri_RNV_Aris_SCO_Eng.pdf.

94 See Alexander Cooley, *Great Games, Local Rules: The New Great Power Contest in Central Asia* (Oxford: Oxford University Press, 2012), pp. 97–115.

95 See Eva Seiwert, 'China's "New International Order": The Shanghai Cooperation Organisation in Afghanistan and Syria', *Europe–Asia Studies*, vol. 76, no. 3, January 2024, pp. 411–32.

96 SCO, 'Soglashenie mezhdu pravitel'stvami gosudarstv-chlenov ShOS o sotrudnichestve v oblasti obespecheniya mezhdunarodnoy informatsionnoy bezopasnosti' [Agreement between the member-state governments of the SCO on cooperation in area of ensuring international information security], 16 June 2009, https://ccdcoe.org/uploads/2018/11/SCO-090616-IISAgreementRussian-1.pdf.

97 See Ali Ahmadi, 'The Shanghai Cooperation Organization Has an Identity Crisis', *World Politics Review*, 18 July 2023, https://www.worldpoliticsreview.com/russia-china-india-iran-shanghai-cooperation-organization-sco/.

98 See President of Russia, 'Obrashcheniye Vladimira Putina v svyazi s nachalom predsedatel'stva Rossii v BRIKS' [Vladimir Putin's address on the occasion of the beginning of Russia's BRICS presidency], 1 January 2024, http://kremlin.ru/events/president/news/73202.

99 See Cynthia Roberts, 'Russia's BRICS Diplomacy: Rising Outsider with

Dreams of an Insider', *Polity*, vol. 42, no. 1, January 2010, p. 57.

100 See Stefan A. Schirm, 'Alternative World Orders? Russia's Ukraine War and the Domestic Politics of the BRICS', *International Spectator*, vol. 58, no. 3, July 2023, pp. 55–73.

101 Karaganov, Kramarenko and Trenin, 'Russia's Policy Toward World Majority', p. 23.

102 Jonathan Corrado and Markus Garlauskas, 'The Arsenal of Autocracy: How North Korean Weapons Fuel Conflict – and How to Stop the Flow', *Foreign Affairs*, 15 February 2024, https://www.foreignaffairs.com/north-korea/arsenal-autocracy.

103 See Phelim Kine, 'Taiwan's Leadership "Extremely Worried" US Could Abandon Ukraine', *Politico*, 23 February 2024, https://www.politico.com/news/2024/02/23/taiwan-leadership-u-s-ukraine-00143047.

104 See Tatiana Stanovaya, 'Russia's Pro-Putin Elites', *Foreign Affairs*, 9 May 2024, https://www.foreignaffairs.com/russia/russias-pro-putin-elites.

Copyright © 2024 The International Institute for Strategic Studies

Ukraine in NATO: Beyond the 'Irreversible Path'

John R. Deni and Elisabeth Nielsen

Although Ukraine did not receive an invitation to join NATO at the July summit in Washington, the Alliance pledged that Ukraine was on an 'irreversible path' to membership.[1] Coupled with concrete steps to further integrate Ukraine, NATO has positioned the country to join very quickly whenever a formal invitation *is* offered. While leaders and experts have debated whether this is a good idea, there has been far less thought given to how the Alliance would need to adapt to Ukraine being a member.[2]

Such speculation may seem premature. Serious negotiations towards a settlement of the war do not appear on the horizon, and it remains unclear what a post-war Ukraine might look like and what its politics might be. Until and unless active fighting ceases, a NATO invitation to Ukraine is highly unlikely. Nevertheless, it would seem imprudent to not think through the likely implications for the Alliance. In the past, significant expansions of NATO membership have compelled the Alliance to change its approach to security. For example, when West Germany joined in 1955, the Alliance shifted its line of forward defence from the Benelux countries and northern France to the inter-German border, requiring new defence concepts and a revised strategy.[3] More recently, when Finland joined in 2023, the Alliance had to adapt recently approved operations plans for northeastern Europe

---

John R. Deni is a research professor of security studies at the US Army War College, a non-resident senior fellow at the Atlantic Council and a non-resident senior fellow at the NATO Defense College. He is the author of *NATO and Article 5* (Rowman & Littlefield, 2017). **Elisabeth Nielsen** was a research intern at the US Army War College's Strategic Studies Institute in summer 2024 and is currently pursuing a degree in international relations and public policy at the College of William and Mary.

Survival | vol. 66 no. 5 | October–November 2024 | pp. 127–146 https://doi.org/10.1080/00396338.2024.2403220

and implement changes in its command structure to facilitate the defence of Finnish territory and its 1,340-kilometre border with Russia.[4]

Given Ukraine's geographic position in Europe, its size and the likelihood that Moscow will remain irredentist in its outlook towards Ukraine, Ukrainian membership will affect NATO profoundly. It is not North Macedonia or Albania. NATO would necessarily need to modify its approach to Euro-Atlantic security. It should consider a number of steps. Firstly, NATO would need to modify its force structure, command structure and force posture to safeguard Ukrainian territorial sovereignty, aiming to deter another Russian invasion and reassure countries seeking to help Ukraine rebuild after the devastation of the war. Secondly, the allies will need to consider how to strengthen Black Sea security in light of its importance to member nations' economic security and what will likely be a resurgence of Russian naval power in the Black Sea after the war is over. Thirdly, NATO should consider beefing up the defence of the 'flank' nations such as the Baltic states, Finland, Norway and Romania, especially the Alliance's response to multidomain attacks and asymmetrical warfare. Finally, the Alliance and especially more capable allies should consider more robust responses to a likely intensification of Russian hybrid activity across the continent.

Defending Ukrainian territory

Ukraine's membership in NATO would add an almost 2,000 km border with Russia – 645 km longer than the Finland–Russia border – and it would more than double the amount of NATO territory contiguous to the Alliance's main adversary. This would pose unique challenges for allied collective defence. The first is securing Ukrainian land borders, which are likely to remain under threat from overt and covert Russian military activities. To counter this, Ukraine would need extensive active and passive border-monitoring capabilities to prevent Russian operatives from infiltrating and to prevent Moscow from taking other steps to destabilise Ukraine, such as sending third-country refugees across the border.

Prior to Russia's full-scale invasion of Ukraine in February 2022, Moscow's depredations in 2014–15 had produced a so-called frozen but in fact quite active low-intensity conflict involving Russian border operations and a Russian-backed separatist insurgency.[5] Neither side pursued meaningful escalation, but through this strategy Russia nonetheless maintained enough pressure to weaken Ukraine and cause significant casualties and physical damage. More than 13,000 people died between the time of Russia's illegal annexation of Crimea in 2014 and its February 2022 invasion.[6]

In addition to monitoring the security and stability of the border, the Alliance would need to anchor the defence of Ukrainian territory in a new or a modified regional-operations plan, just as it did for Finland and Sweden when they joined. A robust operations plan to defend Ukraine would likely rely on in-place forces, as well as reinforcements. For the former, Ukraine would likely need a significant allied military presence on the ground to effectively deter Russia from launching another large-scale attack. The deterrent would be most effective if it included troops from several of the Alliance's leading states, starting with the United States but also including France, Germany, Italy, Spain and the United Kingdom. The presence of these allies on the ground in Ukraine would make it clear to Russia that another invasion would mean a conflict with all of NATO, and in particular many of its largest and most capable members.

The Alliance should consider several factors in crafting its posture inside Ukraine. The first is the array of Russian ground-manoeuvre forces likely to be on the other side of the border in Russia, as well as in Belarus, bearing in mind that the current war's opening moves involved Russian troops attacking Ukraine from Belarusian territory. Prior to the outbreak of war and the reorganisation of Russia's military districts, the Russian Western and Southern military districts bordered Ukraine. In the former Western Military District, the Russian city of Voronezh was home to the 20th Combined Arms Army, composed of two motor-rifle divisions whose subordinate units were based across the region and consisted of roughly 21,000 troops.[7] Meanwhile, the Southern Military District, with headquarters in Rostov-on-Don, included two motor-rifle divisions under the 8th Combined Arms Army, one of them the 150th Motor Rifle Division based at Novocherkassk, just 70 km from the Ukrainian border.[8] Belarus reportedly hosted up to 30,000 Russian troops immediately before the war, though these forces were only temporarily based there, ostensibly for exercises and then as part of the initial invasion force.[9] Otherwise, Russia's official permanent force presence in Belarus appears to consist of fixed-wing combat aircraft, tactical nuclear forces, radar facilities, communications infrastructure and training facilities.[10] Although none of these have major ground-manoeuvre units postured near Ukraine's border and capable of attacking and seizing terrain, Moscow still appears intent on using temporary deployments in Belarus to keep Kyiv off balance.[11] Additionally, and of course depending on the disposition of occupied Ukrainian territory, Moscow may choose to maintain, as opposed to disband, the separatist forces in Donetsk and Luhansk. Based on pre-war manning levels, these could total roughly 30,000 troops.

Prior to the start of the war, in addition to these forces arrayed just across what are likely to be Ukraine's post-war northern and eastern borders, there were other Russian forces in the region that could potentially play important supporting roles – or more. These included a Russian Army Corps in occupied Crimea and a Russian airborne division based in the vicinity of the Kerch Strait. Given pre-war manning levels, these forces together could amount to another 22,000 Russia troops.

Assuming Russia returns to a pre-2022 land-force posture in the regions adjacent to Ukraine – admittedly an open question subject to debate – there could be the equivalent of six manoeuvre divisions plus several special-operations and combat-support units arrayed along Ukraine's northern, eastern and southern borders. With Ukraine in NATO, though, it would be reasonable to posit that Moscow would increase those force levels, assessing that it had to strengthen its defences to deter a Western attack. In any case, with another division's worth of manoeuvre units in the region, there could plausibly be at least 80,000 Russian manoeuvre-unit troops stationed permanently in the vicinity of Ukraine's post-war borders, plus several thousand special operators and combat-support troops, bringing Russian ground-force personnel strength along Ukraine's borders to roughly 90,000.

Conventional military thinking dictates that for an attacker to win, the attacker's forces should be at least three times the size of the defender's forces.[12] This means NATO forces along Ukraine's northern, eastern and southern borders should number at least 30,000 troops to prevent a quick, unforeseen attack from achieving any initial gains. However, to achieve deterrence by denial – that is, to convince leaders in Moscow that a Russian attack on Ukraine would not result in any prompt gains – NATO's force structure in Ukraine should ideally be around 45,000 manoeuvre troops, primarily arrayed along Ukraine's borders with Russia in the north, east and south.

Ukrainian armed forces would naturally constitute most of that force structure, but how much is 'most'? It is difficult to guess what Ukraine's post-war army might look like in terms of size or composition. Even so, it makes sense to figure that it would be much smaller than its wartime size of about 250,000 troops given the human resources necessary to reconstruct Ukraine's economy, yet slightly larger than its pre-war size. In 2021, Ukraine's ground forces consisted of roughly 29 manoeuvre brigades or brigade equivalents, plus eight artillery, surface-to-surface missile,

NATO's force structure in Ukraine should be around 45,000 troops

or multiple-rocket-launcher brigades, for a total troop strength of roughly 95,000.[13] Rounding upward, a post-war Ukrainian manoeuvre-force size of about 100,000 would appear sufficient to deter Russia and defend against an unforeseen attack. But this assumes all those troops would be available all the time, which would be highly unlikely. To be capable of effectively defending Ukraine's frontiers, Ukrainian forces would need to maintain an exceptionally high level of skill and readiness, which can only be achieved by rigorous and regular training. A typical force-generation model entails one unit on duty, one unit recovering from duty, and one unit in training and preparing for duty. Such an A-B-C rotation would yield roughly 33,000 Ukrainian manoeuvre troops available in the field on any given day. That would produce a gap of about 12,000 manoeuvre troops, which could be filled by four to five brigades from Ukraine's new NATO allies.

Commanding and controlling these forces will require NATO to adapt its command structure. Alliance leaders decided in 2018 to add a third joint force command (JFC) – in Norfolk – to the two that already existed in Brunssum, the Netherlands, and Naples, Italy. JFC Norfolk, primarily a maritime-oriented command, has responsibility for transatlantic lines of communication and reinforcement, as well as the Arctic and NATO operations plans for the defence of Iceland and Norway. It is in the process of expanding its capacity and capability, and it will eventually handle operations plans for the defence of Finland and Sweden. For the time being, though, JFC Brunssum is responsible for those two countries, as well as for operations plans covering most of Central and northeastern Europe, while JFC Naples covers operations plans for NATO's southern flank.

This Alliance command structure is arguably inadequate even without adding Ukraine. For example, even when JFC Norfolk achieves the required level of resources, it is difficult to imagine an American three-star admiral based in Norfolk – who is dual-hatted as commander of the US Second Fleet – handling operations plans for defending Finland's border with Russia, roughly 7,250 km to the northeast. As talented as that commander may be, the distance between him or her and the joint forces he or she commands is likely to frustrate efficient and effective operations. Similarly, Brunssum's span of control is strained in both geographic and organisational terms, with responsibility for operations plans covering a massive swath of Central, Eastern, northeastern and (for now) Northern Europe and involving at least half a dozen corps when fully activated.

With Ukraine in NATO, the challenges confronting the Alliance's command structure would grow significantly. To remedy this, the Alliance should be prepared to create at least one additional joint force command in Europe, ideally led by the UK and with responsibility for the operations plans covering all of Scandinavia, Finland, the Baltic Sea and the Arctic.[14] The UK is the natural choice to head such a command given its historically strong role in the Alliance, its naval traditions and its key role as a regional power, including through such frameworks as the Joint Expeditionary Force. Extant Alliance commands located in the UK, such as the Allied Maritime Command or the Allied Rapid Reaction Corps, could form the kernel of this new joint force command. This addition would enable Brunssum to focus on plans covering Poland, the Baltic states and Ukraine. However, it is possible – depending on what the post-war settlement looks like – that even this arrangement, or other proposed changes to NATO's command structure, would prove inadequate to the multidomain challenge posed by an enduringly aggrieved Russia.[15] For this reason, NATO may instead need to create a joint force command focused on Eastern Europe, charged with planning for the defence of Bulgaria, Hungary, Romania, Slovakia, Ukraine, and perhaps someday Moldova, leaving Brunssum to focus on the 'northeastern' countries of the Czech Republic, Estonia, Latvia, Lithuania and Poland.

In addition to establishing an allied troop presence in Ukraine, the Alliance should consider tapping the NATO Security Investment Program (NSIP), which provides funding for collective-defence installations and facilities in allied countries, to help reinforce and construct defensive fortifications near Ukraine's borders with Russia and to develop hardened storage sites for prepositioned equipment in western Ukraine. Depending on where the border between Russia and Ukraine lies at war's end, some defensive fortifications may already exist in the form of trenches, strongpoints and other structures established by Ukrainian forces over the last several months. Key elements of additional defensive fortifications in Ukraine might include tank obstacles, minefields, trenches and surveillance infrastructure to detect and blunt any Russian incursion.

Ukraine's territorial vulnerability extends not only to defence on the ground but also to defence of Ukrainian airspace. By itself, Ukraine's air force is not strong enough to gain air superiority and is susceptible to Russian attacks.[16] Before Russia's invasion of Ukraine, most Ukrainian air-defence systems were of Soviet manufacture. The United States and other NATO allies have since supplied more modern systems, but Ukraine today still relies on a hodgepodge of systems that are insufficient in number, inadequately integrated and difficult to sustain. In some cases, Kyiv has had to rely on 'FrankenSAM' – a mixture of Soviet-vintage and modern Western air-defence systems.[17] Although NATO promised Ukraine more kit, including *Patriot* and National Advanced Surface-to-Air Missile System (NASAMS) defences, the package has fallen short of Kyiv's needs.[18]

To fix this problem, the Alliance would need to significantly expand its NATO Integrated Air and Missile Defence system not merely by incorporating Ukrainian systems but also by ensuring that Ukraine were on a sustainable path towards state-of-the-art inter-operable air- and missile-defence systems operated by highly trained personnel. Ultimately, the goal should be to fully integrate Ukrainian air and missile defence with NATO and especially neighbouring Poland.[19] At the same time, allies should consider expanding and strengthening the Joint Electronic Warfare Core Staff (JEWCS) to better support exercises, as well as both defensive and offensive operations in the electromagnetic spectrum in and over Ukraine.[20] Based at Royal Naval Air Station Yeovilton in Somerset, England, NATO JEWCS provides electronic-warfare expertise and hardware in support of current operations and exercises. It has been integrated into the NATO Command Structure, which will make it eligible for common funding – a necessity for ensuring that it has the most up-to-date equipment.[21]

Beef up Black Sea security

The Black Sea plays a vital economic role for Kyiv, and it will arguably be even more important for rebuilding Ukraine after the war. The Black Sea is also a strategic priority for NATO owing to the crucial role its key ports play in the economies of Bulgaria, Romania and Turkiye, and the military lines of communication that stretch across it.

Rebuilding Ukraine and revitalising regional economies throttled by the war will not be easy. The war has destroyed Ukraine's energy infrastructure, and Russian landmines have reduced the area available for farmland.[22] The United Nations Sustainable Development Fund estimates that Ukraine will need over $486 billion over the course of a decade to rebuild.[23] Much of this could come from Ukrainian exports if security conditions allow. Agriculture is the largest Ukrainian export, accounting for more than $22bn of Ukraine's $36bn in exports in 2023, and more than 90% of Ukrainian agriculture is shipped through the Black Sea.[24] Before the war, Ukraine exported 60% of its goods through the Black Sea, but by 2023 this number had dipped to around 25%.[25] Other things being equal, it is more efficient for Ukraine to send goods through the Black Sea than over land, reducing costs to consumers as well as economically benefiting Ukrainian port cities. But commercial shipping in the area has yet to fully recover, as shipping companies cannot afford the high insurance premiums that war has occasioned.

The Black Sea is critical for Russia as well as for NATO and Ukraine. Since its illegal annexation of Crimea, Moscow has claimed most of the Black Sea as part of its exclusive economic zone.[26] The Black Sea plays a central role in Russian shipping and security, a point Russia recently reinforced by constructing a naval base in Abkhazia.[27] Russian efforts to assert control in the Black Sea have included firing warning shots at and then boarding a Palau freighter in the southwestern portion of the sea.[28] The freighter, manned by Turkish civilians, was heading to the Romanian port of Sulina.

Russia's aggressive stance in the Black Sea is not likely to change if Ukraine joins NATO. There are at least two reasons to think that Moscow may in that case ramp up its provocations in the Black Sea. The first is that with the war over, Turkiye is likely to drop its restrictions on warships transiting the Bosporus, allowing Moscow to increase its naval presence by transferring vessels from its Baltic or Northern fleets.[29] Secondly, NATO's posture in the Black Sea – even in peacetime – is limited by the Montreux Convention, which caps the number, tonnage, weaponry and duration of non-Black Sea states' warships in the Black Sea.[30] Given the small size of Bulgarian and Romanian naval forces – just three surface combatants each – and an almost non-existent Ukrainian fleet, Moscow will probably try to reclaim the advantage it long held over NATO in this region, which many perceive it has lost over the last several years.[31] A rejuvenated Russian Black Sea Fleet could enable Moscow to pressure, harass and otherwise frustrate Western efforts to support Ukraine's reconstruction and integration into the Alliance.

The West is hardly oblivious to these risks. Annual NATO exercises in the Black Sea continue to take place. Bulgaria, Romania and Turkiye have begun joint minesweeping operations to clear Russian mines from the Black Sea and allow for more cargo vessels to navigate the area, and there may be a subtle convergence of US and Turkish strategic approaches to the Black Sea, as both cast a wary eye on any Russian effort to reclaim lost dominance.[32] Yet with Ukraine in NATO, the Alliance would need to significantly increase its presence and role in the Black Sea, and avoid the temptation to once again overlook the region, placate Moscow or defer to Ankara.[33] To build on current efforts, better protect allied commercial activity – especially Ukraine's export routes – and deter and defend against ramped-up Russian aggression following Ukrainian membership, NATO should strengthen its posture in the Black Sea. Due to the Montreux Convention, NATO will need to rely on the navies of Bulgaria, Romania, Turkiye and Ukraine to increase both the number of vessels and the frequency of freedom-of-navigation operations in the Black Sea, specifically in waters bordering the Ukrainian exclusive economic zone. Given Turkish President Recep Tayyip Erdoğan's apparent commitment to balancing Turkiye's relations with Russia and the West, larger, wealthier allies should avoid letting Ankara set the pace, breadth and depth of posture developments by assisting Bulgaria, Romania and Ukraine – bilaterally if necessary. The United States, France, Germany, the UK and others can do this by offering littoral allies recently decommissioned surface combatants, submarines and maritime-patrol aircraft to enhance their capacity, capabilities and inter-operability.[34]

Additionally, NATO should increase the number of exercises in the Black Sea, both to deter Russia and to improve allied inter-operability. Because of Montreux limitations, an expanded exercise programme would have to rely heavily on the navies of littoral allies. But more exercises conducted over shorter periods could also leverage a wider array of non-littoral allies. A more robust exercise programme and a stronger NATO presence in the Black Sea, especially in Ukrainian waters, would go far in facilitating the flow of goods that will be economically vital in the years ahead. Ultimately, this could conserve Western resources by enabling Ukraine to generate more of its own reconstruction revenue though increased Black Sea trade.

Reinforcing the flanks

Russia's reaction to Ukrainian membership in NATO probably would not remain limited geographically to the territory of Ukraine or the Black Sea. In particular, the West should expect Russia to intensify hybrid activities and other military operations designed to intimidate its neighbours while falling short of the magnitude of aggression required to trigger Article 5 mutual-defence action.

These activities could take a variety of forms, some familiar and some novel. For example, over the last several years, Russia has regularly committed airspace violations and conducted electromagnetic-spectrum disruptions across northeastern Europe, some of which have imperilled the safety of civilian airliners and shipping.[35] In the High North, Russian ships were spotted off the Norwegian coast likely conducting espionage activities.[36] After Finland joined NATO, Russian authorities orchestrated the weaponisation of migrants, sending thousands across the border into Finland with the apparent intent of sowing economic and political discord.[37] With Ukraine in NATO, the Alliance should expect this sort of activity to continue and perhaps increase, especially in regions adjacent to Russian territory or easily accessed by Russian air and maritime assets, such as border areas, airspace and maritime domains of Estonia, Finland, Latvia, Lithuania, Norway and Poland.

Currently, NATO maintains a relatively small multinational battlegroup in each of the Baltic states and Poland, as well as in Bulgaria, Hungary, Romania and Slovakia.[38] The allies have also stood up a Baltic Air Policing initiative to patrol the skies above Estonia, Latvia and Lithuania.[39] NATO has plans to scale the forces in Latvia and Lithuania up to brigade level, although doing so will take several years.[40] NATO's multinational battlegroups are still not tasked, structured, equipped or trained to counter or conduct information, electronic or cyber warfare, and the Alliance's approach to air policing still leaves allies vulnerable to airspace violations and potentially catastrophic disruptions of GPS. Were Ukraine to join NATO, the allies would need to prepare for what would likely be more aggressive Russian provocations by modifying the mission sets, rules of engagement and capabilities of its forces in northeastern Europe.

The Alliance should also implement posture adjustments in the flanks to better counter increased Russian aggression. To deter and repel Russian airspace violations across the Baltic region, NATO would have to augment Alliance capabilities in anti-aircraft, anti-surface, anti-submarine and ballistic-missile defence, as well as land attack. The readiest means of doing so would be to urge the United States to reposition two of its four *Aegis* destroyers currently homeported in Rota, Spain, to Sweden's largest naval base, in Karlskrona. To increase situational awareness regarding critical underwater infrastructure in the Baltic and North seas, the Alliance should deploy off-the-shelf uncrewed underwater vehicles.[41] To better focus on the most salient threats, NATO should eliminate its battlegroups in Bulgaria, Hungary and Slovakia, and use those resources to bolster its presence in the remaining forward-operating locations of Estonia, Latvia, Lithuania, Poland and Romania. To better counter Russian uncrewed systems – including those being used today to frustrate NATO's support for Ukraine[42] – NATO should encourage the United States and other allies to field prototype directed-energy, short-range air-defence systems across the flank countries.[43]

On top of changing posture, fielding relevant capabilities and redesigning missions, the Alliance should adjust its prepositioned equipment holdings in the flanks. In the event of an attack on a member state, prepositioned equipment enables a faster allied response, as troops can flow across the Atlantic or across the continent far more quickly than, for example, heavy tanks. Due in part to the demands of arming Ukraine, NATO now lacks the ability to build up substantial prepositioned stocks. Slowly but steadily, though, European and US defence contractors are ramping up production.[44] Relatedly, the US Department of Defense has identified shortfalls of prepositioned air-defence systems and supplies for special operations as funding priorities for 2025.[45] When conditions allow, equipment should also be prepositioned in Nordic member states, affording troops stationed in or deployed to the Nordic and Baltic states easy access to equipment as needed.

Pushing back against hybrid attacks

For many years, the Kremlin has engaged in multifaceted hybrid warfare against the West, especially in the cyber domain, but also in the information space, aimed at undermining Western security through non-kinetic measures.[46] More recently, Moscow's hybrid warfare has taken a more virulent turn by way of sabotage and assassination operations that appear aimed at frustrating Western efforts to arm and train Ukrainian troops.[47] If and when Ukraine joins NATO, the Alliance should expect Russia to double down on hybrid efforts against the West. Moscow could raise hybrid activity as a way of exacting revenge on the West for its support to Ukraine while Russian military forces rebuild. More worrisomely, Moscow might engage in horizontal escalation, targeting sabotage, assassination and other measures on the activities of NATO members beyond arming and training Ukrainian troops. All allies – regardless of their geography or their role in assisting Ukrainian armed forces – are likely to experience increased hybrid attacks.

NATO has been clear that hybrid and cyber attacks can lead to the invocation of the Article 5 mutual-defence clause. However, current NATO strategy relies on a degree of ambiguity to deter Russian hybrid operations, with NATO officials unwilling to clarify exactly what kind of cyber or hybrid attack could trigger that provision. But Article 5 is not the only mechanism that could justify an allied response. If an ally feels threatened, that country could invoke NATO's Article 4, which allows members to 'consult with each other if they believe that their security, political independence or territorial integrity is threatened'.[48] Article 4 was most recently invoked after Russia's full-scale invasion of Ukraine, when several Eastern European nations called for consultations. Activating Article 4 signals allied solidarity to an adversary, and Alliance members would probably need to call on it more frequently if Russia heightened hybrid attacks against Western targets in the event of Ukrainian NATO membership.

Although a NATO state could in theory invoke Article 5 to gain assistance in executing an aggressive response to Russian hybrid operations, as a practical matter, the Alliance eschews offensive hybrid operations, instead favouring intelligence-sharing and linking up allies under attack with those with useful responsive capabilities. In order to better deter, absorb and respond to intensified Russian hybrid activity incident to Ukraine's accession, the Alliance would need to expand this 'matchmaking' activity, and the number of allies with valuable capabilities would need to grow. Offensive cyber and information campaigns, and covert operations directed at adversaries, are sensitive, often risky measures. However, if the Alliance hoped to avoid vertical escalation and more effectively deter and respond to intensified Russian hybrid activity after Ukraine joined, NATO and especially more reluctant allies would to an extent need to acclimate themselves to such operations.[49] Many Ukrainians are fluent in Russian, and some have proven able to infiltrate Russia to engage in covert activity.[50] Ukrainian skills and knowledge of the adversary could significantly increase the Alliance's ability to combat Russian hybrid warfare while avoiding vertical escalation.

*   *   *

Ukraine may well be on a trajectory for eventual membership in NATO. Assuming it does join, Russia will likely confront NATO with a range of challenges – some old and some new – designed not only to signal its displeasure but also to undermine public confidence in the Alliance, destabilise Ukraine and in general fray Western nerves. In the service of these aims, its activities will probably include multidomain provocations, hybrid-warfare initiatives and covert operations across Europe of a range and vigorousness not seen since the Cold War. To counter these threats, maintain transatlantic security and solidarity, and establish the stability necessary for Ukrainian reconstruction, NATO must consider not only the defence of Ukraine's territory and airspace, but also that of its maritime regions, the broader Black Sea and other allies adjacent to Russian territory. And it must anticipate an intensification of covert Russian hybrid activity across the continent. The Alliance would be well advised to begin a full-spectrum, multidomain, transcontinental review of how NATO would fulfil its mission with Ukraine on board.

Notes

[1] NATO, 'Washington Summit Declaration', paragraph 16, 10 July 2024, https://www.nato.int/cps/en/natohq/official_texts_227678.htm.

[2] See, for example, 'Read the Full Transcript of President Joe Biden's Interview with *Time*', *Time*, 5 June 2024, https://time.com/6984968/joe-biden-transcript-2024-interview/; Christopher S. Chivvis, 'Admitting Ukraine to Nato Would Be a Mistake for Both Ukraine and Nato', *Guardian*, 20 June 2024, https://www.theguardian.com/commentisfree/article/2024/jun/20/ukraine-nato-membership; and Kurt Volker, 'Bringing Ukraine into NATO Without World War III', Center for European Policy Analysis, 29 November 2023, https://cepa.org/article/bringing-ukraine-into-nato-without-world-war-iii/.

[3] See Richard L. Kugler, *The Great Strategy Debate: NATO's Evolution in the 1960s* (Santa Monica, CA: RAND, 1991).

[4] See Aurélie Pugnet, 'Finland's Real Integration into NATO Might Take Years, Officials Say', Euractiv, 1 June 2023, https://www.euractiv.com/section/defence-and-security/news/finlands-real-integration-into-nato-might-take-years-officials-say/; and 'Finland Will Host a NATO Land Command and Troops', Reuters, 14

June 2024, https://www.reuters.com/world/europe/finland-will-host-nato-land-command-troops-2024-06-14/.

5   See Erik J. Grossman, 'Russia's Frozen Conflicts and the Donbas', *Parameters*, vol. 48, no. 2, Summer 2018, pp. 51–62.

6   David Carment and Dani Belo, 'Gray-zone Conflict Management: Theory, Evidence, and Challenges', *Journal of European, Middle Eastern & African Affairs*, vol. 2, no. 2, June 2020, pp. 21–41.

7   Konrad Muzyka, 'Russian Forces in the Western Military District', CNA, June 2021, https://www.cna.org/archive/CNA_Files/pdf/russian-forces-in-the-western-military-district.pdf.

8   International Institute for Strategic Studies (IISS), *The Military Balance 2021* (Abingdon: Routledge for the IISS, 2021), p. 167. The 8th Combined Arms Army also includes the 20th Motor Rifle Division, which is based in the Volgograd region roughly 320 km from Ukraine's eastern border.

9   See 'Ukraine Crisis: Russia Keeps Troops in Belarus amid Ukraine Fears', BBC News, 20 February 2022, https://www.bbc.com/news/world-europe-60451955.

10 See 'Belarus Dismantling Three Russian Training Grounds, Satellite Images Show', Radio Free Europe/Radio Liberty, 7 July 2023, https://www.rferl.org/a/belarus-dismantling-russian-training-grounds-satellite-images/32492923.html; Jack Detsch and Robbie Gramer, 'Russia's Nuclear Weapons Are Now in Belarus', *Foreign Policy*, 14 March 2024, https://foreignpolicy.com/2024/03/14/russia-nuclear-weapons-belarus-putin/; Nick Mordowanec, 'Belarus Gives Russia Control of Airfield Less than 20 Miles from Ukraine', *Newsweek*, 7 July 2022, https://www.newsweek.com/russia-control-belarus-zyabrovka-airfield-20-miles-ukraine-1722757; Valentyna Romanenko, 'Number of Russian Troops in Belarus Has Significantly Decreased', *Ukrainska Pravda*, 7 June 2023, https://www.pravda.com.ua/eng/news/2023/06/7/7405794/; and Maria Yeryoma, 'Belarus Weekly: Belarus Allows Russia to Use Two Military Bases for 25 More Years', *Kyiv Independent*, 16 September 2022, https://kyivindependent.com/belarus-weekly-belarus-allows-russia-to-use-two-military-bases-for-25-more-years/.

11 See Brendan Cole, 'Russian Military Transfers to Belarus Reignite Ukraine Attack Fears', *Newsweek*, 16 May 2024, https://www.newsweek.com/belarus-putin-russia-railways-1901285.

12 See, for example, John J. Mearsheimer, 'Assessing the Conventional Balance: The 3:1 Rule and Its Critics', *International Security*, vol. 13, no. 4, Spring 1989, pp. 54–89.

13 IISS, *The Military Balance 2021*, p. 209.

14 See John R. Deni, 'The New NATO Force Model: Ready for Launch?', NATO Defense College, 27 May 2024, https://www.ndc.nato.int/news/news.php?icode=1937.

15 For another example of a proposal to modify NATO's command structure, see Richard D. Hooker, Jr, 'A New NATO Command Structure', Atlantic Council, Issue Brief, May 2024, https://www.atlanticcouncil.org/wp-content/uploads/2024/05/A-New-NATO-Command-Structure.pdf.

16 See Hunter Stoll, John Hoehn and William Courtney, 'Air Defense

Shapes Warfighting in Ukraine', *Real Clear Defense*, 22 February 2024, https://www.realcleardefense.com/articles/2024/02/22/air_defense_shapes_warfighting_in_ukraine_1013615.html.

17 See Julian Kossoff, 'Ukraine Says It Deployed Its "FrankenSAM" Air-defense Systems Made from Stitching Together US and Soviet Weapons', *Business Insider*, 28 December 2023, https://www.businessinsider.com/ukraine-says-using-frankensam-weapons-fusing-us-soviet-weapons-2023-12.

18 See Bryant Harris, 'Biden Unveils Additional Air Defense Aid for Ukraine at NATO Summit', *Defense News*, 9 July 2024, https://www.defensenews.com/pentagon/2024/07/09/biden-unveils-additional-air-defense-aid-for-ukraine-at-nato-summit/; and Warren Murray, 'Ukraine War Briefing: Nato Summit Opens with Patriot Pledges', *Guardian*, 9 July 2024, https://www.theguardian.com/world/article/2024/jul/10/ukraine-war-briefing-nato-summit-opens-with-patriot-pledges.

19 See Olivia Yanchik, 'Ukraine Needs Enhanced Air Defenses as Russia Expands Missile Arsenal', Atlantic Council, 2 March 2024, https://www.atlanticcouncil.org/blogs/ukrainealert/ukraine-needs-enhanced-air-defenses-as-russia-expands-missile-arsenal/.

20 See NATO, 'NATO Joint Electronic Warfare Core Staff (JEWCS)', https://shape.nato.int/page1139304/nato-joint-electronic-warfare-core-staff-jewcs.

21 See '2023 AOC Convention Keynote: Lt. Gen. Lance Landrum, USAF (Ret.) Discusses EW in NATO', *Journal of Electromagnetic Dominance*, December 2023, https://www.jedonline.com/2023/12/20/lt-gen-lance-landrum-usaf-ret-discusses-ew-in-nato/.

22 See John E. Herbst, Olga Khakova and Charles Lichfield, 'Reconstructing Ukraine at War: The Journey to Prosperity Starts Now', Atlantic Council, 7 June 2024, https://www.atlanticcouncil.org/in-depth-research-reports/report/reconstructing-ukraine-at-war-the-journey-to-prosperity-starts-now.

23 UN Sustainable Development Group, 'Ukraine's Recovery and Reconstruction Needs Mount: $486 Billion Needed over Next Decade', 15 February 2024, https://unsdg.un.org/latest/stories/ukraines-recovery-and-reconstruction-needs-mount-486-billion-needed-over-next-decade.

24 Emma Dodd, Caitlin Welsh and Joseph Glauber, 'Setting the Record Straight on Ukraine's Grain Exports', Center for Strategic and International Studies, 2 May 2024, https://www.csis.org/analysis/setting-record-straight-ukraines-grain-exports.

25 Romina Bandura, Ilya Timtchenko and Benjamin Robb, 'Ships, Trains, and Trucks: Unlocking Ukraine's Vital Trade Potential', Center for Strategic and International Studies, 8 April 2024, https://www.csis.org/analysis/ships-trains-and-trucks-unlocking-ukraines-vital-trade-potential.

26 See Matthew Boyse et al., 'The Battle for the Black Sea Is Not Over', Hudson Institute, 16 April 2024, https://www.hudson.org/security-alliances/battle-black-sea-not-over-matthew-boyse-george-scutaru-mykhailo-samus-antonia-colibasanu.

27   See Nicholas Castillo, 'Russia On the Back Foot in the Black Sea: Implications for Georgia and the Caspian Region', Caspian Policy Center, 31 January 2024, https://www.caspianpolicy.org/research/regional-south-caucasus/russia-on-the-back-foot-in-the-black-sea-implications-for-georgia-and-the-caspian-region; 'Russia May Launch Naval Base in Georgian Breakaway Region in 2024', Reuters, 12 January 2024, https://www.reuters.com/world/europe/russia-may-launch-naval-base-georgian-breakaway-region-2024-2024-01-12/; and Logan Williams, 'Construction Accelerates at Planned Russian Navy Base in Disputed Abkhazia', Bellingcat, 30 July 2024, https://www.bellingcat.com/news/uk-and-europe/2024/07/30/construction-accelerates-at-planned-russian-navy-base-in-disputed-abkhazia/.

28   See Guy Faulconbridge, 'Russian Warship Fires Warning Shots at Cargo Ship in Black Sea', Reuters, 13 August 2023, https://www.reuters.com/world/europe/russian-warship-fires-dry-cargo-ship-black-sea-defence-ministry-2023-08-13/.

29   See Heather Mongilio, 'Turkey Closes Bosphorus, Dardanelles Straits to Warships', USNI News, 28 February 2022, https://news.usni.org/2022/02/28/turkey-closes-bosphorus-dardanelles-straits-to-warships. This assumes that Russia has the infrastructure necessary to increase its naval presence in the Black Sea. There is evidence that Russia is already expanding its infrastructure footprint in the region, such as through the construction of a naval base in Ochamchire, Abkhazia. Nevertheless, depending on the post-war disposition of Sevastopol, for example, it is possible the Russian navy will lack sufficient basing access to substantially augment its presence in the region.

30   See League of Nations, 'Convention Regarding the Regime of the Straits, with Annexes and Protocol', 20 July 1936, https://treaties.un.org/doc/Publication/UNTS/LON/Volume%20173/v173.pdf.

31   See Alper Coşkun, 'The Shifting Balance of Power in the Black Sea', GIS, 14 February 2024, https://www.gisreportsonline.com/r/turkey-black-sea/; and Joshua Kucera, 'Erdogan, in Plea to NATO, Says Black Sea Has Become "Russian Lake"', Eurasianet, 12 May 2016, https://eurasianet.org/erdogan-plea-nato-says-black-sea-has-become-russian-lake.

32   See Kemal Kirişci, 'Black Sea Mine Sweeping Aids a Subtle Convergence of Turkish–US Policies', Brookings Institution, 18 June 2024, https://www.brookings.edu/articles/black-sea-mine-sweeping-aids-a-subtle-convergence-of-turkish-us-policies/; US Naval Forces Europe–Africa and U.S. Sixth Fleet Public Affairs, 'U.S. Navy Participates in NATO's Sea Shield 2024 in Constanţa, Romania', 20 April 2024, https://www.navy.mil/Press-Office/News-Stories/Article/3751039/us-navy-participates-in-natos-sea-shield-2024-in-constana-romania/; and Cem Devrim Yaylali, 'Turkey, Bulgaria, Romania Team Up to Clear Black Sea Mines', Defense News, 11 January 2024, https://www.defensenews.

com/global/europe/2024/01/11/
turkey-bulgaria-romania-team-up-to-
clear-black-sea-mines/.

33 See Nick Childs, 'The Black Sea in
the Shadow of War', *Survival*, vol. 65,
no. 3, June–July 2023, pp. 25–36; and
Harlan Ullman, 'NATO Must Seize
the Current Strategic Opportunity
in the Black Sea', Atlantic Council,
19 February 2022, https://www.
atlanticcouncil.org/blogs/ukrainealert/
nato-must-seize-the-current-strategic-
opportunity-in-the-black-sea/.

34 See Gavin Clough, 'To Fend Off
Russia in the Black Sea, the US
and NATO Need to Help Boost
Allies' Naval Power', Atlantic
Council, 10 January 2024, https://
www.atlanticcouncil.org/blogs/
new-atlanticist/to-fend-off-russia-in-
the-black-sea-the-us-and-nato-need-to-
help-boost-allies-naval-power/; Craig
Hooper, 'In a Russia–Ukraine Peace,
Montreux Convention Will Stress
NATO Black Sea Peacekeepers', *Forbes*,
3 July 2023, https://www.forbes.
com/sites/craighooper/2023/07/03/
in-a-russia-ukraine-peace-montreux-
convention-will-stress-nato-black-
sea-peacekeepers/; and Aaron
Stein, 'Side-stepping Turkey: Using
Minesweepers to Increase Allied
Presence in the Black Sea', *War on
the Rocks*, 7 September 2023, https://
warontherocks.com/2023/09/
side-stepping-turkey-using-
minesweepers-to-increase-allied-
presence-in-the-black-sea/.

35 See Jakub Bornio, 'Airspace Violations
in Central and Eastern European
Countries in the Context of the War in
Ukraine', Instytut Europy Środkowej,
17 January 2024, https://ies.lublin.pl/

en/comments/airspace-violations-in-
central-and-eastern-european-countries-
in-the-context-of-the-war-in-ukraine/;
and Daniel Kochis, 'Russian
Recklessness Over the Skies of
Europe', *Real Clear Defense*, 15 May
2024, https://www.realcleardefense.
com/articles/2024/05/15/
russian_recklessness_over_the_skies_
of_europe_1031571.html.

36 See Lili Bayer, 'Russian Ships
Pose Threat in Nordic Waters as
Spies Take More Risks, Norway's
PM Says', *Politico*, 23 April 2023,
https://www.politico.eu/article/
norway-pm-jonas-gahr-store-russia-
intelligence-nordic-seas-war-ukraine/.

37 See Essi Lehto, 'Finland Says
Thousands of Migrants Are
Seeking to Enter via Russia',
Reuters, 20 February 2024, https://
www.reuters.com/world/europe/
finland-says-thousands-migrants-
seek-enter-via-russia-2024-02-20/.

38 NATO, 'NATO's Military Presence in
the East of the Alliance', 8 July 2024,
https://www.nato.int/cps/en/natohq/
topics_136388.htm.

39 NATO, 'Baltic Air Policing', https://
ac.nato.int/missions/air-policing/baltics.

40 See Sean Monaghan et al., 'Is
NATO Ready for War?', Center
for Strategic and International
Studies, June 2024, https://csis-
website-prod.s3.amazonaws.
com/s3fs-public/2024-06/240611_
Monaghan_Ready_War_0.pdf.

41 For an analysis of the threats
to Alliance critical underwater
infrastructure and related recommen-
dations, see Sean Monaghan et al.,
'NATO's Role in Protecting Critical
Undersea Infrastructure', Center for

Strategic and International Studies, 19 December 2023, https://www.csis.org/analysis/natos-role-protecting-critical-undersea-infrastructure.

42 See Joshua Posaner and Cristina Gonzalez, 'Mysterious Drones Keep Watch as Ukrainians Train in Germany', *Politico*, 16 July 2024, https://www.politico.eu/article/drones-ukrainian-troops-german-military-training-eu-military-assistance-mission/.

43 See Colin Demarest, 'US Testing Stryker-mounted Lasers in Iraq amid Middle East Drone Boom', *Defense News*, 22 March 2024, https://www.defensenews.com/battlefield-tech/directed-energy/2024/03/22/us-testing-stryker-mounted-lasers-in-iraq-amid-middle-east-drone-boom/.

44 See Andrew Gray, 'EU Aims to Shift European Arms Industry to "War Economy Mode"', Reuters, 5 March 2024, https://www.reuters.com/world/europe/eu-aims-shift-european-arms-industry-war-economy-mode-2024-03-04/; and Noah Robertson, 'Production of Key Munition Years Ahead of Schedule, Pentagon Says', *Defense News*, 15 September 2023, https://www.defensenews.com/pentagon/2023/09/15/production-of-key-munition-years-ahead-of-schedule-pentagon-says/.

45 See US Department of Defense, 'European Deterrence Initiative', Department of Defense Budget Fiscal Year (FY) 2025, March 2024, https://comptroller.defense.gov/Portals/45/Documents/defbudget/FY2025/FY2025_EDI_JBook.pdf.

46 See, for example, Robert S. Mueller, *Report on the Investigation into Russian Interference in the 2016 Presidential Election* (Washington DC: US Department of Justice, 2019), https://www.justice.gov/archives/sco/file/1373816/dl; and Ian Traynor, 'Russia Accused of Unleashing Cyberwar to Disable Estonia', *Guardian*, 16 May 2007, https://www.theguardian.com/world/2007/may/17/topstories3.russia.

47 See Dan De Luce and Jean-Nicholas Fievet, 'Russia's "Brazen" and Intensifying Sabotage Campaign Across Europe', NBC News, 13 May 2024, https://www.nbcnews.com/news/investigations/russias-brazen-intensifying-sabotage-campaign-europe-rcna147178.

48 NATO, 'The Consultation Process and Article 4', https://www.nato.int/cps/en/natolive/topics_49187.htm.

49 See Henrik Breitenbauch and Niels Byrjalsen, 'Subversion, Statecraft and Liberal Democracy', *Survival*, vol. 61, no. 4, August–September 2019, pp. 31–41.

50 See Adam Entous and Michael Schwirtz, 'The Spy War: How the C.I.A. Secretly Helps Ukraine Fight Putin', *New York Times*, 25 February 2024, https://www.nytimes.com/2024/02/25/world/europe/cia-ukraine-intelligence-russia-war.html.

Copyright © 2024 The International Institute for Strategic Studies

Britain in the Pacific: Staying the Course?

Nick Childs and Callum Fraser

After 14 years out of office, the British Labour Party has inherited a dire economic situation, accompanied by bitter argument over who or what is to blame. It is also grappling with a dynamic global strategic environment that has been transformed during that period. Prime Minister Keir Starmer's top international priority is a reset in the United Kingdom's post-Brexit relations with the rest of Europe and the European Union. Labour has also committed to a 'NATO-first' defence and security policy.[1] What this means in itself and for UK relations with the rest of the world remains unclear. Of particular interest are its implications for defence and military commitments pursuant to the 'Indo-Pacific tilt' unveiled by the Conservative government three years ago.

There was plenty for Labour to be critical, or at least suspicious, of in the tilt. Many saw as it as an example of the Conservatives' party-political, post-imperial, post-Brexit nostalgia, under the even more hubristic-sounding banner of 'Global Britain'. It was also associated with the polarising personality of former prime minister Boris Johnson, with the ill-starred endorsement of his almost equally controversial but far less durable successor, Liz Truss. Yet the strategic rationale for greater UK engagement in the Asia-Pacific region was powerful and remains so.

Nick Childs is IISS Senior Fellow for Naval Forces and Maritime Security. **Callum Fraser** is a British Army Officer, serving with the Royal Gurkha Rifles. He recently completed a 12-month Chief of the General Staff Fellowship at the IISS.

Survival | vol. 66 no. 5 | October–November 2024 | pp. 147–158 https://doi.org/10.1080/00396338.2024.2403226

This article was originally published with errors, which have now been corrected in the online version. Please see Correction (https://doi.org/10.1080/00396338.2024.2413825).

In opposition, Labour's criticism of the basic idea was muted and tended instead to be directed more towards its motivations, its areas of focus and especially the associated defence commitments. As shadow minister, John Healey – now the new secretary of state for defence – was in the vanguard of those calling them unrealistic and warning that they would come at the expense of the UK's contribution to NATO.[2] Indeed, many commentators expressed concern about the opportunity costs of deployments that would have little strategic impact in the region and might only risk UK embroilment in confrontation.[3] Some military officers have had similar misgivings. Moreover, the policy dilemmas that the tilt presented seemed only to be sharpened by the eruption of a crisis much closer to home with Russia's full-scale invasion of Ukraine in February 2022.

In the immediate run-up to the recent UK general election, David Lammy, who would become Labour's foreign secretary, framed the party's approach to foreign policy as one of 'progressive realism', or 'the pursuit of ideals without delusions'.[4] As applied to the tilt, that reads like code for scaling back ambitions, particularly in terms of defence and security commitments, and in light of the government's strained finances and increasing pressure on the defence budget. The tilt has always been about a much broader set of political, diplomatic and economic relationships than just hard-power obligations. But they are all interconnected, and the value of enhanced military re-engagement in helping open the door to improvements in those relationships should not be underestimated. In addition, intensifying some defence and security commitments in the region could advance some of the government's other key strategic ambitions, including those in Europe. Labour has a Strategic Defence Review (SDR) under way and its first full budget looms. These should help clarify where it stands on the Asia-Pacific region and defence as a whole. If it wants to, the new government has the opportunity to take ownership of the tilt, albeit with tough choices.

The arc of history

In 1968, the Labour government, under mounting economic pressure, announced the UK's military withdrawal 'east of Suez' by 1971. At the time, the UK had a range of air, land and naval forces in Asia, including a significant fleet based in Singapore and centred on an aircraft carrier.

The withdrawal was not, in fact, comprehensive. A handful of frigates were kept on briefly in the early 1970s to be replaced for a few more years by a couple of 'gunboats' or utility frigates based in Singapore and also in Hong Kong, where a wider military presence was maintained until the 1997 handover. More significantly, the Royal Navy developed the group-deployment concept, involving the regular dispatch from the UK of a powerful, essentially self-sufficient task group for several months, to 'show the flag' and exercise the Royal Navy's skills at deploying globally.[5] The first of these deployments occurred in 1973. There was also a garrison presence in Brunei that continues to this day, and a framework of continued defence cooperation and regular exercises with Australia, Malaysia, New Zealand and Singapore under the Five Power Defence Arrangements. An enduring naval presence in the Middle East and northern Indian Ocean was also re-established in the early 1980s.

The UK maintained the drumbeat of naval group deployments extending as far as East Asia until 2009. At that point, the demands of the two prolonged campaigns in Iraq and Afghanistan, and mounting resource constraints, were taking their toll. Anything other than occasional single-ship visits was challenging. However, the continuing shift of the global economic centre of gravity eastward, plus the growing resonance of the Asia-Pacific as an important arena of renewed state-based competition, began to draw London's strategic attention again. This predated both Brexit and Global Britain, and was reflected in the language of the 2015 Strategic Defence and Security Review by way of renewed interest in the Gulf and in the Asia-Pacific, particularly increased strategic cooperation with Japan.[6]

In March 2021, the Integrated Review (IR) of Security, Defence, Development and Foreign Policy formally inaugurated the notion of the Indo-Pacific tilt and declared the UK's ambition to establish there 'a greater and more persistent presence than any other European country'.[7] This was no small proclamation given that France's territory in the region totalled nearly a half million square kilometres and its enduring presence there included some 8,000 personnel.

The most specific uplifts in defence commitments, set out in the Defence Command Paper that followed the IR, were naval, consisting of a mixture of persistent, periodic and episodic deployments. This enhanced maritime presence included the persistent assignment to the region from 2021 of the two *River*-class offshore patrol vessels (OPVs) *Spey* and *Tamar*, either to be replaced or supplemented later in the decade by new Type-31 frigates currently under construction, and the periodic deployment from 2023 of a modest amphibious formation dubbed a Littoral Response Group.[8]

What may have raised both eyebrows and expectations the highest was the high-profile operational debut of the Royal Navy's revived aircraft-carrier capability on a major Pacific-focused deployment called Carrier Strike Group 2021 (CSG21), with the anticipation that such missions would be reprised at regular intervals. These deployments have seemed in some ways to further echo the adaptation that followed the retrenchment east of Suez at the end of the 1960s and into the 1970s: deploying gunboats to mark presence and mounting more ambitious group deployments to show the flag and demonstrate a continuing expeditionary capability with global reach. But even with CSG21 still under way, many hoped and expected that the next deployment would occur within two years. In fact, it will be at least four.

The tilt so far

The 2023 IR 'Refresh', to take account of the sharply increased global turbulence in the two years following the original IR, declared that 'we will put our approach to the Indo-Pacific on a long-term strategic footing, making the region a permanent pillar of the UK's international policy'.[9] Although then-prime minister Rishi Sunak declared the tilt realised, some sensed a strategic downgrading: the Refresh eschewed the phrase 'Global Britain', which had been quietly fading from the official lexicon. In the three years since the previous government unveiled the tilt, however, there has been a palpable uptick in UK engagement activity in the region. Significantly, an effectively integrated approach has evolved, providing potentially important guidance for other middle powers from outside the region with similar ambitions.

As the Refresh put it, there has been only a 'modest initial increase' in the UK's regional defence presence, and what has been achieved so far has been 'largely through non-military instruments – such as diplomacy, trade, development, technological exchange and engagement with regional organi-sations'.[10] That said, the word 'initial' in reference to the UK's currently rather light defence presence clearly implies more to come if necessary. For now, the OPVs *Spey* and *Tamar* are helping to coordinate with partners and providing training opportunities across the region that serve the priorities of those part-ners, and to some extent fill a demand for engagement that the United States is not necessarily prioritising. The impact of Britain's vessels in terms of defence diplomacy has exceeded expectations.

Likewise, the Brunei-based battalion continues to run training and engagement drills across the region, from Australia and Papua New Guinea to Thailand and Vietnam. The Littoral Response Group's recent transit around the region has injected a slightly higher level of capability, but this military footprint is not about balance-of-power calculations per se. Instead, it is about presenting the UK as a reliable and trustworthy partner to nations in and beyond the security realm, with skills to share but not necessarily seeking a leadership role.

In contrast to this overall humility, two key collaborations have audaciously melded both economic and security ambitions and have retroactively vindicated the tilt. The first is the Australia–UK–US agreement, known as AUKUS, centred on Australia's intention with American and British help to establish a conventionally armed but nuclear-powered attack-submarine (SSN) capability, and also involving collaboration on other advanced defence technologies.[11] The other is the Global Combat Air Programme (GCAP), bringing together Italy, Japan and the UK to develop a next-generation multi-role fighter and associated systems.[12] The UK's accession to the Comprehensive and Progressive Agreement for Trans-Pacific Partnership (CPTPP) – it is the only non-regional state to join – has also been noteworthy, as has Britain's acceptance as a dialogue partner of the Association of Southeast Asian Nations (ASEAN).[13]

Save for AUKUS, which turned mainly on the UK's ability to supply a suitable nuclear-propulsion technology, these milestones were achieved largely because the UK had promised to be a more robust defence partner in the future. The subsequent expansion of the strategic relationship between London and Tokyo, including a mutual-defence cooperation and access agreement, reinforces the point.[14] Reported alarm in Tokyo when the incoming Labour government's public endorsement of GCAP seemed less enthusiastic than that for AUKUS underscores the sensitivities at play.[15]

The AUKUS agreement has produced perhaps the most significant additional regional defence burden on the UK, and particularly the Royal Navy, since the tilt. In the long term, AUKUS should mean more investment, more jobs and more work for the UK submarine-building industry, and the promise of more and better SSNs for the Royal Navy as well. En route to that future, the UK has agreed to forward-deploy in Australia one SSN on a rotational basis, alongside several from the US Navy, starting in 2027. With a British SSN fleet likely then to consist of just seven boats in total, and with numerous and important demands closer to home, that will be a major challenge for the UK, and one that involves a real capability trade-off.[16]

So far, however, the UK's enhanced defence presence has come at relatively little opportunity cost. The OPVs have delivered beyond expectations, though they may have been low anyway due to the UK's relative absence from the region in the recent past. Returns are therefore likely to diminish. Increasingly, regional allies and partners will be looking for a more purposeful and reliable commitment of capabilities that will contribute to assurance and deterrence, as well as diplomacy. Rather than looking to cut back commitments, the key for the new government should be to acknowledge that the true dividends from the tilt will accrue from sticking with it. Conversely, for the UK to default on expected commitments would risk disappointing allies and partners, to the detriment of British influence, leverage and interests.

Non-binary outlook

The strategic choices here – for example, between the Euro-Atlantic and the Asia-Pacific arenas, and between a regional and continental role and an expeditionary one – may not be as stark or binary as they are often portrayed. For the UK, even a NATO-first role can yield different interpretations, especially now that several of the Alliance's other members have increased their military heft. The British Army certainly needs to rebuild its capability, but potentially for a more agile and flexible role involving missions in which it can poise and flex forces between NATO's key theatres. From this perspective, there may be synergies among capabilities that can add value in both regions, in particular with respect to aircraft carriers, SSNs and new-generation fighter programmes like GCAP. In the latter case, the UK may have found that it has more in common in terms of its future fighter requirements with Japan, another island nation on the other side of the world, than it does with some of its closer European neighbours, including the need for an aircraft with greater range and payload.

The previous British government coined the term 'Atlantic–Pacific' partnerships for its AUKUS and GCAP tie-ups. Security concerns and geo-political challenges of the Euro-Atlantic and Asia-Pacific arenas have indeed become more intertwined by virtue of strengthened ties between China, Iran, North Korea and Russia, as well as shifting and fluid allegiances among geographically dispersed sections of the global community, particu-larly in the Global South.

At the 2016 IISS Shangri-La Dialogue in Singapore, Jean-Yves Le Drian, France's then-defence minister and subsequently its foreign minister, unveiled a proposal for a coordinated European presence in Asian seas.[17] It struggled to make headway because regional interests were not clear to many European capitals. Since then, several of the UK's European neigh-bours have become more cognisant of the increased stakes that they have in the Asia-Pacific region and are undertaking their own variations of the tilt themselves, likewise with enhanced defence deployments in the face of limited resources.[18] In 2024, the German navy deployed to the region for only the second time in two decades – the first being a mere two years ago – and the Italian navy sent a carrier strike group.[19] The rising presence of European ministerial delegations at the Shangri-La Dialogue is further evi-dence of their growing engagement. Less clear is what role the Europeans can play.

In its Strategy for Cooperation in the Indo-Pacific, published in September 2021, the European Commission spoke of the importance of a 'meaningful' European naval presence in the region and said the EU would explore ways to ensure enhanced naval deployments[20] – an ambi-tion underlined in the 2022 EU Strategic Compass document.[21] The 2023

Anglo-French summit yielded a new pledge by London and Paris to coordinate aircraft-carrier deployments, in part as a basis for a sustained European, if not an EU, maritime presence in the Indo-Pacific.[22] One ready path to a Labour reset with Europe would be through greater – defence and especially naval – cooperation in the Indo-Pacific. That will not be an easy course to navigate. Acknowledging that Europe has a greater stake in Asia-Pacific stability is not the same as aligning approaches towards the US, China and other players in the region. For most European countries, a commitment in the Western Pacific is an ambition too far, the Indian Ocean being the practical extent of their reach. The best chance for the Europeans to have impact and influence in the Asia-Pacific may lie in acting together. Yet this also has its limits, not least because, for the most part, they remain commercial rivals in the region.

Keeping up appearances

The defence-commitment element of the tilt will remain a critical under-pinning, and sustaining a credible level of commitment in terms of force requirements is likely to get harder, notwithstanding the potential mitigating effect of new technology and innovation.

Propelling the tilt was then-prime minister Boris Johnson's promise of a significant injection of extra defence funding and his declared ambition to bolster the Royal Navy 'to restore Britain's position as the foremost naval power in Europe'.[23] His government contemplated increasing the destroyer and frigate strength of the fleet by some 25% by the mid-2030s.[24] It is somewhat ironic that, in the late 1960s when the then-Labour government was announcing the end of a British role east of Suez on grounds of cost, Britain indisputably possessed the most powerful Western European naval fleet.

The CSG21 deployment, while impressive, took a significant slice of the Royal Navy's combat and support resources to deliver. Even then, to help fill some gaps, the UK turned to allies, including the US Marine Corps, for a squadron of Lockheed Martin F35B *Lightning* II fighters because the UK itself did not yet have enough jets to provide a fully effective carrier air group. An aircraft carrier is a unique hard- and soft-power tool, with extraordinary resonance for a deterrent role in the Asia-Pacific region. But at a point when even the US Navy is struggling to meet all its commitments and turning more and more to allies and partners, for the UK to adopt an integrated deterrence approach looks not merely viable but logical.

The UK's critical challenge is to achieve the right balance between integrated and sovereign capabilities so as to add value without overstretching limited resources or descending to mere tokenism. A middle power like the UK will always face significant constraints. But the ladder of capability ambitions in the original IR still looks like a good prescription for the tilt: the persistent presence of OPVs and later frigates, the periodic deployment of a tailored amphibious group and the episodic dispatch of a carrier group. Augmenting these components would be the AUKUS-linked, forward-deployed SSN.

The problem is that the Royal Navy will struggle even more to deliver CSG25 than it did CSG21. The fleet has shrunk rather than grown, as older ships have been mothballed before new ships arrive. Moreover, the building programme for the future will surely come under scrutiny in the SDR. This means Labour will need to directly and specifically answer questions about where defence in general and the Indo-Pacific in particular are situated in its list of priorities. This includes clarifying its general-election pledge to 'set out the path to spending 2.5% of GDP on defence'.[25] The primary institutional focus will remain NATO, the main geographical focus the Euro-Atlantic, and the key procurement focus the capability shortfalls exposed by the Russia–Ukraine war.

To safeguard the tilt, the SDR should define the UK's role as a leading NATO and European player, and its role as an effective Indo-Pacific one, in a way that maximises the synergies between them. This will still require difficult strategic choices. Some have argued that an Indo-Pacific tilt that focuses more on the Gulf and the northwest Indian Ocean is more logical and achievable, and that at present Washington might value it more than a full Pacific tilt. Looking farther out, however, the more distant horizons may eclipse the Middle East as a strategic priority for the UK, as well as the United States and other key allies and partners.

The tilt has already illuminated the virtues of an integrated approach to strategy and has helped deliver a patchwork of new relationships that has enhanced the UK's standing and interests. But the key concern is what next. A key piece of the puzzle is the relationship with China. Labour derided the Conservatives' approach as lurching and inconsistent, but virtually all Western nations have struggled to formulate a coherent and durable approach to China, which has itself presented a moving target. While London does not share Washington's perspective, it is probably closer to Washington and other key Indo-Pacific partners such as Australia and Japan than it is to most other European countries. Labour has embraced a formula that has been adopted in many forms in different capitals – to 'co-operate where we can, compete where we need to, and challenge where we must'.[26] The trick, of course, is turning that buzz phrase into policy and strategy. Labour has pledged to audit the UK's China policy and place it on a different footing. Some may anticipate that Labour will emphasise 'cooperate' more than 'compete'. But China's assertiveness and the regional mood music may push in the other direction, urging a hard-power defence commitment. Labour may be compelled to specify what action it is prepared to entertain if one of the region's flashpoints flares into confrontation.

*   *   *

Although 'Global Britain' has faded from government rhetoric in recent years, the UK has retained highly ambitious global objectives for a nation of its size and material strength. There is no sign that Labour wants to step back from that overall level of ambition. However, the demands of the Russia–Ukraine war are pressing, the shrinking size and excessive commitment of the UK armed forces are palpable, and China is becoming more strategically shrill. Something may have to give. At the same time, the issue of whether the UK can continue to enjoy influence in the Indo-Pacific without compromising its Euro-Atlantic security priorities may not be as stark as some have portrayed it. Up to now, Labour's chief legacy in the region has been its decision to withdraw east of Suez under economic pressure to meet the Cold War requirement of concentrating resources on the challenge of the Warsaw Pact in Europe. Today, it may need to grapple with how to sustain and reinforce a strategic return to the region.

Notes

1 John Healey and David Lammy, 'This Labour Government Will Have a "NATO First" Defence Strategy', *Telegraph*, 8 July 2024, https://www.telegraph.co.uk/politics/2024/07/08/labour-government-nato-first-defence-strategy/.

2 See Cristina Gallardo, 'Labour Urges "Realism" on UK's Indo-Pacific Military Ambitions', *Politico*, 9 March 2023, https://www.politico.eu/article/labour-john-healey-defense-uk-military-indo-pacific-aukus/.

3 See, for example, David Blagden, 'Written Evidence Submission from Dr David Blagden (University of Exeter) for an Inquiry of the UK House of Commons' Defence Select Committee on "The Navy: Purpose and Procurement"', 8 June 2021, https://committees.parliament.uk/writtenevidence/36594/pdf/?_gl=1*d7lc8e*_up*MQ..*_ga*Mjg4NzcwMDcyLjE3MjUyMjgwODc.*_ga_9684J19FT4*MTcyNTIyODA4Ni4xLjAuMTcyNTIyODE0Mi4wLjAuMA.

4 David Lammy, 'The Case for Progressive Realism', *Foreign Affairs*, vol. 103, no. 3, May/June 2024, pp. 125–35.

5 See Edward Hampshire, *The Royal Navy in the Cold War Years 1966–1990: Retreat and Revival* (Barnsley: Seaforth Press, 2024), pp. 112–16.

6 See UK Government, 'National Security Strategy and Strategic Defence and Security Review 2015: A Secure and Prosperous United Kingdom', November 2015, pp. 58–9, https://assets.publishing.service.gov.uk/media/5a81a100e5274a2e8ab5504e/52309_Cm_9161_NSS_SD_Review_PRINT_only.pdf.

7 UK Government, 'Global Britain in a Competitive Age: The Integrated Review of Security, Defence, Development and Foreign Policy 2021', March 2021, p. 62, https://assets.publishing.service.gov.uk/media/60644e4bd3bf7f0c91eababd/Global_Britain_in_a_Competitive_Age-_the_Integrated_Review_of_Security__Defence__Development_and_Foreign_Policy.pdf.

8 See Ministry of Defence, 'Defence in a Competitive Age', March 2021, p. 32, https://assets.publishing.service.gov.uk/media/6063061e8fa8f55b6ad297d0/CP411_-Defence_Command_Plan.pdf.

9 UK Government, 'Integrated Review Refresh 2023: Responding to a More Contested and Volatile World', March 2023, https://assets.publishing.service.gov.uk/media/641d72f45155a2000c6ad5d5/11857435_NS_IR_Refresh_2023_Supply_AllPages_Revision_7_WEB_PDF.pdf.

10 *Ibid.*, p. 7.

11 See White House, 'Joint Leaders Statement on AUKUS', 15 September 2021, https://www.whitehouse.gov/briefing-room/statements-releases/2021/09/15/joint-leaders-statement-on-aukus/.

12 See UK Government, 'PM Announces New International Coalition to Develop the Next Generation of Combat Aircraft', 9 December 2023, https://www.gov.uk/government/news/pm-announces-new-international-coalition-to-develop-the-next-generation-of-combat-aircraft.

13 See ASEAN, 'Joint Communiqué of the 54th ASEAN Foreign Ministers' Meeting', 2 August 2021, https://asean.org/wp-content/uploads/2021/08/Joint-

Communique-of-the-54th-ASEAN-Foreign-Ministers-Meeting-FINAL.pdf.

14 See Japan Ministry of Foreign Affairs, 'Signing of Japan–UK Reciprocal Access Agreement', 11 January 2023, https://www.mofa.go.jp/erp/we/gb/page1e_000556.html.

15 See Stuart Lau, 'Japan Wants Reassurance Britain's New Government Has Its Back', *Politico*, 30 July 2024, https://www.politico.eu/article/japan-want-indo-pacific-reassurance-britain-uk-new-labour-government/.

16 See Nick Childs, 'The AUKUS Anvil: Promise and Peril', *Survival*, vol. 65, no. 5, October–November 2023, pp. 7–24.

17 See Jean-Yves Le Drian, 'The Challenges of Conflict Resolution', speech at the IISS Shangri-La Dialogue, Fourth Plenary Session, Singapore, 5 June 2016, https://www.iiss.org/en/events/shangri-la-dialogue/archive/shangri-la-dialogue-2016-4a4b/plenary4-6c15/drian-5b52.

18 See Ben Schreer, 'Coming of Age? European Defence Engagement in the Indo-Pacific', IISS Online Analysis, 22 May 2024, https://www.iiss.org/online-analysis/online-analysis/2024/05/coming-of-age-european-defence-engagement-in-the-indo-pacific/.

19 See Alessio Patalano, 'What Is an Italian Carrier Strike Group Doing in the Indo-Pacific?', *War on the Rocks*, 29 August 2024, https://warontherocks.com/2024/08/what-is-an-italian-carrier-strike-group-doing-in-the-indo-pacific/.

20 See European Commission, High Representative of the Union for Foreign and Security Affairs, 'The EU Strategy for Cooperation in the Indo-Pacific', 16 September 2021, https://www.eeas.europa.eu/sites/default/files/jointcommunication_2021_24_1_en.pdf.

21 See Council of the European Union, 'A Strategic Compass for Security and Defence', 21 March 2022, https://data.consilium.europa.eu/doc/document/ST-7371-2022-INIT/en/pdf.

22 See UK Prime Minister's Office, 'France–UK Joint Leaders' Declaration', 10 March 2023, https://www.gov.uk/government/publications/uk-france-joint-leaders-declaration/uk-france-joint-leaders-declaration.

23 UK Prime Minister's Office, 'PM Statement to the House on the Integrated Review: 19 November 2020', 19 November 2020, https://www.gov.uk/government/speeches/pm-statement-to-the-house-on-the-integrated-review-19-november-2020.

24 *Ibid.*

25 Labour Party, 'Change: Labour Party Manifesto 2024', p. 15, https://labour.org.uk/wp-content/uploads/2024/06/Labour-Party-manifesto-2024.pdf.

26 *Ibid.*, p. 120.

Copyright © 2024 The International Institute for Strategic Studies

Mirage of Coercion: The Real Sources of China's Influence in the Middle East and North Africa

Dale Aluf

As China extends its geopolitical reach into the Middle East and North Africa, misconceptions about its strategic priorities and oversimplifications regarding the mechanisms of power in global politics today seem to have obscured the true character of Beijing's influence.

This is hardly surprising. External perceptions of China's foreign policy are often mired in contradictions and polarised into extremes. Some analysts join Brahma Chellaney to warn of a 'hegemonic sphere of trade, communication, transportation, and security links' advancing China's 'neocolonial designs' grounded in a realpolitik framework that ignores China's distinct culture and context.[1] Others overemphasise China's uniqueness, often drawing on history to illustrate that the Chinese are inherently averse to global hegemony.[2] Regarding the Middle East, analysts tend to oscillate between extremes of viewing China as an all-powerful entity with substantial regional clout or minimising its significance and asserting that its influence is, in fact, quite limited. The Israel–Hamas war has brought these misinterpretations into sharp relief.

Coercion and economic diplomacy

It is notable that Chinese influence in the region lacks the coercive dimensions seen elsewhere. China at various times has tried to punish Australia, Canada, Norway, Taiwan and others. Such punitive actions are absent in

Dale Aluf is the founder of Political Mind. He is also a research fellow at SIGNAL Group, for which he served as Research Director from 2017 to 2024. His research examines the impact of China's rise on the Middle East and North Africa.

Survival | vol. 66 no. 5 | October–November 2024 | pp. 159–182 https://doi.org/10.1080/00396338.2024.2403227

its approach to the Middle East and North Africa. This difference is easier to understand if we appreciate how Beijing prioritises its strategic interests and how these interests relate to the region.

Echoing the Confucian adage, 'to put the world in order, we must first put the nation in order', Beijing privileges domestic stability within its foreign-policy framework. Certain actions, such as the arrest of prominent Chinese citizen Meng Wanzhou by Canada in 2018, Australia's push for an investigation into China's handling of the COVID-19 outbreak or then-US House speaker Nancy Pelosi's visit to Taiwan in 2022 harboured the potential to inspire internal dissent, erode national pride and threaten the legitimacy of the Chinese Communist Party, elevating them to matters of critical national-security concern. China's behaviour in such cases is thus largely a product of its anxiety over its own unity and prosperity.

While these episodes demonstrated Beijing's increasing resort to punitive economic statecraft on issues that it considers as threatening to its core interests, China's leadership is, in fact, risk averse. This is especially true in a region as complex and volatile as the Middle East, where China's understanding of local dynamics is still evolving. The Chinese are scholars of history, and previous interventions by foreign powers in the region, often with costly and unintended consequences, have served as a cautionary tale. China is wary of being ensnared in disputes that diverge significantly from its core interests. It has therefore prioritised a less forceful form of geo-economics in that part of the world.

A web of interdependence

China has emerged as the largest trading partner of, and a significant source of investment, infrastructure and technology for, most Middle Eastern and North African states. To date, 21 Arab states, along with the Arab League, have signed onto Xi Jinping's Belt and Road Initiative (BRI).[3] China also enjoys 'strategic partnerships' with Iraq, Jordan, Kuwait, Morocco, Oman, Qatar, Tunisia, Turkiye and Syria; 'comprehensive strategic partnerships' with Algeria, Bahrain, Egypt, Iran, Saudi Arabia and the United Arab Emirates (UAE); and a 'comprehensive innovation partnership' with Israel.[4] Between 2017 and 2022, Chinese trade with the Middle East doubled from

$262.5 billion to $507.2bn, according to Chinese customs data.[5] Meanwhile, Arab and Middle Eastern countries saw Chinese BRI investments increase by around 360% from 2020 to 2021.[6] In the first half of 2022, the Middle East received around 57% of global BRI investments.[7] In the realm of technology, Chinese firms have rolled out fifth-generation telecommunication networks (5G), undersea cables, data centres and surveillance systems, becoming integral to smart-city projects such as Saudi Arabia's NEOM and Morocco's Tangier Tech City.[8]

Around 6,000 Chinese businesses operate in the UAE, another 1,500+ are registered in Egypt, and Morocco's Tangier Tech City is expected to host around 200 Chinese companies once Chinese contractors complete its construction.[9] As of mid-2017, there were reportedly 84 projects being executed by Chinese companies in Kuwait, valued at $18.12bn.[10] In Oman, China's investment had reached $193 million by the first quarter of 2023.[11] Meanwhile, China has invested more than $70bn in Algerian public-development projects, while China's investments, mergers and acquisitions in Israel's tech sector amounted to 449 deals worth roughly $9.14bn by the close of 2020.[12]

As China has expanded its maritime influence, investing in more than 100 ports across 63 nations, the region has welcomed upwards of 20 Chinese port projects.[13] With roughly 60% of China's exports to Europe transiting the Suez Canal, these assets serve as critical logistical nodes empowering China to exert substantial control over key segments of the supply chain.[14] This includes more effective management of both outbound trade routes, essential for its export economy, and inbound logistics, crucial for securing a continuous supply of vital resources such as energy from the Middle East.

China imports more oil than any other nation in the world, and Middle Eastern countries consistently rank among China's top ten suppliers. Despite a recent spike in crude imports from Russia that displaced Saudi Arabia as China's leading supplier earlier this year, almost half of China's oil imports still originate in six Middle Eastern countries: Iraq, Kuwait, Oman, Qatar, Saudi Arabia and the UAE.[15] Qatar alone accounts for 26.6% of China's imports of liquefied natural gas (LNG) and 16% of China's total natural-gas (pipeline and LNG) imports.[16] In November 2022, QatarEnergy signed a 27-year deal to supply China's Sinopec with 4m metric tons of LNG annually. In June 2023, QatarEnergy signed an identical deal with China National Petroleum Corporation (CNPC).[17]

By 2030, China is expected to rely on imports for more than 80% of its oil and 60% of its natural gas.[18] It may be willing and able to purchase cheap energy from Russia, but pipeline capacity currently limits the extent to which China can effectively diversify these supplies in the short to medium terms.[19] Even if Beijing seeks to engage in diversification in the long term, this is unlikely to extinguish its thirst for Middle Eastern energy. As Center for Strategic and International Studies analyst Anthony Cordesman pointed out in 2021, 'China and Asia will have a sharply growing dependence on MENA [Middle Eastern and North African] and Gulf petroleum exports that may well extend through 2050'.[20]

Shifts in technology and financial cooperation

As tensions with the West have escalated, Middle Eastern and North African countries have become increasingly important for Chinese tech companies. Western apprehensions about Chinese technology, spurred by a US-led campaign against firms such as Huawei and ZTE, saw many capitals close the door to Chinese digital innovations and infrastructure.[21] Yet with the exception of Israel, which has followed a similar trajectory to its Western allies – albeit more cautiously and with substantially less gusto – much of the region has continued to welcome Chinese involvement in their technology ecosystems.[22]

Still, while China's presence in the region's digital infrastructure is certainly growing, it remains many clicks away from dominating the West's presence. Western tech companies are deeply embedded in the region, and despite governments having been explicit about their aversion to picking sides in the US–China rivalry, some companies have indeed succumbed to US pressure.[23] In December 2023, G42, a leading Gulf artificial-intelligence company, announced that it would be phasing Chinese hardware out of its systems to secure continued access to US-made semiconductors.[24] Following the announcement, the company's chief executive, Peng Xiao, told the *Financial Times*: 'For better or worse, as a commercial company, we are in a position where we have to make a choice.'[25]

Finance capital is another realm undergoing a shift. While the region has long been a significant recipient of Chinese investment, economic and geopolitical trends are gradually altering this dynamic. Both structural and cyclical factors have seen China's economy turn for the worse. Foreign direct investment into China has declined dramatically, reaching its lowest level in 25 years by the second quarter of 2023.[26] This downturn in China's economic fortunes is having a ripple effect on its overseas investments. The Middle East is no exception.

While BRI deals agreed with Middle Eastern countries in the first half of 2023 reached $40bn, according to data from the American Enterprise Institute, this remains well below the $100bn or more invested annually before the COVID-19 pandemic. Beyond the BRI, the outlook for foreign investment remains bleak. According to CEIC data, China's overall direct investment in eight key Middle Eastern countries (excluding Israel and Iran) dropped by around one-third in 2021 compared to the previous year. In 2022, China failed to rank among the top ten investors in Arab countries in capital-expenditure terms for the first time since 2018.[27]

As China seeks new sources of finance capital, the Gulf Cooperation Council countries have much to offer. The sovereign-wealth funds of Bahrain, Kuwait, Oman, Qatar, Saudi Arabia and the UAE are together worth an estimated $4 trillion, and are expected to grow to about $10trn by 2030. Nicolas Aguzin, the former chief executive of the Hong Kong Stock Exchange, expects that somewhere between 10% and 20% of these funds will be relocated to China by the end of the decade.[28] This $1–2trn will likely be sufficient to offset the losses from China's Western financiers.[29]

When Xi visited Riyadh in December 2022 to participate in a China–Arab States Summit, a China–Gulf Cooperation Council Summit and a China–Saudi summit, China signed 40 agreements with Saudi Arabia in sectors ranging from energy to emerging technology.[30] The total value of these agreements is reported to be around $30bn.[31] This burgeoning financial relationship has inspired 'Chinese firms [to] flock to Saudi Arabia in [a] Middle East gold rush', according to the media company Caixin.[32]

This reorientation in finance capital has been accompanied by a parallel trend in trade relations. A November 2023 report by David Goldman, the deputy editor at the *Asia Times*, pointed out that 'China now exports more to the Muslim world ($42 billion a month) than to the United States ($38 billion a month)'.[33] While these figures include countries outside the Middle East and North Africa, such as Malaysia and Indonesia, the influence of Middle Eastern countries in these predominantly Muslim Asian states cannot be ignored by Beijing.

Security concerns

Despite the many benefits emanating from deepening economic entanglement, Chinese investment has simultaneously created an imperative to safeguard these interests in a region prone to violence and conflict. What's more, China's growing economic presence in the region has been accompanied by an influx of Chinese citizens, further exacerbating Beijing's predicament. In 2022, China's ambassador to the UAE, Zhang Yiming, told Gulf News that the Chinese population in the UAE had reached 400,000, accounting for around 4% of the country's total population.[34] One Israeli scholar has estimated that the total number of Chinese citizens residing in the Middle East exceeds one million.[35]

Over the past two decades, Chinese citizens, businesses, peacekeepers and government facilities have been the targets of terrorism in a range of countries including Afghanistan, Iraq, Jordan, Mali, Pakistan, Somalia, Sudan, Syria and Yemen.[36] Before Libya descended into civil war during the Arab Spring, China had invested $18.8bn there, where more than 75 Chinese companies were operating.[37] As the country crumbled in 2011, China evacuated more than 35,000 of its citizens and incurred billions of dollars in damage to its facilities. More recently, as of August 2024, four Chinese nationals had been killed in the Israel–Hamas war, two remained missing and several others had been injured.[38]

While these events occurred far from China's borders, they nonetheless affected domestic stability. The Chinese government has experienced substantial domestic blowback for failing to protect its citizens abroad.[39] Influential private companies and state-owned enterprises alike have demanded that China's leadership improve the security of Chinese nationals living abroad by helping to mediate domestic and international armed conflicts.[40] Xi has not ignored these calls. Since launching the BRI, China has expanded its mediation efforts from just three conflicts in 2012 to nine in 2017, spanning a broad range of regions and actors.[41]

Even so, China's military capabilities in the region are comparatively limited – unlike those of the US, which maintains more than 40,000 troops and two aircraft-carrier strike groups in the Middle East.[42] China's base in Djibouti, which houses an estimated 200 marines, along with a rather modest naval deployment in the Gulf of Aden, might be sufficient to protect goods in transit from piracy or to help evacuate Chinese nationals.[43] However, Beijing's nascent military presence currently presents no credible threat to regional states or their proxies. China has thus been reluctant to involve itself militarily beyond its immediate neighbourhood, relying on US forces to protect its interests in far-flung regions like the Middle East. Yet, amid rising tensions between the two great powers, China's leadership has come to view its dependence on the American security umbrella as a vulnerability. In 2021, China completed a pier large enough to accommodate aircraft carriers at its Djibouti naval base, a sign of plans to expand its regional military presence and project power beyond its traditional operating areas of the East and South China seas.[44]

America's dominant position in the Middle East poses a further strategic conundrum for Beijing, which assesses that any future confrontation could result in US Central Command (CENTCOM) blockading Chinese energy shipments that transit critical maritime choke points such as the Suez Canal, the Bab el-Mandeb Strait and the Strait of Hormuz. As US General Erik Kurilla confirmed in a March 2023 congressional hearing: 'We could end up holding a lot of [the Chinese] economy at risk in the CENTCOM region … Seventy-two percent of all Chinese oil is imported … That can make them vulnerable.'[45] China itself identified shipping lanes as a security vulnerability as early as 2003, when then-president Hu Jintao identified China's 'Malacca dilemma'.[46] In a March 2023 interview with the *Financial Times*, a Chinese security analyst reiterated Beijing's anxieties surrounding energy security, explaining: 'The fact that the US has influence, or even control, over certain countries in the Middle East poses a risk to China.'[47]

Transnational risks

Even if the US persists in safeguarding Chinese interests in the region, the challenges posed to China's domestic stability from terrorism, separatism and extremism are not contained by borders. China's leadership has long feared that radical forces based in the region will stoke separatist, Islamist sympathies among its 11m-strong Uyghur minority. As Chinese scholar Xiaodong Zhang wrote back in 1999, 'in both international and internal affairs, Islam challenges Chinese policy-making ... China must soberly consider and work out a strategy and policy to deal with the key area of Islam – the Middle East.'[48] This imperative has encompassed a need for China to balance its relations among rival regional powers such as Saudi Arabia, Iran and Turkiye, the first two being major exporters of Islamic thought and ideology, and Turkiye being linked to China's Uyghur population.[49]

It has been suggested that China's support for the Palestinians, which it has demonstrated both in its rhetoric and in its voting pattern at the United Nations, has been intended to enhance China's profile among the Muslim-majority countries in the Middle East, as well as those in its neighbourhood – particularly Indonesia and Malaysia.[50] Indeed, in the months before the outbreak of the ongoing Israel–Hamas war, there was speculation that China's growing clout in the Middle East was challenging America's long-standing regional dominance.[51] These sentiments were not entirely unfounded: China brokered a Saudi–Iranian rapprochement in 2023, and that same year it hosted Palestinian Authority President Mahmoud Abbas. Israeli Prime Minister Benjamin Netanyahu had planned to visit in October – preceding his expected trip to Washington.[52] China's Foreign Affairs Minister Wang Yi even declared that China's actions were driving 'a wave of reconciliation' across the region.[53]

Hamas's invasion of Israel on 7 October and the subsequent conflict have since cast doubt on Beijing's diplomatic clout.[54] Many framed China's subdued reaction to the war and failure to condemn Hamas as evidence that Beijing has little power to effect any meaningful regional change, especially when it comes to resolving the decades-long Israeli–Palestinian conflict. Some analysts have argued that Chinese statements about the conflict, while not insignificant, 'amount to hollow platitudes', and have described China's five-point peace plan as generic and unmemorable.[55] Still, others have clung to the conviction that China harbours sufficient leverage to pressure Iran and other states to prevent the conflict from engulfing the entire region. Washington even raised the issue with Wang Yi during his three-day visit to America in late October 2023.[56] Before the visit, US Senator Chuck Schumer went so far as to imply that China should use its relationship with Iran to pressure Hamas.[57]

Certainly, China has zero tolerance for terrorism at home, and has therefore pursued a series of policies in Xinjiang that have drawn intense international scrutiny. Yet in summer 2019, Bahrain, Egypt, Iran, Iraq, Saudi Arabia, Sudan, Syria, the UAE and Yemen were among the 45 countries that signed a statement in defence of China's policies in Xinjiang.[58] It seems reasonable to surmise that China's investment and technology links, which have helped regional countries to reduce their reliance on the West, played a role in garnering support for Beijing's policies. At the same time, it is important to acknowledge that many Sunni Arab states share a common threat perception with China towards radical Islam. Egyptian President Abdel Fattah al-Sisi has called for a revolution in Islam and initiated curricular reforms, legislative action against the Muslim Brotherhood and steps to diminish the authority of Al-Azhar University – all sources of intolerant interpretations of Islam.[59] The UAE shares similar sentiments and has even established a Ministry of Tolerance and Coexistence.[60] Bahrain, Jordan, Morocco, Oman and Saudi Arabia have likewise sought to eradicate extremism within their borders. At the ninth ministerial meeting of the China–Arab States Cooperation Forum in 2020, China and Arab League members adopted the Amman Declaration, in which all parties agreed to denounce terrorist activities in all forms and combat extremist ideology, serving to further align Arab countries' interests with – or at least mute their criticism of – China's stance on Xinjiang.[61]

Turkiye has been among the few Muslim-majority countries to have confronted Beijing about its Xinjiang policies. In February 2019, in response to rumours about the death of Abduréhim Héyit, a renowned Uyghur musician and poet in detention in Xinjiang, the Turkish Foreign Ministry voiced staunch criticism of Beijing's treatment of Uyghurs.[62] Accordingly,

Turkiye became one of the few states in the region to have received punitive action from China – which targeted Turkiye's tourism industry through travel warnings issued by China's central government.[63] However, by 2021 Turkiye had changed its tune, cracking down on Uyghur protests after receiving complaints from China's central government. That year, the Turkish lira had plunged following changes in the central bank's leadership and policy, losing 44% of its value.[64] In June 2019, China's central bank had transferred $1bn-worth of funds to Turkiye – facilitated by a currency-swap agreement reached in 2012.[65] The timing was no coincidence: the package was approved just a few months after the Xinjiang spat and coincided with the run-up to the Turkish municipal elections. By 2021, Turkiye's central bank had agreed with China to increase the existing currency-swap facility from $2.4bn to $6bn.[66]

The apparent shift in Turkiye's stance on the Uyghur issue may be seen as connected to its economic circumstances and reliance on Chinese investment. Some outlets even declared that Turkiye was becoming a Chinese client state.[67] However, this risks overlooking the likelihood that Turkish President Recep Tayyip Erdoğan made a calculated decision to use the Uyghur issue as a bargaining chip. After all, Ankara had weaponised its interdependence with other countries in the past, as when Erdoğan threatened to flood Europe with refugees in 2016 after the European Union floated the idea of suspending Turkiye's candidacy for EU membership amid the Syrian refugee crisis.[68]

The agency of smaller states

Turkiye's strategic manoeuvring in its dealings with China illuminates an often underappreciated dynamic in international relations: that even small states have agency in their interactions with so-called great powers. It also raises the question of who's manipulating whom. There are several examples of Middle Eastern countries manoeuvring Beijing in pursuit of their own interests and aspirations. Among these, Saudi Arabia's success in co-opting China to advance the Kingdom's technoscientific agenda stands out. As the authors of a Carnegie Endowment for International Peace study put it, 'the partnership was born from the technoscientific and developmental needs of the Saudi state itself', rather than being an attempt by China to exert greater influence.[69]

Saudi Arabia's 'Vision 2030' plan was vital in lending clarity to the Kingdom's national-development priorities and guiding cooperation with China. Accordingly, Riyadh welcomed Chinese expertise across sectors such as renewable energy, space technology and digital infrastructure. Moreover, by encouraging technology transfer and localisation, Saudi Arabia succeeded in bolstering its domestic capabilities while reducing reliance on external expertise. This proactive engagement was reinforced by significant investments in institutional capacity, enabling Saudi Arabia to more effectively guide the trajectory of its partnership with Beijing.

The Saudis aren't the only ones playing this game. Egypt's strategic position in relation to the Suez Canal has benefited Cairo as Chinese fears about maritime choke points have catalysed a steady stream of Chinese investment in Egyptian infrastructure and digitisation projects. Egypt and Algeria have also sought to compel Chinese tech firms such as Huawei to localise production and capacity-building.[70] However, such efforts have produced only mixed results, as companies like Huawei typically find ways to maintain their technological edge while falling short of enacting meaningful local capacity-building.

Indeed, China is not averse to manoeuvring Middle Eastern states for its own ends. Its dealings with Iran are a case in point. The two countries announced a 25-year, $400bn deal in 2021. To meet the commitment, China would need to invest $16bn each year, yet Chinese annual investment since the agreement's signing has barely reached $185m.[71] Chinese scholar Wu Bingbing and former Iranian ambassador to China Mohammad-Hossein Malaek have both since admitted that the deal was more a strategy to encourage deeper cooperation with Saudi Arabia than a real commitment to deepening bilateral ties between China and Iran – a diplomatic manoeuvre that Wu dubbed 'positive balancing'.[72]

China currently accounts for upwards of 30% of Iran's bilateral trade portfolio, while Iran represents less than 1% of China's.[73] Thus, China appears to possess considerable leverage over Iran. But even with economic incentives or threats from a powerful nation like China, there is no guarantee that Tehran will acquiesce to demands that might conflict with its national interests. As Professor Brantly Womack has observed, 'asymmetric relations can rarely be forced by the stronger side'.[74] Iran's historical experiences of colonialism and imperialism have instilled in its leadership a strong sense of national pride, a penchant for independence and a tendency towards resisting external pressure. What's more, Iran has developed strategies to assert its interests despite its weaker position by leveraging its regional influence, advancing its nuclear programme and using asymmetrical-warfare tactics – all of which serve to offset direct economic or diplomatic pressures.[75] Likewise, many other regional states have embraced a multi-vector foreign policy, engaging with multiple actors including India, Japan, Russia, South Korea and the United States.[76] Such diversification serves as a safeguard against becoming overly dependent on any single country, thus preserving states' sovereignty and enhancing their strategic flexibility. Beyond diversification, the Saudis, Egyptians, Emiratis and others have employed an 'omni-alignment' strategy to navigate the US–China rivalry, leveraging their relations with one great power to extract concessions from the other.[77] On a deeper level, these moves may reflect a belief that a reorganisation of the global order is under way, one that will produce a more multipolar structure.

Towards multipolarity

China's intensified diplomatic and economic engagement with the region since 2018 is part of a broader attempt to rally the so-called Global South as a counterweight to the US-led alliance network.[78] Doing so serves to advance Beijing's vision of a multipolar world order in which China is not beholden to the Western-dominated institutions that currently form the backbone of the post-war system. To this end, China has doubled down on efforts to expand the Shanghai Cooperation Organisation (SCO) and BRICS – a multilateral grouping comprising Brazil, Russia, India, China and South Africa that 'aims to promote peace, security, development and cooperation' and establish 'a more equitable and fair world'.[79]

At the 2022 Dushanbe Summit, Iran became the SCO's ninth member state, while Egypt, Qatar and Saudi Arabia were admitted as dialogue partners. Bahrain, Kuwait and the UAE have all since applied to join the organisation as dialogue partners. At a summit in Johannesburg in August 2023, BRICS members agreed to admit Egypt, Iran, Saudi Arabia and the UAE in 2024. The admission of key Middle Eastern powers into the SCO and BRICS is a significant development for China as it seeks to garner support for its vision for international and security governance, as articulated in its Global Development and Global Security initiatives.[80] Arab countries have already expressed their support for these initiatives at events like the China–Arab States and China–Gulf Cooperation Council summits in December 2022.[81]

Meanwhile, China has been seeking to leverage its multilateral engagements to reduce America's dominance over the global financial system, create financial channels less vulnerable to US and European sanctions, and promote the Chinese yuan's internationalisation. The proposal to establish a BRICS currency, however unrealistic, along with speculation that China and Saudi Arabia may create a petro-yuan to replace the petro-dollar, are emblematic of these efforts.[82] In November 2020, the People's Bank of China and the Saudi Central Bank reached a local-currency-swap agreement worth CNY50bn ($6.93bn).[83]

Analysts continue to frame these developments as a sign of China's growing regional clout.[84] However, the enthusiasm of many such states to join the SCO and BRICS, sign currency-swap agreements, welcome Chinese infrastructure projects and involve China in their weapons-development programmes is not merely the product of Chinese manoeuvring. Rather, each country has its own interests that it is seeking to secure. Engaging with China is, as noted, but one component of a multi-vector foreign policy involving cooperation with a range of actors from West to East.[85]

Making sense of the mirage

China's influence in the Middle East and North Africa is neither the all-encompassing force that many analysts fear, nor entirely benign. It is both far more complex and less formidable than often perceived. Yet a blend of China's self-aggrandising rhetoric and Western apprehensions often serves to distort perceptions of Beijing's conduct. Chinese economist Yao Yang has admitted that 'even we [Chinese] don't believe much of what we say', adding that China's 'goal is not to defeat liberalism, but instead to say that what we have can be as good as what you have'.[86] While China is actively working to cultivate asymmetries in its favour and leverage them to reach its goals, this rhetoric suggests an effort to enhance strategic positioning rather than to achieve outright domination. It is important to differentiate between China's rhetorical assertions of influence and the actual extent of its diplomatic and strategic capabilities. It is equally important to appreciate that perceptions of Chinese activities are influenced by Western analysis that often inflates the China challenge and portrays it as an existential threat.

This pattern is evident in the Saudi–Iran rapprochement, where China's role, though much publicised, was relatively minor compared to the groundwork laid by Oman and Iraq.[87] Tehran and Riyadh undoubtedly had their own reasons for affording Beijing the honour of taking the credit, but these were mostly overlooked in the media's telling of the story. As such, the agency of these regional powers was largely ignored.

China's goal to establish a new security architecture in the Middle East under its Global Security Initiative (GSI) also exemplifies this disconnect. While the initiative was presented with ambitious rhetoric, it remains nebulous, even to many within China. Nevertheless, this has not deterred various scholars from engaging in extensive speculation about the potential challenges the proposal could pose to the Middle East and the global order more generally.[88] Such assessments are not necessarily unwarranted. The GSI's amorphous nature resembles the BRI in its early days, reflecting the often improvisational nature of Chinese policymaking. Yet the BRI did ultimately take shape in the form of a range of development projects. Each port, subsea cable and smart city constructed in the Middle East or elsewhere advances Beijing's interests. The incremental approach China often employs – a strategy of very gradually working to tilt asymmetries in its favour – warrants close monitoring.

When it comes to the Israel–Hamas war, China has no tangible leverage over Israel and little to gain from the Palestinians beyond appeasing the Muslim world or portraying the US in a negative light. Still, China has indicated that a resolution to the Israel–Palestine question is a central goal of the GSI. Rhetoric aside, Beijing's involvement in the conflict will likely remain marginal for the foreseeable future. That does not mean that it cannot create challenges for Israel, the US or others in the region. Beijing's insistence that the Israel–Palestine conflict must be brought under the auspices of the United Nations, its promotion of the concept of 'indivisible security' and its calls to establish a nuclear-free zone in the Middle East all run counter to Israeli interests. What's more, implementation of a regional security architecture that sidelines the Abraham Accords would run counter to the interests of numerous countries, including Bahrain, Egypt, Israel, Morocco, Saudi Arabia, Sudan, the UAE and the US.

Overestimating a threat confounds policymakers' abilities to respond effectively and can lead to undesirable outcomes. Underestimating a threat can be equally dangerous. As China continues to define its role in the region, observers and policymakers alike must discern the realities of its influence, steering clear of both undue alarmism and complacency.

Notes

1 Brahma Chellaney, 'China's Debt-trap Diplomacy', Australian Strategic Policy Institute, 24 January 2017, https://www.aspistrategist.org.au/chinas-debt-trap-diplomacy/.

2 These pundits point to Zheng He's 1405–33 naval expeditions to the Caspian Sea, East Africa, the Red Sea and the Persian Gulf – notable for their emphasis on economic engagement and eventual peaceful withdrawal – as evidence of this reluctance. See Dawn Murphy et al., 'Ask the Experts: Is China's Growing Influence in the Middle East Pushing Out the United States?', London School of Economics and Political Science, 5 December 2022, https://blogs.lse.ac.uk/cff/2022/12/05/ask-the-experts-is-chinas-growing-influence-in-the-middle-east-pushing-out-the-united-states/.

3 State Council Information Office of the People's Republic of China, 'BRI Brings Development of China and Middle East Closer than Ever', *China Daily*, 10 May 2023, http://english.scio.gov.cn/m/beltandroad/2023-05/10/content_85278499.htm.

4 See Camille Lons et al., 'China's Great Game in the Middle East', European Council on Foreign Relations, 21 October 2019, https://ecfr.eu/publication/china_great_game_middle_east/; State Council of the People's Republic of China, 'China, Tunisia Establish Strategic Partnership', 31 May 2024, https://english.www.gov.cn/news/202405/31/content_WS6659ae71c6d0868f4e8e7b3a.html; State Council Information Office of the People's Republic of China, 'China, Bahrain Establish Comprehensive Strategic Partnership', 1 June 2024, http://english.scio.gov.cn/m/topnews/2024-06/01/content_117228629.htm; and State

Council Information Office of the People's Republic of China, 'Xi, Assad Jointly Announce China–Syria Strategic Partnership', 22 September 2023, https://english.www.gov.cn/news/202309/22/content_WS650d7c21c6d0868f4e8dfae0.html.

5   The State Council of the People's Republic of China, 'Sino Trade Volumes Soar with Middle East, Africa', *China Daily*, 17 July 2023, https://english.www.gov.cn/news/202307/17/content_WS64b49b48c6d0868f4e8ddd72.html.

6   Christoph Nedopil Wang, 'Brief: China Belt and Road Initiative (BRI) Investment Report 2021', Green Finance and Development Center, 2 February 2022, https://greenfdc.org/brief-china-belt-and-road-initiative-bri-investment-report-2021/.

7   Christoph Nedopil Wang, 'Brief: China Belt and Road Initiative (BRI) Investment Report H1 2022', Green Finance and Development Center, 24 July 2022, https://greenfdc.org/china-belt-and-road-initiative-bri-investment-report-h1-2022/.

8   See Dale Aluf, 'China's Tech Outreach in the Middle East and North Africa', *Diplomat*, 17 November 2022, https://thediplomat.com/2022/11/chinas-tech-outreach-in-the-middle-east-and-north-africa/; and Dale Aluf, 'China's Subsea-cable Power in the Middle East and North Africa', Atlantic Council, 30 May 2023, https://www.atlanticcouncil.org/in-depth-research-reports/issue-brief/chinas-subsea-cable-power-in-the-middle-east-and-north-africa/.

9   See Ralph Jennings, 'China–Middle East to Step Up Trade amid Strained Ties with Western Partners', *South China Morning Post*, 14 September 2023, https://www.scmp.com/economy/china-economy/article/3234552/china-middle-east-aim-lift-trade-new-heights-2030-amid-strained-ties-western-partners; and Melissa Hancock, 'China Shows Faith in Egypt with Deeper Investment', Arabian Gulf Business Insight, 15 November 2023, https://www.agbi.com/analysis/egypt-china-investment-belt-road/.

10 'Chinese Projects in Kuwait Hit 84', *Kuwait Times*, 20 August 2017, https://kuwaittimes.com/chinese-projects-kuwait-hit-84/.

11 Jomar Mendoza, 'Oman Among the Top Destinations of China's Overseas Direct Investment', *Oman Observer*, 15 May 2023, https://www.omanobserver.om/article/1137193/business/economy/oman-among-the-top-destinations-of-chinas-overseas-direct-investment.

12 On Algeria, see John Calabrese, '"The New Algeria" and China', Middle East Institute, 26 January 2021, https://www.mei.edu/publications/new-algeria-and-china. On Israel, see Doron Ella, 'Chinese Investments in Israel: Developments and a Look to the Future', Institute for National Security Studies, 1 February 2021, https://www.inss.org.il/wp-content/uploads/2021/02/special-publication-010221.pdf.

13 John Calabrese, 'China's "Pearl": The UAE amid Great-power Rivalry', Middle East Institute, 30 November 2021, https://www.mei.edu/publications/chinas-pearl-uae-amid-great-power-rivalry.

14 Samuel Shen, Casey Hall and Ellen Zhang, 'Red Sea Shipping Attacks

Pressure China's Exporters as Delays, Costs Mount', Reuters, 22 January 2024, https://www.reuters.com/world/red-sea-crisis-pressures-chinas-exporters-ship ping-delays-costs-mount-2024-01-19/.

15   Andrew Hayley, 'Russia Remains China's Top Crude Supplier in July Despite Narrower Discounts', Reuters, 20 August 2023, https://www.reuters.com/business/energy/russia-remains-chinas-top-crude-supplier-july-despite-narrower-discounts-2023-08-20/.

16   Erica Downs, Robin Mills and Shangyou Nie, 'Unpacking the Recent China–Qatar LNG Deals', Center on Global Energy Policy, Columbia University, 10 July 2023, https://www.energypolicy.columbia.edu/unpacking-the-recent-china-qatar-lng-deals/.

17   Maha El Dahan, Louise Heavens and Sharon Singleton, 'QatarEnergy, TotalEnergies Sign 27-year LNG Supply Agreement', Reuters, 11 October 2023, https://www.reuters.com/markets/commodities/qatarenergy-totalenergies-sign-27-year-lng-supply-agreement-2023-10-11/.

18   See Qiang Wang, Shuyu Li and Rongrong Li, 'China's Dependency on Foreign Oil Will Exceed 80% by 2030: Developing a Novel NMGM-ARIMA to Forecast China's Foreign Oil Dependence from Two Dimensions', Energy, vol. 163, 15 November 2018, pp. 151–67; and ChinaPower, 'How Is China's Energy Footprint Changing?', https://chinapower.csis.org/energy-footprint/.

19   See Carol Zu, 'Russia Crude Oil Pipeline Capabilities to Mainland China – The ESPO Crude Oil Pipeline', S&P Global, 1 April 2022, https://www.spglobal.com/commodityinsights/en/ci/research-analysis/espo-crude-oil-pipeline.html.

20   Anthony H. Cordesman, 'China, Asia, and the Changing Strategic Importance of the Gulf and MENA Region', CSIS, 15 October 2021, https://www.csis.org/analysis/china-asia-and-changing-strategic-importance-gulf-and-mena-region.

21   See Katharina Buchholz, 'Which Countries Have Banned Huawei?', Statista, 30 January 2020, https://www.statista.com/chart/17528/countries-which-have-banned-huawei-products/.

22   See Dale Aluf, 'Israel–China Relations amid the Sino-US Rivalry', Asia Times, 11 February 2023, https://asiatimes.com/2023/02/israel-china-relations-amid-the-sino-us-rivalry/.

23   See Zainab Fattah, 'Top UAE Official Warns on Risk of "Cold War" Between China, U.S.', Bloomberg, 2 October 2021, https://www.bloomberg.com/news/articles/2021-10-02/top-uae-official-warns-on-risk-of-cold-war-between-china-u-s.

24   Michael Peel and Simeon Kerr, 'UAE's Top AI Group Vows to Phase Out Chinese Hardware to Appease US', Financial Times, 7 December 2023, https://www.ft.com/content/6710c259-0746-4e09-804f-8a48ecf50ba3.

25   Ibid.

26   See Scott Kennedy et al., 'Experts React: China's Economic Slowdown: Causes and Implications', CSIS, 30 August 2023, https://www.csis.org/analysis/experts-react-chinas-economic-slowdown-causes-and-implications;

and Suzanne Woolley and Claire Ballentine, 'China's Foreign Investment Gauge Declines to 25-year Low', Bloomberg, 7 August 2023, https://www.bloomberg.com/news/articles/2023-08-07/china-foreign-investment-gauge-at-25-year-low-amid-high-tensions.

27 See Nathaniel Taplin, 'China's Middle East Clout Has Limits – WSJ', *Wall Street Journal*, 12 November 2023, https://www.wsj.com/world/middle-east/chinas-middle-east-clout-has-limits-af5cc396.

28 Sarmad Khan, 'China to Receive up to $2tn in Middle East Sovereign Investments by 2030, HKEX CEO Says', National, 12 June 2023, https://www.thenationalnews.com/business/markets/2023/06/12/china-to-receive-up-to-2tn-in-middle-east-sovereign-investments-by-2030-hkex-ceo-says/.

29 Chris Devonshire-Ellis, 'Foreign Investment into China Falls as Capital Sources Change', China Briefing, 30 October 2023, https://www.china-briefing.com/news/foreign-investment-into-china-falls-as-capital-sources-change/.

30 Adam Lucente, 'Saudi Arabia, China Sign Over 40 Deals During Xi's Visit', Al-Monitor, 9 December 2022, https://www.al-monitor.com/originals/2022/12/saudi-arabia-china-sign-over-40-deals-during-xis-visit.

31 Aziz El Yaakoubi and Eduardo Baptista, 'China's Xi on "Epoch-making" Visit to Saudi as Riyadh Chafes at U.S. Censure', Reuters, 7 December 2022, https://www.reuters.com/world/chinas-xi-starts-epoch-making-saudi-visit-deepen-economic-strategic-ties-2022-12-07/.

32 Zhai Shaohui and J. Zhang, 'In Depth: Chinese Firms Flock to Saudi Arabia in Middle East Gold Rush', Caixin Global, 4 May 2023, https://www.caixinglobal.com/2023-05-04/in-depth-chinese-firms-flock-to-saudi-arabia-in-middle-east-gold-rush-102042468.html.

33 David P. Goldman, 'China's Imperial Model and the Muslim World', *Asia Times*, 4 November 2024, https://asiatimes.com/2023/11/chinas-imperial-model-and-the-muslim-world/.

34 Xuena Zhang, 'The 400,000 Chinese Expatriates' Community in the UAE: What Makes Them Build Lives in the UAE', Gulf News, 11 May 2023, https://gulfnews.com/uae/the-400000-chinese-expatriates-community-in-the-uae-what-makes-them-build-lives-in-the-uae-1.1683715608053.

35 Mordechai Chaziza, 'China's Overseas Police Service Stations in the Middle East', *Diplomat*, 29 June 2023, https://thediplomat.com/2023/06/chinas-overseas-police-service-stations-in-the-middle-east/.

36 See Dawn Murphy, 'China's Approach to International Terrorism', United States Institute of Peace, 2 October 2017, https://www.usip.org/publications/2017/10/chinas-approach-international-terrorism; and 'Rescue Underway for Kidnapped Chinese in Iraq', China.org.cn, 12 April 2004, http://www.china.org.cn/english/China/92780.htm.

37 Frederic Wehrey and Sandy Alkoutami, 'China's Balancing Act in Libya', Carnegie Endowment for International Peace, 10 May 2020, https://carnegieendowment.

org/2020/05/10/china-s-balancing-act-in-libya-pub-81757.

38 Foreign Ministry of the People's Republic of China, 'Foreign Ministry Spokesperson Mao Ning's Regular Press Conference on October 16, 2023', https://www.fmprc.gov.cn/eng/xwfw_665399/s2510_665401/2511_665403/202310/t20231016_11161588.html.

39 See Mathieu Duchâtel, Oliver Bräuner and Zhou Hang, 'Protecting China's Overseas Interests', Stockholm International Peace Research Institute, Policy Paper 41, June 2014, https://www.sipri.org/sites/default/files/files/PP/SIPRIPP41.pdf.

40 See Mikko Huotari et al., 'China's Emergence as a Global Security Actor: Strategies for Europe', Mercator Institute for China Studies, MERICS Paper on China no. 4, July 2017, p. 34, https://merics.org/sites/default/files/2020-04/China%27s%20Emergence%20as%20a%20Global%20Security%20Actor.pdf.

41 Helena Legarda and Marie L. Hoffman, 'China as a Conflict Mediator: Maintaining Stability along the Belt and Road', IISS Online Analysis, 22 August 2018, https://www.iiss.org/online-analysis/online-analysis/2018/08/china-conflict-mediation-belt-and-road/.

42 Statistics on the US military presence in the Middle East are taken from Jacob Knutson, 'Where U.S. Troops Are Stationed in the Middle East', Axios, 31 October 2023, https://www.axios.com/2023/10/31/american-troops-middle-east-israel-palestine.

43 See David P. Goldman, 'China's Influence in the Middle East and the Strategic Considerations Underlying

It', *Jerusalem Strategic Tribune*, August 2023, https://jstribune.com/goldman-chinas-influence-in-the-middle-east/.

44 See Tsukasa Hadano, 'China Adds Carrier Pier to Djibouti Base, Extending Indian Ocean Reach', Nikkei Asia, 27 April 2021, https://asia.nikkei.com/Politics/International-relations/Indo-Pacific/China-adds-carrier-pier-to-Djibouti-base-extending-Indian-Ocean-reach.

45 US House Armed Services Committee, 'Full Committee Hearing: U.S. Military Posture and National Security Challenges in the Greater Middle East and Africa', 23 March 2023, https://armedservices.house.gov/hearings/full-committee-hearing-us-military-posture-and-national-security-challenges-greater-middle.

46 See Mohit Choudhary, 'China's Malacca Bluff: Examining China's Indian Ocean Strategy and Future Security Architecture of the Region', *Journal of Indo-Pacific Affairs*, vol. 6, no. 1, 2023, pp. 99–108.

47 Kathrin Hille, 'China Casts Itself as Middle East Peacemaker with Global Ambition', *Financial Times*, 14 March 2023, https://www.ft.com/content/9d832121-022b-4b56-bf84-95a237e698e8.

48 Xiaodong Zhang, 'China's Interests in the Middle East: Present and Future, *Middle East Policy*, vol. 6, no. 3, 1999, p. 150, https://mepc.org/journal/chinas-interests-middle-east-present-and-future.

49 See Peter G. Mandaville (ed.), *Wahhabism and the World: Understanding Saudi Arabia's Global Influence on Islam* (New York: Oxford University Press, 2022); Shabnam Moinipour, 'The Islamic

Republic of Iran's Export of Human Rights Violations Through Proxies: Yemen and the Case of the Bahá'ís', *Religion & Human Rights*, vol. 17, no. 2, 15 July 2022, pp. 65–81; and Nilgün Eliküçük Yıldırım, 'Legitimation, Co-optation, and Survival: Why Is Turkey Silent on China's Persecution of Uyghurs?', *Democratization*, vol. 31, no. 6, 2023, https://doi.org/10.1080/13510347.2023.2293154.

50 In a 2023 lecture, Singaporean diplomat Bilahari Kausikan noted that 'Muslim politicians in Malaysia and Indonesia [are competing] to make political capital out of the Gaza war, adding to existing inter-ethnic and inter-religious stresses in their societies'. He elaborated that 'over the last 40 years or so, the traditional syncretic and open Southeast Asian understanding of Islam has been steadily displaced by narrower, more essentialist, often Wahhabist, interpretations from the Middle East'. Hamas has a significant presence in Malaysia. For an abridged version of his remarks, see Bilahari Kausikan, 'The Gaza War and East Asia', *Jerusalem Strategic Tribune*, December 2023, https://jstribune.com/kausikan-the-gaza-war-and-east-asia/.

51 See Ben Hubbard and Amy Qin, 'As the U.S. Pulls Back from the Mideast, China Leans In', *New York Times*, 2 February 2022, https://www.nytimes.com/2022/02/01/world/middleeast/china-middle-east.html; and Erin Hale, 'Can China Replace the US in the Middle East?', Al-Jazeera, 25 April 2023, https://www.aljazeera.com/features/2023/4/25/can-china-replace-the-us-in-the-middle-east.

52 See Vivian Wang, 'Hosting Palestinian Leader, Xi Pushes China as Peacemaker for Israel', *New York Times*, 14 June 2023, https://www.nytimes.com/2023/06/14/world/asia/china-mahmoud-abbas-xi-jinping.html; and Dale Aluf, 'Of Course Netanyahu Must Go to China', China Project, 10 July 2023, https://thechinaproject.com/2023/07/10/of-course-netanyahu-must-go-to-china/.

53 'China Sees Iran–Saudi Arabia Relations Improving – Foreign Ministry', Reuters, 21 August 2023, https://www.reuters.com/world/china-sees-iran-saudi-arabia-relations-improving-foreign-ministry-2023-08-21/.

54 See James Pomfret, Joe Cash and Chen Lin, 'Middle East Crisis Exposes Limits of China's Diplomatic Ambitions', *Japan Times*, 10 October 2023, https://www.japantimes.co.jp/news/2023/10/10/asia-pacific/politics/china-diplomacy-ambitions-test/; and Jean-Loup Samaan, 'Israel–Hamas War Testing Credibility of China's Middle East Strategy', ThinkChina, 20 November 2023, https://www.thinkchina.sg/israel-hamas-war-testing-credibility-chinas-middle-east-strategy.

55 See Andrew Scobell, 'What China Wants in the Middle East', United States Institute of Peace, 1 November 2023, https://www.usip.org/publications/2023/11/what-china-wants-middle-east.

56 See Demetri Sevastopulo, 'US Urges Beijing to Temper Iran's Response to Israel–Hamas War', *Financial Times*, 28 October 2023, https://www.ft.com/content/badc81e7-e804-4de2-86f4-d737bb6744d7.

57 See Eric Olander, 'China's Response to the Israel–Hamas War', China Global South Project, 21 November 2023, https://chinaglobalsouth.com/podcasts/chinas-response-to-the-israel-hamas-war/.

58 See Catherine Putz, '2020 Edition: Which Countries Are For or Against China's Xinjiang Policies?', *Diplomat*, 9 October 2020, https://thediplomat.com/2020/10/2020-edition-which-countries-are-for-or-against-chinas-xinjiang-policies/.

59 See Sarah Feuer, 'New Egyptian Legislation Aims to Reduce Al-Azhar's Authority', Washington Institute for Near East Policy, 20 August 2020, https://www.washingtoninstitute.org/policy-analysis/new-egyptian-legislation-aims-reduce-al-azhars-authority.

60 See 'UAE Creates Ministers for Happiness and Tolerance', BBC, 9 February 2016, https://www.bbc.com/news/world-middle-east-35531174.

61 See 'China, Arab Countries Adopt Declaration, Action Plan to Deepen Cooperation', Xinhua News, 7 July 2020, http://www.xinhuanet.com/english/2020-07/07/c_139195393.htm.

62 Ondřej Klimeš, 'China's Tactics for Targeting the Uyghur Diaspora in Turkey', *China Brief*, vol. 19, no. 19, 1 November 2019, https://jamestown.org/program/chinas-tactics-for-targeting-the-uyghur-diaspora-in-turkey/.

63 See Dorian Jones, 'Turkish–Chinese Tensions Escalate Over Uighurs', VOA News, 13 February 2019, https://www.voanews.com/a/turkish-chinese-tensions-escalate-over-uighurs/4785303.html.

64 Ece Toksabay and Tuvan Gumrukcu, 'Turkey's Lira Logs Worst Year in Two Decades Under Erdogan', Reuters, 31 December 2021, https://www.reuters.com/markets/europe/turkeys-lira-weakens-fifth-day-monetary-policy-worries-2021-12-31/.

65 Kerim Karakaya and Asli Kandemir, 'Turkey Got a $1 Billion Foreign Cash Boost from China in June', Bloomberg, 9 August 2019, https://www.bloomberg.com/news/articles/2019-08-09/turkey-got-1-billion-from-china-swap-in-june-boost-to-reserves.

66 Ezgi Erkoyun and Jonathan Oatis, 'Turkish Central Bank Says Larger Swap Agreement with China Recorded in Accounts', Reuters, 15 June 2021, https://www.reuters.com/article/turkey-cenbank/turkish-central-bank-says-larger-swap-agreement-with-china-recorded-in-accounts-idUSS8N2JI01G/.

67 Ayca Alemdaroglu and Sultan Tepe, 'Erdogan Is Turning Turkey into a Chinese Client State', *Foreign Policy*, 16 September 2020, https://foreignpolicy.com/2020/09/16/erdogan-is-turning-turkey-into-a-chinese-client-state/.

68 See 'Turkey's Erdogan Threatened to Flood Europe with Migrants: Greek Website', Reuters, 8 February 2016, https://www.reuters.com/article/idUSKCN0VH1R0/.

69 Mohammed Al-Sudairi et al., 'How Saudi Arabia Bent China to Its Technoscientific Ambitions', Carnegie Endowment for International Peace, 1 August 2023, https://carnegieendowment.org/2023/08/01/how-saudi-arabia-bent-china-to-its-technoscientific-ambitions-pub-90301.

70 See Tin Hinane El Kadi, 'How Huawei's Localization in North Africa Delivered Mixed Returns', Carnegie Endowment for International Peace, 14 April 2022, https://carnegieendowment.org/2022/04/14/how-huawei-s-localization-in-north-africa-delivered-mixed-returns-pub-86889.

71 Saeed Azimi, 'Iran's Special Relationship with China Beset by "Special Issues"', Bourse and Bazaar Foundation, 16 February 2023, https://www.bourseandbazaar.com/articles/2023/2/16/special-issues-on-the-agenda-as-irans-raisi-visits-beijing.

72 See Thomas Des Garets Geddes, 'China's Middle East Policy by Peking University Prof. Wu Bingbing', Sinification, 20 October 2023, https://www.sinification.com/p/chinas-middle-east-policy-by-peking; and 'China Uses 25-year-deal with Iran to Get More from Saudis – Ex-diplomat', Iran International, 17 January 2023, https://www.iranintl.com/en/202301177404.

73 Jon B. Alterman, 'Chinese and Russian Influence in the Middle East', Statement before the House Foreign Affairs Subcommittee on the Middle East, North Africa, and International Terrorism, CSIS, 9 May 2019, https://www.congress.gov/116/meeting/house/109455/witnesses/HHRG-116-FA13-Wstate-AltermanJ-20190509.pdf.

74 Brantly Womack, 'Asymmetry Theory and China's Concept of Multipolarity', *Journal of Contemporary China*, vol. 13, no. 39, 7 August 2006, https://doi.org/10.1080/10670560420002119942.

75 See Michael Eisenstadt, 'Iran's Gray Zone Strategy: Cornerstone of Its Asymmetric Way of War', Washington Institute for Near East Policy, 19 March 2021, https://www.washingtoninstitute.org/policy-analysis/irans-gray-zone-strategy-cornerstone-its-asymmetric-way-war.

76 See Dale Aluf, 'Middle Eastern Countries Are Rebalancing Relations with the US and China', *Diplomat*, 5 May 2023, https://thediplomat.com/2023/05/middle-eastern-countries-are-rebalancing-relations-with-the-us-and-china/.

77 See Michael Singh, 'The Middle East in a Multipolar Era: Why America's Allies Are Flirting with Russia and China', *Foreign Affairs*, 7 December 2022, https://www.foreignaffairs.com/middle-east/middle-east-multipolar-era.

78 See Masahiro Okoshi, 'China Eyes Global South, Not West, to Expand Influence: Expert', Nikkei Asia, 20 March 2023, https://asia.nikkei.com/Politics/International-relations/US-China-tensions/China-eyes-Global-South-not-West-to-expand-influence-expert.

79 South African Government, 'Fifth BRICS Summit: General Background', https://www.gov.za/events/fifth-brics-summit-general-background.

80 See Dale Aluf, 'China Ramps Up Its Efforts to Shape a Multipolar World', China Project, 31 March 2023, https://thechinaproject.com/2023/03/31/china-ramps-up-its-efforts-to-shape-a-multipolar-world/.

81 See 'China, Arab States Agree to Strengthen Cooperation, Promote Strategic Partnership', Xinhua, 10 December 2022, https://english.news.cn/20221210/8b60dbccf6664f69873dacbc0515c775/c.html.

82 See Rachel Savage, 'What Is a BRICS Currency and Is the U.S. Dollar in Trouble?', Reuters, 24 August 2023, https://www.reuters.com/markets/currencies/what-is-brics-currency-could-one-be-adopted-2023-08-23/.

83 Joe Cash, 'China, Saudi Arabia Sign Currency Swap Agreement', Reuters, 20 November 2023, https://www.reuters.com/markets/currencies/china-saudi-arabia-central-banks-sign-local-currency-swap-agreement-2023-11-20/.

84 See, for example, Hasan Alhasan, 'With BRICS Expansion, China and Middle Eastern Powers Draw Closer', IISS Online Analysis, 31 August 2023, https://www.iiss.org/en/online-analysis/online-analysis/2023/08/with-brics-expansion-china-and-middle-eastern-powers-draw-closer/.

85 See Samuel Ramani, 'A Middle Path for Saudi Arabia: How Does the War in Ukraine Affect Saudi Foreign Policy?', Gulf International Forum, https://gulfif.org/a-middle-path-for-saudi-arabia-how-does-the-war-in-ukraine-affect-saudi-foreign-policy/.

86 Quoted in Jessica Chen Weiss, 'Even China Isn't Convinced It Can Replace the U.S.', New York Times, 4 May 2023, https://www.nytimes.com/2023/05/04/opinion/china-us-world-order.html.

87 See Ali Mamouri, 'Explainer: How Iraq Planted the Seeds for China's Saudi–Iran Deal', Al-Monitor, 18 March 2023, https://www.al-monitor.com/originals/2023/03/explainer-how-iraq-planted-seeds-chinas-saudi-iran-deal; and Yasmine Farouk, 'Riyadh's Motivations Behind the Saudi–Iran Deal', Carnegie Endowment for International Peace, 30 March 2023, https://carnegieendowment.org/2023/03/30/riyadh-s-motivations-behind-saudi-iran-deal-pub-89421.

88 See, for example, Tuvia Gering, 'Full Throttle in Neutral: China's New Security Architecture for the Middle East', Atlantic Council, 15 February 2023, https://www.atlanticcouncil.org/in-depth-research-reports/issue-brief/full-throttle-in-neutral-chinas-new-security-architecture-for-the-middle-east/.

Copyright © 2024 The International Institute for Strategic Studies

Unpalatable Options: Confronting the Houthis

Thomas Juneau

The attacks by the Houthis, an armed group that emerged in northwest Yemen and now forms its de facto governing authority in Sanaa, the capital, have significantly impeded commercial shipping in the Red Sea and the Gulf of Aden. This represents a threat to the global economy: the Bab el-Mandeb Strait, which links the Gulf of Aden to the southern Red Sea, is one of the world's most crucial maritime choke points, normally accounting for about 12% of global-trade transits daily. As a result of Houthi attacks, the number of ships transiting the Red Sea and the Suez Canal to the Mediterranean Sea has dropped, by one count, by up to 90%.[1] There is, of course, a legitimate and unresolved debate about what degree of American involvement in the Middle East US interests there warrant. Especially after the strategically costly invasion and occupation of Iraq, many US analysts have advocated restraint in the region. Yet the Houthi attacks damage the security of the global commons, which is a vital American interest. And no country other than the United States has the capability to address this threat.

Washington, however, faces unpalatable options. There is no prospect in the short to medium terms for a peace process in Yemen that could lead to a decrease in the Houthi threat to Red Sea shipping. The Houthis have practically won the war in Yemen and are now militarily dominant in the

Thomas Juneau is a professor at the Graduate School of Public and International Affairs at the University of Ottawa and a non-resident fellow at the Sana'a Center for Strategic Studies.

Survival | vol. 66 no. 5 | October–November 2024 | pp. 183–200 https://doi.org/10.1080/00396338.2024.2403228

country; they are in no mood to compromise with domestic rivals or regional powers. Although the war in Gaza between Israel and Hamas is a stated pretext for the Houthi attacks, it is unlikely that its end will conclusively eliminate the problem. The Houthis now understand that threatening shipping in the Red Sea effectively pressures their adversaries – Israel, Saudi Arabia and the United States – and will continue to do so unless checked. The current approach of limited American–British airstrikes, which started in January 2024, is inadequate, but the two most obvious military alternatives – no airstrikes or more airstrikes – are arguably worse.

The United States should at a minimum continue its current efforts to contain the Houthis, centred on airstrikes, protecting commercial ships in the Red Sea and interdicting the smuggling of Iranian weapons to the Houthis. This alone, however, would merely lock Washington into an open-ended commitment to stave off the Houthis. A more ambitious and long-term strategy would see the United States help rebuild the internationally recognised government of Yemen, which nominally brings together anti-Houthi factions but is, in practice, fragmented and weak. Though a long-term endeavour with uncertain prospects, this is the only option that could conceivably modify the balance of power in Yemen and limit the Houthis' freedom of action. Without such an effort, they will undoubtedly consolidate power. This would be a tragedy for the Yemeni people given the brutality of the Houthis, and a perennial danger for regional security given their proven aggression and regional ambitions.

The ascent of the Houthis

The Houthis emerged in the 1980s and 1990s in northwest Yemen amid growing resentment against economic, cultural, religious and political marginalisation of the Zaydi Shi'ites at the hands of the central government. Led by the al-Houthi family, the movement was able to mobilise widespread frustration among the Zaydi, who are a small minority among Shi'ites worldwide but comprise 35–40% of Yemen's population and are a majority in the mountainous, poor northwest. For about a thousand years, a Zaydi imamate, or kingdom, had ruled parts of northwest Yemen until the last one was overthrown by republican forces during Yemen's civil war in 1962–70.[2]

The Houthi movement, which now refers to itself as Ansar Allah, or Partisans of God, steadily morphed into an armed insurrection, engaging in six increasingly violent rounds of fighting between 2004 and 2010. The Houthis then took advantage of the instability resulting from the Arab uprisings in Yemen in 2011 to further expand their influence in northwest Yemen. In the wake of a failed national-dialogue process, they emerged from their stronghold and seized the capital, Sanaa, in 2014.[3] Alarmed with the Houthis' growing power and their increasingly close ties to Iran, Saudi Arabia, as head of a coalition of ten states, launched a military intervention in Yemen in 2015. Riyadh's objectives were to roll back Houthi gains and to reinstate the internationally recognised government.

The Houthis have now won the civil war in Yemen and repelled their vastly more powerful neighbour to the north.[4] They are the de facto governing authority in the northwest quadrant of Yemen. They do not control the entire country, but have held the capital since 2014, and more than half the population lives under their authority. No actor or coalition inside the country will be able to challenge their position politically or militarily for the foreseeable future.

Iran started providing modest quantities of small arms to the Houthis around 2009, viewing them as a potentially attractive partner owing to their shared opposition to Saudi Arabia and a US-dominated regional order. As the Houthis' momentum continued after the 2011 uprising, Tehran steadily increased its support.[5] After 2015, as Saudi Arabia became bogged down in a costly and unwinnable war in Yemen, Iran upgraded support for the Houthis to a main priority, providing not only more light weapons but also parts for missiles, drones and other weapons systems, as well as training to assemble and use them. This changed the regional security dynamics.

While Iranian support has been essential to the growth in Houthi power, it is only half the story. The weakness of anti-Houthi forces since 2014 has arguably played an equally important role. The internationally recognised government, now led by an eight-man Presidential Leadership Council bringing together a balance of Saudi- and Emirati-backed factions, is weak, corrupt and fragmented. It is, in practice, a disparate collection of warlords, tribal militias and remnants from the pre-war national army barely held together by Saudi pressure and a loosely shared opposition to the Houthis. Its leaders distrust one another and, in some cases, do not even view the fight against the Houthis as their key priority.[6]

Despite their dominance, the Houthis face several obstacles. Yemen, already the Arab world's poorest country before 2014, has been economically ravaged by a decade of war. The Houthis, moreover, have shown themselves to be abysmal economic managers. Rumblings of discontent in Houthi-controlled areas have risen, especially as Houthi governance has become increasingly brutal, corrupt and obscurantist.[7] Nevertheless, the Houthis' position remains secure insofar as they face no competitor capable of challenging them.

No prospects for peace

In April 2022, the Houthis and Saudi Arabia agreed to a truce, and both sides have since, for the most part, adhered to it. The stated objective is for the cessation of violence to provide the political space for the two sides to negotiate a permanent end to the war. Talks have been disrupted by the Hamas attacks against Israel on 7 October 2023 and the war in Gaza that followed, but both sides remain committed to the process. The Houthis, however, see it solely as a vehicle for consolidating their domination of Yemen. Because they have de facto won the war, they are not interested in discussing the formation of a national-unity government or in thoroughgoing reconciliation. On account of their military dominance, they have been intransigent and unwilling to offer concessions to either Saudi Arabia or their domestic rivals.

Saudi Arabia appreciates this reality, having decisively failed to achieve its two war objectives of rolling back Houthi gains and reinstating the internationally recognised government. After nine years of war, the Houthis are far more powerful than they initially were, and they are firmly in control of the capital and the northwest, while the coalition has been unable to challenge them. The negotiations have therefore centred on the terms of Riyadh's withdrawal from its failed intervention and its efforts to minimise its losses. Riyadh primarily hopes to convince the Houthis to refrain from attacking its territory with missiles or drones again, allowing Crown Prince Muhammad bin Salman to put the war behind him and remove it as a drain on the country's coffers and energies. Yet the negotiations have been prolonged in part because the Houthis, understanding Saudi weakness and desperation, have consistently tried – and often succeeded – to force Saudi Arabia to revise its demands downward.[8]

If Saudi–Houthi talks succeed, the Houthis will consolidate and legitimise their power and gain recognition as the governing authority in northwest Yemen. This result will afford them the leeway to continue expanding the territory under their control and with it their regional power and role. The central city of Marib, one of the last strongholds of the internationally recog-nised government, will likely be in their cross hairs soon after (and perhaps before) the completion of the talks. Marib sits at a strategic crossroads of east–west and north–south roads, and the area holds some of Yemen's hydrocarbon reserves. And, as recent events in the Red Sea demonstrate, the consolidation of Houthi power domestically would provide them with more space to expand their regional role.

The Houthis as a regional power

The realist theorist Robert Gilpin famously noted that one of the cardi-nal rules of international politics is that capabilities shape intentions, and growing capabilities therefore shape growing ambition.[9] As their strength has grown domestically, the Houthis have sought to play a more assertive regional role. They aim to position themselves as a regional power aligned with Iran and its network of non-state armed partners such as Hizbullah and Hamas.[10]

Geography has been especially helpful to the Houthis. Unlike Lebanon, Yemen does not share a border with Israel, lying about 2,000 kilometres away. This gives the Houthis a comfortable margin of manoeuvre that other Iran-backed groups do not have: the Houthis can provoke Israel while remaining shielded by distance. This bolsters Houthi perceptions that they have less to lose than others from ramping up the confrontation with Israel. Compounding their audacity has been the hubris arising from their mili-tary victory. Houthi rhetoric has come to display excessive self-confidence and a sense of untouchability.[11] An exclusionary ideology and world view have also fuelled Houthi ambition. Abdulmalik al-Houthi, the movement's military and political leader, is fiercely nationalist and xenophobic. He holds supremacist views that place the Houthis at the top of a highly stratified social hierarchy and has, for instance, openly proclaimed his ambition to seize Mecca from Saudi Arabia.[12]

Thanks largely to Iranian support, the Houthis now possess a significant stockpile of cruise and ballistic missiles, as well as drones that can strike deep into Saudi Arabia and the United Arab Emirates (UAE). This is a major worry for both countries. The UAE's ability to attract trade, investment and foreign workers depends substantially on its reputation as a haven of stability in a turbulent region. As for Saudi Arabia, while Crown Prince Muhammad bin Salman's foreign policy was at first reckless, most visibly in the war in Yemen and the blockade of Qatar, more recently he too has prioritised trade and the promotion of investment and tourism, which he regards as essential to his ambitious agenda of domestic socio-economic reforms.[13] The threat of missile or drone strikes and wider hostilities imperils both countries' respective visions.

The Houthis have paid Iran outsize dividends on a limited investment. The amount of military and other support Tehran provides is impossible to quantify precisely, but it probably adds up to no more than the low hundreds of millions of dollars per year.[14] Yet it has secured for Iran a partner that has defeated Saudi Arabia, now controls Yemen's capital, has emerged as a regional power and, by virtue of the shipping attacks, has afforded Iran and Hizbullah some limited cover for their restraint against Israel over the course of the Gaza war. Iran's most important objective in Yemen now is to advance the consolidation and legitimisation of Houthi rule.[15] It will therefore support the political process between the Houthis and Saudi Arabia as long as it leads in that direction. It will not hesitate to act as a spoiler if it perceives otherwise. Tehran opposes efforts to promote national reconciliation or an eventual unity or coalition government, since this would dilute Houthi power.

A long-term threat to the Red Sea

The war in Gaza that started in October 2023 has presented the Houthis with an opportunity to further expand their regional influence. Early on, mostly in autumn 2023, they struck Israel directly with missiles and drones.

As of 1 May, according to the Congressional Research Service, they had hit Israel at least 53 times.[16] This marked an expansion of their range: until then, their maximum known reach was about 1,500 km, enough to hit the UAE and deep in Saudi Arabia but short of the roughly 2,000 km needed to strike southern Israel. The symbolism was powerful but the military impact limited, as Israel's advanced air defences easily thwarted relatively rudimentary missiles and drones launched individually. More broadly, however, the Houthi threat from the south heightens the risk that Israeli defences could be overwhelmed in the event of an all-out war during which Iran and its other partners, in addition to the Houthis, could all target Israel simultaneously.

During the war in Gaza, the Houthis have slowed the pace of direct attacks on Israel and shifted to targeting shipping in the Red Sea and the Gulf of Aden. According to the Yemen Conflict Observatory, between October 2023 and mid-June 2024 there were 92 recorded Houthi attacks in these waters.[17] A June 2024 report by the US Defense Intelligence Agency (DIA) assessed that the Houthi threat had affected at least 29 companies across more than 65 countries and caused insurance premiums for Red Sea transits to rise more than sevenfold. According to the DIA, container shipping through the Red Sea, which accounted for about 15% of total global maritime trade prior to October 2023, had fallen by 90% between December 2023 and February 2024. Shipping companies were compelled to reroute vessels around the Cape of Good Hope, adding several days and about $1m to the cost of a voyage between Europe and Asia.[18]

The Houthis, then, have clearly shown that they have the intent and capability to obstruct shipping in the Red Sea. They have become a limited maritime power of sorts by virtue of an arsenal of ballistic and cruise missiles and aerial, surface and underwater drones that they have used to target ships, even though their effectiveness and reliability have been variable. They carried out a helicopter-borne capture of one ship. Media reporting suggests that their targeting has improved, notably through better use of intelligence and reconnaissance. This, again, is in part the result of Iranian support: they have reportedly set up a joint-operations room with Hizbullah in Beirut, where Iran shares intelligence with them.[19] While actual attacks have remained sporadic and in some cases haphazard, they have continued to have considerable political impact.

The Houthis claim that the Red Sea attacks are intended to protest Israel's war in Gaza and the United States' support for Israel, and they have said that they would stop only when the Gaza war stopped. This suggests to some that the solution to the crisis is not American-led airstrikes on Yemen but a ceasefire in Gaza. The logic is appealing, but it does not hold up. Houthi leaders have said that they would stop attacks once Israel's 'aggression' in Gaza stops, and they are likely to interpret this term broadly to cover more than the current round of fighting and include Israel's continuing occupation of Palestinian territories.[20]

While it is true that Houthi ideology embraces a significant anti-Israeli and anti-Semitic component – their sloganeering includes the chants 'Death to Israel' and 'A curse upon the Jews' – the war in Gaza has been a pretext for the Houthi attacks much more than their cause. The Red Sea campaign has allowed them to mobilise and exploit strong pro-Palestinian feelings among Yemenis to consolidate their power and boost recruitment.[21] At the regional level, the Houthis have similarly positioned themselves as champions of the Palestinian cause, significantly raising their status against rivals and adversaries that have not taken clear public stances in opposition to Israel.

These strategic benefits, combined with the Houthis' expansionist and ambitious world view and their hubris, strongly suggest that the jeopardy the Houthis pose to Red Sea shipping will not subside with an eventual ceasefire in Gaza. They will at least threaten to use force in the Red Sea again should they wish, for example, to pressure Israel or the United States to advance a stalled post-war political process in Gaza or to gain concessions from Saudi Arabia in talks on Yemen.

Bad options

The United States faces a distinctly unappealing set of options for dealing with the long-term Houthi threat to maritime commerce. There are three broad options, along a continuum. At the extremes, Washington could either do nothing or adopt a strategy of full-scale opposition to the Houthis. The middle road would be containment involving limited airstrikes and maritime interdiction.

Doing nothing would avoid a new quagmire of open-ended combat in Yemen with at best uncertain chances of success while denying the Houthis propaganda gains from anti-American resistance. But this would forswear any firm deterrent against the Houthis and signal to their partners in the Iran-led 'axis of resistance', as well as others thinking about emulating them, that attacks on the global commons could go unpunished.

A prolonged, intensive air campaign targeting Houthi military sites, leaders and broader infrastructure would be equally unappealing. While it would diminish Houthi capabilities, it would also risk escalatory Houthi retaliation, including against American assets in the region, such as military bases in the Gulf. It could also draw resistance from Saudi Arabia and the UAE, which would fear retaliatory Houthi attacks on their own territory. Furthermore, large-scale airstrikes probably would not defeat or fully deter the Houthis, and would provide them with a massive propaganda boost.

The intermediate option represents what the United States, with the United Kingdom, has been doing since January 2024: a limited campaign of airstrikes targeting Houthi military sites, especially those that facilitate missile and drone launches, and occasional strikes against weapons factories through *Operation Poseidon Archer*. But most analysts assess that continued operations along these lines are unlikely to do enough damage to compel the Houthis to stop them.[22] The dispersal of Houthi military sites and infrastructure throughout the country, often in urban areas or difficult terrain, makes them difficult to completely destroy and, according to satellite-imagery analysis, they are expanding underground military facilities.[23] After 20 years of fighting, first against the Yemeni government and then against Saudi Arabia, they are also battle-hardened and not easily discouraged.

In addition, the air campaign has strengthened the Houthis domestically, inspiring strong pro-Palestinian feelings in the Yemeni population and effectively casting political opponents who object to Houthi aggression in the Red Sea as American lackeys.[24] If or when a ceasefire comes in Gaza, the Houthis will be able to claim credit with some plausibility, further lifting their domestic and regional standing. The Houthis have also perceived Washington's reluctance to escalate as signalling a lack of resolve.[25] Airstrikes, even in a limited campaign, further push the Houthis closer to Iran. Thus, if the United

States simply keeps doing what it's been doing, it could find itself locked into an indefinite low-level confrontation with the Houthis with no exit strategy or prospect for success and an indefinite risk of escalation.

Constraints on US options

Three factors severely limit the American margin of manoeuvre. Firstly, the United States' two main regional partners in Yemen – Saudi Arabia and the UAE – have often been working at cross purposes, hampering their ability to build a united anti-Houthi front. The UAE officially supports the internationally recognised government, though it is directly aligned with only certain factions, such as the separatist Southern Transitional Council, and opposes others, such as Islah, a Saudi-backed Islamist party loosely linked to the Muslim Brotherhood and a key member of the anti-Houthi bloc. Individual Presidential Leadership Council members, half of whom are supported by the Saudis and the other half by the Emiratis, retain control of their own military units or militias, and resist forming a unified force to fight the Houthis. For years, armed clashes and sustained threats between these actors have benefitted the Houthis.[26]

Secondly, prospects for a viable US-supported peace process in Yemen are dim because the United States lacks a reliable partner on the ground. A notional means of mitigating the threat posed by the Houthis would be for Washington to support a peace process in Yemen aimed at national reconciliation and post-war reconstruction. But in the absence of a strong counterweight to the now militarily and politically dominant Houthis, the outcome of any such process would undoubtedly be the consolidation of Houthi power and the further marginalisation of the country's disparate anti-Houthi factions. The United States could choose to provide support to specific anti-Houthi factions, such as the National Resistance Forces based in southwestern Yemen, propping them up so that they can fight the Houthis and deter them from continuing their attacks in the Red Sea, but their leader is Tareq Saleh, the nephew of the former president Ali Abdallah Saleh. His association with the former regime and its dismal record on corruption and governance makes the National Resistance Forces an unappealing alternative from both a popular and a strategic perspective. Supporting them would likely reinforce the fragmentation that is one of the root causes of instability in Yemen.

The United States could also consider backing the Southern Transitional Council, which controls a chunk of territory in southern Yemen, mostly around Aden, and commands effective militias.[27] In practice, however, this would come at a high cost. The Southern Transitional Council seeks independence for the south, so supporting it would de facto weaken the idea of the Yemeni state itself. A possible counter-argument could be that after years of war and with southerners more mobilised than at any time since reunification, that idea has become a fiction. This raises a difficult question, which Washington will probably want to punt forward for now, but which will not go away: whether the United States could eventually support southern independence as a counterweight to the long-term inevitability of a Houthi-dominated, hostile north Yemen.

Thirdly, the challenge for the United States is steepened by the reality that the Houthis have gained the ability to deter Saudi Arabia and the UAE from ramping up support for their preferred Yemeni partners. In early 2022, for instance, the Giants Brigade, a fairly effective UAE-backed militia based in the southwest, started advancing against Houthi positions around Marib. In response, the Houthis hit an industrial area close to Abu Dhabi airport with drones. The attack caused minimal damage, but the message was clear and strong: should the UAE support groups attacking the Houthis, the latter would hit back directly at critical Emirati infrastructure. Because UAE prosperity is partly premised on its image of stability, its leaders want to avoid Houthi retaliation. The Giants Brigade therefore withdrew, and has not seriously threatened the Houthis since. By this same logic, the UAE and Saudi Arabia have refrained from becoming members of the US-led coalition to counter Houthi attacks in the Red Sea: both strongly oppose the Houthis and suffer from their efforts to hamper maritime traffic, but they also do not want to provoke Houthi retaliation.

Living with the Houthis

The United States wants to avoid becoming bogged down in another unwinnable war in the Middle East, but it also has a strong interest in preventing the Houthis from sustaining or increasing the threat they pose. Saudi Arabia and the UAE oppose Houthi actions in the Red Sea, but are limited by the Houthis' ability to retaliate against them, as well as being constrained by the strong pro-Palestinian feelings of their populations, which curtail their political leeway for suppressing a group that has successfully positioned itself as a champion of the resistance. Iran wants to avoid escalation to wider regional war, but it also benefits from the growth of the Houthis' power and is unlikely to pressure them to relent. Fuelled by hubris and ambition, the Houthis eagerly step into this balance of caution. To complement the limited airstrikes started in January 2024, Washington and its allies and partners could, in the shorter term, broaden their containment strategy and, in the longer term, aim to build the internationally recognised government as a genuine alternative to the Houthis.

A more comprehensive containment strategy could include several elements in addition to airstrikes. The United States and its allies have little choice but to commit to an open-ended engagement to escort and defend ships in the Red Sea, notwithstanding the costly asymmetry of deploying high-end naval vessels to defend commercial ships against the Houthis' rudimentary and inexpensive drones and missiles.[28] To make allied efforts more effective, the US would ideally merge its *Operation Prosperity Guardian* with the European Union's *Operation Aspides*. This is highly unlikely, but the two operations could at least coordinate more closely. As both missions are overstretched, the effort would also benefit from additional military participants. While many countries are reluctant to formally join any prospective coalition efforts for political reasons, some that are heavily incurring the commercial costs of the Houthi attacks, such as India, which has unilaterally deployed its own ships in the region, might be willing to coordinate more fully on an ad hoc basis.

The United States should also intensify measures to interdict smuggled Iranian supplies to the Houthis, which constitute their chief lifeline. Iran has mostly used two routes – the first through the Persian Gulf and then by land through Oman and eastern Yemen to Houthi-controlled territory, the second via the Arabian Sea in small fishing vessels, often to the coast of Somalia for subsequent transhipment. According to media reports, the Houthis have reportedly also established networks for smuggling weapons and fighters through Djibouti.[29] Securing the participation of more allies and partners in anti-smuggling efforts would enhance both their legitimacy and their effectiveness.

Perhaps the principal stumbling block to military efforts to suppress Houthi attacks in the Red Sea is the Gulf Arab states' reluctance to take ownership of the problem for fear of Houthi retaliation. To diminish it, Washington should continue to bolster the Saudis' and Emiratis' air defences and increase its support for their navies and coastguards, which have historically been neglected.[30]

Finally, Washington and its partners should tighten and refine efforts to deny the Houthis access to foreign currency and global financial networks. A delicate balance is required. The Trump administration designated the Houthis a Foreign Terrorist Organization, which imposed obstacles to the delivery of humanitarian assistance and made dealings with the Houthis more difficult.[31] In 2021, the Biden administration sensibly changed their status to Specially Designated Global Terrorist, which involves a less stringent set of penalties while still limiting Houthi funding by freezing any assets they may have within the United States' jurisdiction and restricting their access to financial markets. Further fine-tuning may be necessary to avoid interfering with Saudi Arabia's eventual payment of civil servants' salaries in Houthi-controlled areas, which is integral to its effort to negotiate a withdrawal from the war.[32]

A lasting dispensation

In the longer term, the United States and its allies need to rethink their relationship with and support for the internationally recognised government of Yemen. Efforts to build it into a credible alternative to the Houthis have failed, yet doing so remains the only feasible means of incentivising them to negotiate.

Because the fragmentation of anti-Houthi forces and their utter inability to form a united front has been crucial to Houthi success, US support must be conditioned on greater unity. It must especially avoid the trap of backing individual factions within the government, which would only strengthen the centrifugal forces that have impeded anti-Houthi efforts since 2014. The focus should be on unifying and reinforcing the severely depleted national forces – including the army and what is left of the navy and coastguard – that remain loyal to the recognised government through the provision of weapons, training and advice. Washington and its partners should also increase economic and humanitarian aid in areas under the government's control. Further, the United States and its allies need to improve their performance on the information-operations front, where they are badly losing the narrative battle against the increasingly effective Houthi propaganda machine.[33] In particular, they should more forcefully emphasise the brutality and corruption of Houthi rule, and its inconsistency with the resistance narrative they are promoting.

A possibility that warrants some attention is that of 'flipping' the Houthis. Some prominent Yemeni analysts believe that it is possible, and perhaps even probable, that Riyadh could eventually convince them to jettison their partnership with Iran in favour of a more cooperative relationship with Saudi Arabia. The proposition is not illogical. There is a history of shifting tribal alliances in Yemen. Saudi Arabia supported the royalists, loosely the predecessors of the Houthis as the Zaydi rulers of north Yemen, during the Yemeni civil war of the 1960s, while Gamal Abdel Nasser's Egypt supported republican forces, who eventually won.[34] In 2014, Ali Abdallah Saleh, who had lost the presidency in 2012 but retained the loyalty of several units in the armed forces, decided to join the Houthis, enabling their takeover of Sanaa. Their alliance of convenience lasted three years, until the Houthis assassinated Saleh in 2017. Furthermore, the Houthis' most important challenge in post-war Yemen will be economic, and Saudi Arabia has far more to offer than Iran in that regard.[35]

There are, of course, significant countervailing considerations. Ties between the Houthis and Iran have become deeply institutionalised and will not be easily broken. Moreover, hardliners tightly aligned with Iran now dominate the Houthis, having sidelined pragmatic elements more inclined to consider such a drastic shift. In addition, should a Saudi–Houthi rapprochement become plausible, Iran would most likely encourage the formation of hardline splinter groups that it would continue supporting. Iran's foothold in northwest Yemen would not disappear, even if its overall influence in the Houthi movement would be diminished.

* * *

The United States faces a choice in Yemen. Given its other strategic challenges, containment is the default option. But this would leave Yemen fragmented and most Yemenis living under brutal Houthi rule while failing to extinguish the threat that the Houthis pose to regional security. The more ambitious path of increasing support for the internationally recognised government would encounter major obstacles and face steep odds. At the same time, it could keep American diplomatic entanglement at a tolerable level by focusing support on a potentially viable partner on the ground. Even partial success could tilt the internal balance of power in Yemen and provide the internationally recognised government with greater leverage for inducing the Houthis to compromise by, among other things, standing down in the Red Sea.

Notes

1   Defense Intelligence Agency, 'Yemen: Houthi Attacks Placing Pressure on International Trade', 13 June 2024, https://www.dia. mil/Portals/110/Images/News/ Military_Powers_Publications/ YEM_Houthi-Attacks-Pressuring-International-Trade.pdf.

2   See Marieke Brandt, *Tribes and Politics in Yemen: A History of the Houthi Conflict* (Oxford: Oxford University Press, 2017).

3   See Marie-Christine Heinze (ed.), *Yemen and the Search for Stability: Power, Politics and Society After the Arab Spring* (London: I.B. Tauris, 2018).

4   See Thomas Juneau, 'Saudi Arabia's Costly War in Yemen: A Neoclassical Realist Theory of Overbalancing', *International Relations*, 13 February 2024, https://journals.sagepub.com/ doi/epub/10.1177/00471178241231728.

5   See Thomas Juneau, 'How War in Yemen Transformed the Iran–Houthi Partnership', *Studies in Conflict and Terrorism*, vol. 47, no. 3, July 2021, pp. 278–300.

6   See Veena Ali-Khan, 'Yemen's Troubled Presidential Leadership Council', International Crisis Group, 4 May 2023, https://www.crisisgroup. org/middle-east-north-africa/gulf-and-arabian-peninsula/yemen/ yemens-troubled-presidential-leadership-council.

7   See Maysaa Shuja Al-Deen, 'Crafting a Police State: Houthis Tighten Grip amid Red Sea Attacks', Sana'a Center for Strategic Studies, 9 April 2024, https:// sanaacenter.org/the-yemen-review/ jan-mar-2024/22292.

8   See Thomas Juneau, 'Negotiating Saudi Arabia's Defeat and the

Houthi Victory in Yemen', *War on the Rocks*, 15 May 2023, https://warontherocks.com/2023/05/negotiating-saudi-arabias-defeat-and-the-houthi-victory-in-yemen/.

9   See Robert Gilpin, *War and Change in World Politics* (Cambridge: Cambridge University Press, 1981).

10 See Daniel Sobelman, 'Houthis in the Footsteps of Hizbullah', *Survival*, vol. 65, no. 3, June–July 2023, pp. 129–44.

11 See Scott Peterson, 'Gaza War: Why Houthis Pose a Stubborn Challenge to US in Red Sea', *Christian Science Monitor*, 4 January 2024, https://www.csmonitor.com/World/Middle-East/2024/0104/Gaza-war-Why-Houthis-pose-a-stubborn-challenge-to-US-in-Red-Sea.

12 See Abdulghani Al-Iryani, 'The Saudi Overture to the Houthis', Sana'a Center for Strategic Studies, 14 November 2022, https://sanaacenter.org/the-yemen-review/october-2022/18992.

13 See Kristian Coates Ulrichsen, 'De-risking the Neighbourhood: The Security Politics of Saudi Vision 2030', in Eleonora Ardemagni (ed.), *The Security Side of Gulf Visions: Adapting Defence to the Connectivity Age* (Milan: ISPI, 2024), pp. 21–32.

14 See Juneau, 'How War in Yemen Transformed the Iran–Houthi Partnership'.

15 See Thomas Juneau, 'Iran's View of Houthi Attacks in the Red Sea: Protecting Gains and Limiting Costs', Sana'a Center for Strategic Studies, 9 April 2024, https://sanaacenter.org/the-yemen-review/jan-mar-2024/22296.

16 Christopher M. Blanchard, 'Houthi Attacks in the Red Sea: Issues for Congress', Congressional Research Service, updated 1 May 2024, https://crsreports.congress.gov/product/pdf/IN/IN12301.

17 Armed Conflict Location & Event Data Project (ACLED), 'Red Sea Attacks Dashboard', accessed 21 June 2024, https://acleddata.com/yemen-conflict-observatory/red-sea-attacks-dashboard/#1707908374225-329692ad-51d5.

18 Defense Intelligence Agency, 'Yemen: Houthi Attacks Placing Pressure on International Trade'.

19 See, for example, 'Hizbullah Chief Meets Hamas, Islamic Jihad Officials, Agrees to "Keep Coordinating"', Al Fassel, 25 October 2024, https://alfasselnews.com/en_GB/articles/gc1/features/2023/10/25/feature-02.

20 See Faozi Al-Goidi, 'Houthis Involvement in Gaza War: A Tactical Move?', Middle East Council on Global Affairs, 7 December 2023, https://mecouncil.org/blog_posts/houthis-involvement-in-gaza-war-a-tactical-move/.

21 See Shuja Al-Deen, 'Crafting a Police State'.

22 See, for example, Gregory Johnsen, 'The Houthis Escalate and Expand the War', Arab Gulf States Institute in Washington, 18 June 2024, https://agsiw.org/the-houthis-escalate-and-expand-the-war/.

23 See Fabian Hinz, 'Yemen's Houthis Are Going Underground', International Institute for Strategic Studies, Military Balance Blog, 29 April 2024, https://www.iiss.org/en/online-analysis/military-balance/2024/04/yemens-houthis-are-going-underground/.

24 See Giorgio Cafiero, 'The Unintended Consequences of Biden's Approach to Yemen', *Amwaj*, 19 February 2024, https://amwaj.media/article/the-unintended-consequences-of-biden-s-approach-to-yemen.

25 See Farea Al-Muslimi, 'The Houthis Won't Back Down After US and UK Strikes on Yemen', Chatham House, 12 January 2024, https://www.chathamhouse.org/2024/01/houthis-wont-back-down-after-us-and-uk-strikes-yemen.

26 See Afrah Nasser, 'Divergent Saudi–Emirati Agendas Cripple Yemen's Presidential Leadership Council', Arab Center, 15 May 2024, https://arabcenterdc.org/resource/divergent-saudi-emirati-agendas-cripple-yemens-presidential-leadership-council/.

27 See Thomas Juneau, 'The UAE and the War in Yemen: From Surge to Recalibration', *Survival*, vol. 62, no. 4, August–September 2020, pp. 183–208.

28 See Rudy Ruitenberg, 'French Navy Defends Use of Million-euro Missiles to Down Houthi Drones', *Defense News*, 11 January 2024, https://www.defensenews.com/global/europe/2024/01/11/french-navy-defends-use-of-million-euro-missiles-to-down-houthi-drones/

29 See Gordon Lubold, 'How an Iranian-backed Militia Ties Down U.S. Naval Forces in the Red Sea', *Wall Street Journal*, 12 June 2024, https://www.wsj.com/world/middle-east/how-an-iranian-backed-militia-ties-down-u-s-naval-forces-in-the-red-sea-3821056c.

30 See Eleonora Ardemagni, 'Saudi Arabia Has a Red Sea Vision, Not Yet a Strategy', Arab Gulf States Institute in Washington, 17 May 2024, https://agsiw.org/saudi-arabia-has-a-red-sea-vision-not-yet-a-strategy/.

31 See 'What the Designation of "Terrorist" Means for Yemen's Houthis', Al-Jazeera, 18 January 2024, https://www.aljazeera.com/news/2024/1/18/what-the-designation-of-terrorist-means-for-yemens-houthis.

32 See 'US Seeks to Block Houthi Revenues in Possible Threat to Yemen Truce: Report', Al-Jazeera, 6 June 2024, https://www.aljazeera.com/news/2024/6/6/us-seeks-to-block-houthi-revenue-in-possible-threat-to-yemen-truce-report.

33 See Burhan Ahmed, 'Houthi Media: A Study in Ideological Warfare', Sana'a Center for Strategic Studies, 5 June 2024, https://sanaacenter.org/publications/analysis/22797.

34 See Asher Orkaby, *Beyond the Arab Cold War: The International History of the Yemen Civil War, 1962–68* (Oxford: Oxford University Press, 2017).

35 See, for instance, Sarah Phillips, *Yemen's Democracy Experiment in Regional Perspective: Patronage and Pluralized Authoritarianism* (New York: Palgrave Macmillan, 2008).

Copyright © 2024 The International Institute for Strategic Studies

Review Essay

Is a Visionary Defence Bureaucracy Possible?

Paul Fraioli

Unit X: How the Pentagon and Silicon Valley Are Transforming the Future of War
Raj M. Shah and Christopher Kirchhoff. London: Scribner, 2024.
£20.00. 336 pp.

In 2013, a working group of eminent faculty members at Harvard began meeting regularly to discuss the rise of China and the evolving relationship between Beijing and Washington. The group included Deng Xiaoping's biographer and several former US government officials – an acting secretary of state, a treasury secretary, a vice chairman of the Joint Chiefs of Staff and a long-time diplomat who is now the American ambassador to China. Xi Jinping had only just taken power, but it had already become clear that he was something more than a replacement-rate bureaucrat. When the conversation at one meeting turned to China's state-owned enterprises and the obvious ways that Beijing had been leveraging massive government investments in the private sector for strategic purposes, the tone was one of resignation. US officials, the group agreed, would have no idea how to comparably coordinate with the private sector even if they wanted to. If Washington ever had 'industrial policy' muscles, they had long since atrophied.[1]

Paul Fraioli is IISS Senior Fellow for Geopolitics and Strategy, and Editor of *Strategic Comments*.

Survival | vol. 66 no. 5 | October–November 2024 | pp. 201–208   DOI 10.1080/00396338.2024.2403229

DIUx

The US Department of Defense does, of course, have vast experience working with the private sector on strategically significant projects, having forged symbiotic relationships with 'defence primes' Boeing, General Dynamics, Lockheed Martin, Northrop Grumman and RTX Corporation over the course of decades. Yet corporate actors outside this circle have often found the Pentagon inscrutable and seen few paths to profitability in working with the world's largest bureaucracy.[2] By the middle of the last decade, the consequences were becoming clear. Much of the technology used by US forces

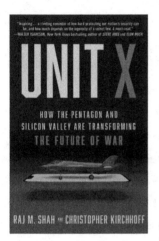

was beginning to look obsolete compared with devices and software available at Walmart. More concerningly, there was a risk that as China spent significant sums to acquire new military capabilities, it might be able to integrate cutting-edge technology from the private sector into weapons and operational systems to its advantage in a future conflict.

In February 2015, then-president Barack Obama appointed Ash Carter secretary of defense. A physicist and academic, and earlier the deputy secretary of defense, he had a widely known impatience for bureaucracy and was particularly frustrated by the slow pace of technological change in government. That April, he gave a speech at Stanford University highlighting the 'need to drill holes in the wall … between the Department of Defense and the commercial and scientific sector'.[3] By August, he had announced the creation of Defense Innovation Unit Experimental (DIUx), a new office based in Silicon Valley meant to connect the Pentagon with entrepreneurs, start-ups and commercial technology firms. The office was initially a conspicuous failure: staffers had little experience working outside of Washington, and responsibility had been delegated so far down in the Pentagon's organisational chart that it took six months to deliver furniture and install internet service. Sceptical onlookers in Silicon Valley were vindicated.

Hoping to confer credibility on the office, Carter appointed Raj M. Shah and Christopher Kirchhoff to fix its problems and publicly relaunch it. Shah was a technology entrepreneur and a former F-16 pilot in the Air National Guard. Kirchhoff had served as a senior civilian advisor in the Pentagon and a National Security Council staffer. Carter granted the pair extraordinary bureaucratic powers: a direct reporting line to the secretary's office, control over budgeting and hiring and the effective authority to waive Pentagon rules that got in their way. In *Unit X: How the Pentagon and Silicon Valley Are Transforming the Future of War*, Shah and Kirchhoff recount how the office nearly failed again despite enjoying these powers, how it clawed the relatively small sum of $30 million from sceptical congressional staffers in 2016 and how that budget has grown to $983m today.

Bureaucratic politics

Shah and Kirchhoff bear scars from their time battling what they call the 'military-industrial auto-immune system' (p. 59). In several instances, they learned of an unconscionably outdated piece of technology playing a critical role in military operations, with the fix years behind schedule and millions of dollars over budget. In 2016, for example, they found that at the Combined Air Operations Center in Qatar, the Air Force was planning more than 1,500 in-air refuelling flights daily over Afghanistan, Iraq and Syria using a manual algorithm and magnets on a map superimposed on a whiteboard. The inefficiency of the process cost the Pentagon more than $5m weekly. Shah exclaimed that the contractors tasked to computerise the process 'have been working for eight years and they have little to show for it. They've burned three-quarters of a billion dollars. We can hire coders in Silicon Valley and get this whole thing done in one-tenth the time and one-tenth the cost' (p. 59). His forecast proved prescient, and he was later able to persuade senator John McCain to kill the legacy contract and award the project to DIUx. This victory came at a cost, however, as it signalled the degree to which Shah and Kirchhoff could threaten established ways of doing business.

According to Shah, 'in Washington it's a zero-sum game. It's not like Silicon Valley, where folks can expand the pie by working together. In D.C., power is budget and people. The only way to expand is to take something from someone else. This leads to monumental infighting' (p. 227). In some ways, the book fits comfortably into a well-known genre: that of Washington memoir. It lionises friends, settles scores and tallies accomplishments. But it also chronicles two notable moments. In the first, Shah and Kirchhoff faced off against two particularly ruthless staffers on the House Committee on Appropriations anonymised as 'Evelyn and Ed', who cut the DIUx budget to zero just as it was launching. The fact that Carter had given the authors carte blanche within the Pentagon was irrelevant; Evelyn and Ed cared only about what DIUx would do for their boss's home state of Indiana. The second moment arose after Carter's sudden death from a heart attack in 2022. Shah and Kirchhoff offer an acid description of a defence-prime lobbyist, standing at the entrance to the Washington National Cathedral at his funeral, 'glad-handing people and handing out business cards' while flaunting Stars and Stripes lapel pins (p. 220).

The bureaucratic conflicts at the heart of the book, though plentiful, are ultimately overshadowed by the remarkable innovations that DIUx delivered to soldiers. These include miniature cloud-penetrating radar satellites for use in North Korea (which is overcast roughly 200 days a year), software modifications enabling the safe use of Chinese drones by US forces in Afghanistan, and flying electric cars scheduled to enter service in the US Air Force in 2025.[4]

Ukraine as proving ground

The book traces the waxing and waning of the Pentagon's support for DIUx during the administrations of Obama, Donald Trump and Joe Biden. Shah and Kirchhoff argue that after receiving strong support from Carter and Trump's defense secretary Jim Mattis, who was so enthused he removed the 'x' from the office's name, DIU was deprioritised at least until Russia's full-scale invasion of Ukraine in 2022 (p. 153). While both men left government in 2018, they continued to work on defence-technology issues – Shah by investing in start-ups and Kirchhoff by participating in national-security commissions with Eric Schmidt, former chief executive of Google and later chairman of the Defense Innovation Board.

The authors point to the war in Ukraine as a turning point for DIU in several ways. Firstly, it launched a 'new gold rush in Silicon Valley', with venture capitalists willing to invest in defence-related start-ups (p. 190). This was powered by outrage at Russia's aggression and the fact that a sustained conflict created the circumstances for products to be tested and sold en masse.

Secondly, major technology firms such as Amazon and Microsoft pitched in, the former by preserving all Ukrainian government records on a suitcase-sized hard drive and then uploading them to the cloud. The authors note that in 2018, some large firms, Google in particular, resisted partnering with the Pentagon owing to the risk that their products would be used in war. This echoes criticisms made by others, such as Palantir founder Alex Karp.[5]

Thirdly, many of the technologies DIUx had brought into the Pentagon earlier found their way onto the battlefield in Ukraine. Capella Space, a start-up that had received foundational funding from the office to build the cloud-penetrating satellites for North Korea, deployed them to track the Russian invasion. Biden cited Capella Space images in February 2022 to make the case that the invasion was imminent. In addition, drone-hacking techniques developed by DIUx-funded companies for use in Afghanistan informed the intense digital arms race that arose between Russian and Ukrainian forces as their efforts to target each other with uninhabited systems intensified.

In Washington, the lessons learned from the Russia–Ukraine war are up for debate and rhyme with earlier disagreements about 'revolutions in military affairs'.[6] Eric Schmidt sees the war as a vindication of his view that technologists will be essential to wars of the future: 'ten programmers can change the way thousands of soldiers operate' (quoted on p. 212). Others believe that commercial technology is not a significant factor compared with traditional factors such as mass, combined-arms manoeuvre and the availability of ammunition. Under Secretary of Defense for Acquisition and Sustainment William LaPlante said in an interview that 'the tech bros aren't helping us too much in Ukraine … It's hardcore production of really serious weaponry. That's what matters' (quoted on p. 213).

The Pentagon's own acquisition plans suggest that there is some truth in both views. In 2023, Deputy Secretary of Defense Kathleen Hicks announced 'Replicator', an initiative that calls for the Pentagon to take an idea – say, for a new weapon or platform – and deliver it to the battlefield with unprecedented speed: 18–24 months. In its first iteration, the pro-gramme is developing technology to launch autonomous drone swarms (aerial, maritime surface and subsurface, and in space) that could be used in a crisis in the Taiwan Strait. At least three contracts have been awarded, and some capabilities are expected to be available by August 2025. In a similar vein, Secretary of the Air Force Frank Kendall stated in 2023 that the service intends to buy 'one thousand to two thousand supersonic drones that would fly as autonomous wingmen alongside fighter aircraft' – an idea incubated at DIU (p. 228).

*   *   *

Unit X relays an anecdote that shows how intuition often fails us when we think about exponential change. Imagine that Lake Michigan – with a surface area the size of Croatia – were emptied of water. One ounce of water is then added in the year 1940 and the amount of water in the lake doubles each year thereafter. By 1970, there would be enough water present for a residential swimming pool. By 2010, after 70 years, there would be only a few inches of water in scattered spots on the bottom of the lake. But by 2020, there would be 40 feet of water, and by 2025 the lake would be full. The point is that it is hard to know when the tipping point will occur.

After leaving DIU, Kirchhoff spent time working on artificial intelligence (AI), among other things serving as an outside contributor to the National Security Commission on AI chaired by Schmidt. Perhaps the most impor-tant recommendation in the commission report, issued in March 2021, was to on-shore the production of semiconductors in the US. Just over a year later, Congress passed Biden's CHIPS Act, which seeks to do just that, while also initiating 'industrial policy' measures that would have seemed shock-ing to the 2013 Harvard working group.

The pace of future policy surprises in this direction – and indeed whether we see major changes at all – will depend on the development of large lan-guage models. The exponential growth of model capabilities, which has held constant over roughly the last decade, could plateau unexpectedly due to constraints on chips, power or training data, or other factors impeding returns to scale. But many prominent technologists have said that they see no sign of this happening.[7] Growth for even a few more years could yield something close to artificial general intelligence, which would have unpredictable – but likely very significant – implications for US national security. The tipping point is unknown. Against this uncertainty, an optimist would view the story of DIU as a proof of concept: when the stakes are high, government officials can figure out whom to call in the private sector and mobilise resources quickly. A pessimist, however, would emphasise the DIU's long and difficult birth and take it as a warning that counterproductive bureaucratism in the Pentagon endures.

Notes

[1] This challenge is discussed in David C. Gompert, 'Spin-on: How the US Can Meet China's Technological Challenge', *Survival*, vol. 62, no. 3, June–July 2020, pp. 115–30; and David C. Gompert, 'Winning the US–China Technology Race', *Survival*, vol. 66, no. 4, August–September 2024, pp. 77–84.

[2] The primes earned $188.9 billion in combined defence-related revenue in 2022. See Stockholm International Peace Research Institute, 'The SIPRI Top 100 Arms-producing and Military Services Companies in the World, 2022', https://www.sipri.org/visualizations/2023/sipri-top-100-arms-producing-and-military-services-companies-world-2022.

[3] US Department of Defense, 'Remarks by Secretary Carter at the Drell Lecture Cemex Auditorium, Stanford Graduate School of Business, Stanford, California', 23 April 2015, https://www.defense.gov/News/Transcripts/Transcript/Article/607043/remarks-by-secretary-carter-at-the-drell-lecture-cemex-auditorium-stanford-grad.

[4] The latter are known as 'electric vertical take-off and landing' (eVTOL) vehicles.

[5] See Maureen Dowd, 'Alex Karp Has Money and Power. So What Does He Want?', *New York Times*, 17 August 2024, https://www.nytimes.com/2024/08/17/style/alex-karp-palantir.html.

[6] See, for example, Richard Hundley, *Past Revolutions, Future Transformations: What Can the History of Revolutions in Military Affairs Tell Us About Transforming the U.S. Military?* (Santa Monica, CA: RAND Corporation, 1999).

[7] See, for example, Leopold Aschenbrenner, 'Situational Awareness: The Decade Ahead', June 2024, https://situational-awareness.ai/wp-content/uploads/2024/06/situationalawareness.pdf; and 'What If Dario Amodei Is Right About A.I.?', The Ezra Klein Show, *New York Times*, 12 April 2024, https://www.nytimes.com/2024/04/12/opinion/ezra-klein-podcast-dario-amodei.html?showTranscript=1.

Copyright © 2024 The International Institute for Strategic Studies

Book Reviews

South Asia
Teresita C. Schaffer

Dethroned: The Downfall of India's Princely States
John Zubrzycki. London: C. Hurst & Co., 2023. £25.00. 360 pp.

John Zubrzycki is an Australian diplomat-turned-journalist, who has written about Indian history and is particularly drawn to somewhat quirky topics. *Dethroned* fits this pattern. The authoritative volume on the incorporation of the princely states into independent India is – and remains – V.P. Menon's *The Story of the Integration of the Indian States*. Menon, who served as secretary to the government in the Ministry of States, was a central player in this drama, along with Sardar Vallabhbhai Patel, the deputy prime minister. Where Menon provided a rich historical background on each of the states, Zubrzycki has focused more on the personalities. He also brings the story up to the final act, the abolition of the princes' 'privy purses', the subsidy they received from the Government of India for about a quarter-century.

Dethroned is engagingly written, and Zubrzycki has an eye for great stories. What he describes with particular sensitivity is the princes' attitude toward the British Raj, and specifically toward the monarchy. He paints a picture of princes who looked on the British monarch as a fellow royal, and their ally in the turbulent world they inhabited. This British Crown was sympathetic to its 'brother monarchs', but its fraternal affection stopped well short of a real commitment to the Indian princes' future welfare. The book's recounting of the back and forth between Menon and Patel, who represented the Government of India and were responsible for the newly independent country's security, and the soon-to-depart British civil servants is particularly interesting.

Zubrzycki writes at the end of his prologue that the story of the princely states is an integral part of Indian history and 'deserves to be told' (p. 14). He tells it well. Integrating the princely states was a tremendous accomplishment for India, and completing the process with 562 princes in two years was extraordinary. It is a sign of Menon's and Patel's success – and India's – that, 75 years after partition, only a handful of princely families remain household names today.

Read this book for the colour and the lore, and for a good understanding of how India's current political masters – the civil service and the political leadership – relate to the princes whose day as rulers is past. The handful who retain an important place in the governing set-up are able to do this because they have integrated into the Indian political system. If Zubrzycki wants to write a sequel, he might describe how this process worked.

The Return of the Taliban: Afghanistan After the Americans Left
Hassan Abbas. New Haven, CT: Yale University Press, 2023.
£16.99/$26.00. 320 pp.

Hassan Abbas has written extensively on South Asia, and especially on Pakistan and Afghanistan. Brought up in Pakistan, he served in that country's Police Service, then came to the United States for graduate studies. He is now a professor of International Security Studies and chair of the Department of Regional and Analytical Studies at the National Defense University in Washington DC.

Abbas has brought his diverse background to bear on this highly readable analysis of the much-misunderstood Taliban movement. Few of those who have tried to explain the Taliban to a Western audience can boast the breadth of interviews and depth of background knowledge that he offers. He situates the Taliban in the turbulent political and social setting of Afghanistan, but goes on to convincingly puncture some of the most hallowed myths about its modus operandi. The movement's rigid adherence to a stern Islamic ideology, for example, has not prevented its younger leaders from becoming quite adept at communicating with modern tools such as social media.

Abbas covers a wide range of topics. Three in particular fascinated me. The first is the Taliban's view of what government is supposed to do, as revealed both in interviews and in a volume published by the Taliban's first chief justice. Basically, Taliban leaders were supposed to make a quick transition from promoting fighting to the opposite – keeping the peace. The objectives of government, not surprisingly, all derive from what their interpretation of Islam requires. On this point, the areas of apparent Taliban consensus do not necessarily represent the only view among strict Islamic scholars. In practice, however, this pushes over half the population to the periphery of social life – women, but also Shi'ites and other minority communities within Islam. Finance does not appear to be high on the governance agenda, and the concept of representing 'all the people' is virtually absent. The whole governing structure is geared toward reinforcing all these aspects of 'God's rule'.

Secondly, despite this dogmatic and all-encompassing ideology, the movement and its governing structure are a hotbed of intense rivalries. The ones Abbas describes stem from ideological disputes, personal competitions and controversial allies outside the Taliban fold (such as Pakistan, pp. 126–8) – and not, in his telling, so much from family feuds. These rivalries exert pressure on the leadership in multiple directions. He concludes that they are 'inherently contradictory' (p. 146).

Thirdly, Afghanistan's relationship with Pakistan is as tangled with the Taliban in power as it was under other governments. Pakistan has been willing to use its ties with the Taliban to enhance Islamabad's influence in Kabul. However, the top tier of Taliban leaders has no interest in appearing as Pakistani stooges, and Pakistan has had real domestic problems with militant groups such as the Tehrik-e-Taliban Pakistan (Pakistan Taliban Movement), which have been a threat to law and order. Pakistan has made agreements with some of the 'freelance' groups, such as the one led by the late Nek Muhammad Wazir. These agreements undercut the authority of local *maliks* (tribal leaders). Most of these agreements were soon broken, and even during their short life, they tended to enhance militant power within Pakistan (pp. 180 ff.)

The chapter on the Taliban's international relationships does not provide much hope that the Taliban will modernise its basic ideas through contact with the outside world. It will use some of its tools – the internet, for example (p. 241) – but the mindset will not soon change.

The Taliban will evolve as its internal and external rivalries play out. The book includes a 'who's who' of the current government – but that too will inevitably change. Still, *The Return of the Taliban* is an excellent source of perspective on the things that aren't likely to change. The author's dedication foreshadows this: 'To the women of Afghanistan.'

Sheikh Abdullah: The Caged Lion of Kashmir
Chitralekha Zutshi. New Haven, CT: Yale University Press, 2024.
£25.00/$35.00. 376 pp.

Sheikh Abdullah, the iconic Kashmiri leader, devoted much of his life to advancing the cause of the Kashmiri people, especially the Muslims of the Kashmir Valley. Kashmir is well known as the most durable dispute between India and Pakistan, but surprisingly little is known about Sheikh Abdullah beyond the realm of dedicated specialists. Chitralekha Zutshi's new biography of him brings out what a complex and contradictory person he was. The introductory chapter sums it up well, quoting Pandit Kashyap Bandhu's description of a man whose 'conscience was Muslim, his heart was Kashmiri, and his brain was secular' (p. xxviii). In the end, weaving those strands together proved to be more than even this larger-than-life character could manage.

Abdullah came from a humble background. He was educated at prestigious Muslim institutions in Lahore and Aligarh, where he was exposed to the big ideological debates of the time. He also founded Kashmir's first political organisation at age 25 – and was arrested for the first time for protesting against Kashmir's princely ruler. This was a kind of 'coming of age' for Indian politicians of his generation. He established himself as a commanding presence – he was tall, and above all a riveting orator. He basked in the adulation of other Kashmiris, but also alienated those who would challenge his claim to leadership.

By the time he was 30, however, the internal contradictions that dogged his political life had crystallised. He was devoted to Islam, but represented a secular Kashmiri nationalism. Kashmir, for him, meant the overwhelmingly Muslim Kashmir Valley, but he claimed to speak for the entire state, including its Hindu residents. And, attracted by the revolutionary ideologies then circulating, he struggled to relate them to the Kashmiris' problems.

Over the last decade of the British Raj and the first of Indian and Pakistani independence, he came to know those who led each country's national movements, and to have a surprisingly warm relationship with Jawaharlal Nehru, which led him to lean toward accepting Kashmir's accession to India for much of the rest of his career.

From 1953 onward, he spent more time in jail than out. He made agreements with the Indian government that got him out of prison and allowed him to become chief minister of Jammu and Kashmir for a couple of years, but the tensions and ambiguities in his persona left him embittered and diminished. He died unhappily in 1982.

Professor Zutshi's biography draws on an impressive array of sources, most importantly the memoir Abdullah wrote later in life. He was known by his Kashmiri admirers as the Sher-e-Kashmir, the 'lion of Kashmir'. The story Zutshi tells is of a man done in by his internal contradictions. The newly independent Indian government was fundamentally opposed to his goal of loosening the ties between Kashmir and the Indian state and granting Kashmiris a more generous form of self-determination – but his own inability to sort out his priorities among the causes he had espoused was the major factor in making him, as the subtitle has it, a 'caged lion'.

What also comes through clearly is that, despite his warm relationships with Independence-era leaders like Nehru, Sheikh Abdullah's inability to consolidate his position was in fact the outcome the Indian government sought. The same is true of the fact that no one has had anything like his centrality in Kashmiri politics. It is hard to be optimistic about the future of Kashmir, caught between two unsatisfied would-be rulers, but this book is a good way into a better understanding of the problem.

Days of Opportunity: The United States and Afghanistan Before the Soviet Invasion
Robert B. Rakove. New York: Columbia University Press, 2023.
£30.00/$35.00. 488 pp.

Robert Rakove is a scholar of US foreign relations, who focuses primarily on the Cold War. This book is an effort to explain what he refers to as the 'Afghan Cold War' – US policy toward Afghanistan between 1923 and 1979. Starting in the 1920s, geography led Afghanistan to be seen from both Moscow and Washington as a 'buffer land' and, especially after the Second World War, as a potential showcase for both East and West. This book fills an important gap: all but the last decade or so of the period it covers is little known even by many South Asia watchers.

As the subtitle indicates, Rakove approaches his subject mainly from the perspective of how the Cold War guided US and Russian relations with Afghanistan. On the US side, it is to an important extent the story of using economic aid as a vehicle to build a political relationship that would keep Afghanistan generally oriented toward the West, although its geography precluded aiming at membership in the ring of alliances around the Soviet Union's southern border.

Two major problems complicated this approach. Firstly, both sides were ambivalent about the relationship. Afghanistan's experience with non-neighbouring countries, especially in the early part of the story, consisted mainly of resisting wars of conquest. (The author rejects the title 'graveyard of empires', but there is much truth to it.) As for the US, in the early days, the idea of using economic aid as a lure was unfamiliar, and Washington was not enthusiastic about trying something novel and expensive in a remote and very poor country. After 1947, another reason for US ambivalence was added: Afghanistan's fraught relations with the newly independent Pakistan, a US ally, and Kabul's habit of stirring up separatist sentiment among the Pashto-speaking population next door.

A second obstacle became even more apparent once the Cold War began in earnest. The US was not very good at delivering development with economic aid. To be fair, that is difficult under the best of circumstances. In this case, one US engineering company (Morrison-Knudsen or MK) was present in Afghanistan throughout the time covered by this book. MK's Helmand Valley project became a byword for poorly executed work with huge cost overruns. This was further complicated by an Afghan government which had little experience administering the far-flung activities of a modern state with a heavily illiterate workforce. As time went on, the tension between potential development priorities (infrastructure, as in the Helmand Valley? Education? Health? A railway, as one US envoy suggested?) coupled with continuing ambivalence in Washington made the economic-aid agenda almost impossible.

The book also recounts the experience of the early US envoys to Afghanistan, their efforts to convince the Afghan government to work with the US, and their tussles with their bosses in Washington, who were more concerned about more pressing foreign-policy issues. The US diplomatic goals were confronted with their Russian counterparts' mirror-image objectives. Keeping Americans out of the border areas of northern Afghanistan was high on the Russian list. Interestingly, the author concludes – correctly, I believe – that the closest these strategies came to success was in creating an odd kind of unacknowledged cooperation between the two superpowers.

Another fascinating strand in this account is Afghanistan's experiment with constitutional democracy. Unfortunately, that was undone by a combination of rivalry within the extended royal family and leftist political movements, the forerunners of those who invited the Soviet army to invade on Christmas Day, 1979.

The one thing that Rakove might have dealt with a bit more clearly is the deep poverty of the country. Understanding this would have made a successful US diplomatic approach much more realistic – and of course it still forms the backdrop for the tragedy of Taliban rule. Some things don't change.

Pakistan and American Diplomacy: Insights from 9/11 to the Afghanistan Endgame
Ted Craig. Lincoln, NE: Potomac Books, 2024. $34.95. 296 pp.

Ted Craig served twice in the US embassy in Pakistan as a US Foreign Service officer during the period his book covers. This volume adds to the already considerable literature on US–Pakistan diplomacy (to which my late husband and I have also contributed with our 2011 book *How Pakistan Negotiates with the United States*). During his time in and around Pakistan, he became a fan of the country's great national passion. He uses cricket as a kind of metaphor for his story.

He covers all the high points one would expect: the two-plus decades of US–Pakistan relations that went from testy to angry and back again; the attempted 'reset' of the Trump era (including Imran Khan's visit to Donald Trump's White

House, where Trump made an unscripted offer to mediate the Kashmir dispute); the poisonous effect of the 'Afghanistan connection' on the US–Pakistan relationship; and Pakistan's long-standing and understandable obsession with India.

The final part of the book, leading up to and through the US exit from Afghanistan, is by far the strongest – Craig offers a fast-paced and exciting account of that time. He conveys the muddled communications within the US government that preceded the exit. He also passes on some stories that are somewhere between intelligence and rumour about would-be go-betweens.

He punctuates this account with accounts of legendary cricket matches won and lost. I'm afraid much of this went over my head. Americans would describe it as 'inside baseball', an explanation that goes too deeply into the arcane aspects of an unfamiliar game. This is often the fate of sports metaphors that wander away from their home fields. I'm sure *Survival* has many readers who will find the cricket metaphor more appealing than I did, however.

Craig introduces the concluding section of the book with an account of the 2019 World Cup at Lord's Cricket Ground, which Pakistan did not win – but neither did India. By this time, Khan was prime minister of Pakistan, and had been elected with a majority of seats in parliament, in contrast to the handful of seats he had earlier enjoyed. The conventional wisdom in Pakistan was that the military's support helped push him across the finish line.

Craig's final observations offer useful and sometimes provocative food for thought. He notes that neither the United States nor Pakistan enjoyed, by the end of the period covered, the leverage it had earlier had with the other. This reflected growing US worries about the apparent nexus between the Pakistan army and various Islamist movements, along with the rise of China, which he describes as '[Pakistan's] preeminent patron' (p. 218). But while US–Pakistan ties were a lower priority, both countries, Craig argues, still needed each other.

Craig wisely stops well short of predicting smooth sailing. His book came out before Pakistani politics took a few more important turns. By the time of Khan's ouster from power in August 2022, he had lost the favour of the Pakistan military. In February 2024, elections were held – and Khan was behind bars, his party banned. As often happens in Pakistan, a number of party personalities found a home in another party. Those that went on to run as independents advertised their association with Khan, and brought home a substantial plurality in parliament. It took some time for them to form a government; when they did, it was led by the party that the army had helped to push out before Khan came to office – and they had the support of Khan's 'non-party'.

None of this invalidates Craig's conclusions, but it is a useful reminder that the iron law of Pakistani politics is, 'you never know!'

Middle East
Ray Takeyh

The Caliph and the Imam: The Making of Sunnism and Shiism
Toby Matthiesen. Oxford and New York: Oxford University
Press, 2023. £25.00/$36.99. 944 pp.

Toby Matthiesen is quickly establishing himself as one of the more interesting historians of the Middle East. His previous book on Shi'ites in Saudi Arabia (*The Other Saudis*) remains the best treatment of this important subject. He has widened his lens in *The Caliph and the Imam*, grappling with the sectarian divisions that have plagued the region starting when the Prophet Muhammad was alive and continuing through to the Arab Spring. His thesis, that the sectarian divide was present from the beginning but became much more toxic after European colonial powers carved up the Middle East, is as provocative as it is insightful.

The question of who should succeed the Prophet Muhammad led to a division between those who thought the leadership of Islam should remain within his family and those favouring his companions. At the outset, the dispute was limited to succession and there was otherwise little doctrinal difference among Muslims, but scriptural interpretation became more disputatious as the followers of caliphs (Islamic leaders selected by the community's elite) and imams (leaders who were descended from Muhammad's son-in-law Ali) lined up on the opposite sides. Matthiesen can be a bit too generous toward those rulers, downplaying the intolerance evident in the early multinational Islamic empires.

The advent of the state system in the modern Middle East was bound to feature sectarian divides. The Europeans certainly tried to empower minorities in their respective mandates: the French relied on Christians, Druze and Alawites in the management of the Levant, and the British empowered Sunnis in Shi'ite-dominated Iraq. This was the old divide-and-rule tactic, but to be fair, any modern state system was bound to exacerbate sectarian tensions as the allocation of resources inevitably discriminated among tribe and sect.

In the twenty-first century, the Iraq War stands as the conflict that did the most to worsen sectarian tensions. It did so by empowering Iraqi Shi'ites and creating a weak administrative structure. Iran did all it could to accentuate these divisions and project its power into this charged arena. Today, Iran stands as the most consequential regional actor, primarily because the traditional bulwarks of Arabism, Syria and Iraq, are too shattered and divided to assert their power. Meanwhile, Egypt is too inward-looking to exert much influence.

Still, it seems that most inhabitants of the region would like to move beyond ancient hatreds and create inclusive governing compacts. The Arab Spring did not begin as a sectarian crusade, but it soon became one as the rulers in both Syria and the Gulf states took a page from the European imperial powers and turned their political adversaries into sectarian agents. This was unfortunate, but perhaps all too inevitable in a region where states feel free to intervene in the affairs of their neighbours and use their populations against them. *The Caliph and the Imam* is a hefty read, but all too rewarding for those who wish to understand how we got here.

The Achilles Trap: Saddam Hussein, the C.I.A., and the Origins of America's Invasion of Iraq
Steve Coll. New York: Penguin Press, 2024. $35.00. 576 pp.

The Iraq War will not be redeemed by historians, and George W. Bush's presidency will not undergo a reassessment in which his decisions on Iraq will be seen as prudent in retrospect. But it is important to remember that the 2003 invasion of Iraq had deep roots in America's tumultuous relationship with Saddam Hussein beginning with his ascension to power in 1979. In his compulsively readable history of these events, Steve Coll revisits familiar pastures and emerges with new and valuable insights. *The Achilles Trap* will stand as the standard work on Iraq for some time to come, not least because of its author's ability to introduce characters and set scenes in a vivid manner.

Saddam's Iraq was not always seen as a menace requiring invasion and occupation. As Iran's Islamists came to power determined to export their revolution throughout the region, Saddam was seen as a sturdy barrier against such forays, and Iraq the only country that could contain the Persians, the Gulf monarchies being too weak to do so. Coll demonstrates that during the Iran–Iraq War, Washington tilted toward Iraq by providing it with intelligence that pinpointed the position of Iranian detachments. This was critical to Iraq's battlefield triumphs. Some of those successes came through the use of chemical weapons that Washington knew about but chose to ignore.

One of the most intriguing aspects of this account is the sheer intellectual poverty of America's approach to Iraq after its expulsion from Kuwait. Bill Clinton was a new type of Democrat, one that took a dim view of so-called 'backlash states', revisionist regimes at odds with the prevailing post-Cold War mood for democratic enlargement. It is important to stress that Clinton was the first president to openly call for regime change in Iraq when he penned the Iraq Liberation Act in 1998. Subsequent criticism by the Democratic Party's luminaries of the Iraq War should not absolve them of their complicity in that folly.

The 9/11 tragedies and the Iraq War are inseparable. A traumatised nation wanted its revenge, and since Osama bin Laden proved elusive and bombing a primitive Afghanistan unsatisfactory, Iraq loomed large. Historians will always be puzzled by the way a large segment of the American public and their elected representatives concluded that a disarmed, dispossessed and dismembered Iraq posed an existential threat to a superpower. This is more than a story of a hubristic America believing that it could condition outcomes in distant lands. Coll affirms the emerging historiographical consensus that this was Bush's war.

Although it was fashionable at the time to blame a cabal of neo-conservatives pulling a benighted Bush into war, the president was the driver of his policy. He later proved incurious about the war he had instigated. During the first three years of the war, the president paid scant attention to the shambolic occupation and rarely took command of the deteriorating situation in Iraq. He started a war, then neglected it and finally lost it.

Wars of Ambition: The United States, Iran, and the Struggle for the Middle East
Afshon Ostovar. Oxford and New York: Oxford University Press, 2024. £22.99/$29.99. 360 pp.

Writing about recent events that have been thoroughly covered in the press is challenging, with presentism a constant danger. Journalists at times try to add something to our knowledge by interviewing policymakers who may wish to either settle scores or burnish their reputations. Historians might sniff around archives for a new twist on old stories. *Wars of Ambition* is a competent but familiar recapitulation of what the Middle East has gone through during the past two decades. It is a useful reminder to a public that so easily forgets.

The starting point of this book is necessarily America's invasion of Iraq. It was at that time that a superpower known for its pragmatism and caution tried to purposely destabilise a region whose existing order it found deficient. The 9/11 tragedies had traumatised Americans and emboldened them to think that they could refashion the Middle East in the United States' democratic image. But not all acts of destructive creation work. The shattering of Iraq presaged the collapse of the regional state system as the Arab Spring provoked its share of insurrections, rebellions and civil wars. It created much mayhem, but no enduring liberal order.

The author is most persuasive in outlining Iran's inner workings and approach to its chaotic region. The Islamic Republic projects its power by using a multinational proxy force to do its bidding on the cheap. This is imperialism at its best, affordable and effective. Anti-Americanism remains at the core of the theocratic regime's international orientation. And for the first time, Iran has attracted great-power patrons to help turbocharge its regional assaults: China provides the necessary economic cushion, while Russia is a reliable source of arms, and possibly nuclear technologies.

Although Iran is in the title, it is missing from large chunks of the book. The author spends much time chronicling Arab upheavals, civil wars and inter-state conflicts. There isn't much new here as the author relies on press accounts and secondary literature. The United States oscillates between ham-fistedness and hesitancy. Neither posture serves the region well, but we are well beyond believing that a determined United States can tame a stubborn region. For the specialist, these historical excursions can be taxing, although a general reader may benefit from this compact history lesson.

Wars of Ambition can be an unsettling book. It demonstrates that while America lost its way in the post-9/11 Middle East, its principal antagonist found a way to fill all the vacuums it created. The theocratic regime's principal weakness is at home, as its sullen population finds that even cheap imperialism can be too much to bear.

What Really Went Wrong: The West and the Failure of Democracy in the Middle East
Fawaz A. Gerges. New Haven, CT: Yale University Press, 2024.
£20.00/$28.00. 336 pp.

What Really Went Wrong is a peculiar book, more of a provocation than a work of history. It resurrects two important figures from the 1950s Middle East, Iranian prime minister Mohammad Mossadegh and the Egyptian strongman Gamal Abdel Nasser, and claims that if America had only refrained from plotting against them, all would be well in the region today. Thus, author Fawaz Gerges liberally connects time and space, forgetting that history is shaped by contingency and chance, and is rarely so predetermined.

The book starts by chronicling the rise of Mossadegh and the oil-nationalisation crisis. This episode has long been fetishised by historians as there was American complicity in the coup that eventually overthrew Mossadegh in August 1953. Along the way, Gerges follows the well-trodden path of absolving Mossadegh of all his sins, which included rigging elections, arresting his political opponents and defying the country's constitution. Mossadegh was a Persian patriot who genuinely abhorred foreign manipulation of Iran, but he was bedevilled by his own misapprehensions. Having alienated much of the Iranian establishment that was still invested in the monarchy, his downfall was all but inevitable no matter what the CIA did.

Too often, historians draw a line between the coup of 1953 and the 1979 revolution, as if the intervening quarter-century did not happen. If the coup is the original sin, the revolution is the necessary expiation. But what happened between the two events had much to do with why the Iranians revolted. To suggest otherwise is to substitute polemics for sound reasoning.

Gerges is on more solid ground in dissecting Nasser's tumultuous tenure. The rise of post-colonial nationalism was seen as an opportunity by American cold warriors, who wanted to channel that force in an anti-communist direction. In Egypt, this resulted in a typical clash between a superpower and a local actor with differing priorities. Nasser was not blameless, as he did plenty of lying in assuring Americans of his willingness to make peace with Israel in exchange for aid and arms. It is hard to see how a leader with an authoritarian personality could be considered an agent of democratisation, and as with Mossadegh, Nasser was undone by his own misjudgements. In 1967, Israeli armour ended his aspirations to make Egypt the most consequential of the radical Arab states.

In the end, *What Really Went Wrong* misuses historical evidence to justify a tendentious claim. If America is to be blamed for all that has gone wrong in the region, then history has to be written in a casual, if not lazy, way. The Middle East certainly suffered during the Cold War, but hardly as much as East Asian states affected by the devastating wars in Korea and Vietnam. Yet Asia has made an economic and political recovery. The problems of the Middle East today are the result of the poor choices its leaders made in combination with the effects of the Cold War, a theme too frequently missing from the literature.

How Sanctions Work: Iran and the Impact of Economic Warfare

Narges Bajoghli et al. Stanford, CA: Stanford University Press, 2024. $24.00. 212 pp.

In the aftermath of the Cold War, sanctions became America's preferred method of dealing with recalcitrant regimes. War was too costly to an American public looking for its peace dividend. Iran, as the authors of this book note, is one of the most sanctioned nations in the international system. The costs and consequences of the financial penalties that have been layered onto Iran are the subject of *How Sanctions Work*.

It is important to stress that sanctions are not without their share of moral concerns. In the bluntest terms, the logic of sanctions is to hurt the many to change the minds of a few. Sanctions, if effectively applied, tend to lower the national standard of living, diminish the middle class and shrink the economy. The hope is that, once faced with such deprivations, the targeted regime will backtrack, amend its ways and come to terms with the international community. The question that lingers is what happens if ruling elites prove insensitive to the sufferings of their constituents. In this way, the offending behaviour of the regime remains unadjusted while the masses continue to suffer.

The Islamic Republic has invited its share of sanctions. The United States imposed its first sanctions on Iran shortly after the 1979 revolution, when militant students held American diplomats hostage for 444 days. Since then, successive administrations have tried to temper Iran's behaviour by imposing an ever-expanding array of sanctions. At times, these penalties have been multilateral and enshrined in international law through United Nations Security Council resolutions. These sanctions were not without their successes: former Iranian president Hassan Rouhani has admitted that Iran negotiated an arms-control agreement with the United States in 2015 in order to revive foreign investment in Iran.

The problem with any mature sanctions regime is that it is nearly impossible to fully lift. This was a complaint of the Islamic Republic, which claims that it offered nuclear concessions quickly, but that sanctions were never fully lifted. The international financial community usually takes a while to warm up to rogue states seeking to mend their ways. Meanwhile, an Iranian regime that continued to sponsor terrorism hardly warranted a clean bill of health.

The authors cover all this in a succinct and accessible manner. They remain critical of sanctions both in terms of their efficacy, which they challenge, and their cost, which they do not dispute. Left unsaid is how the United States should deal with a regime that it suspects is building atomic bombs. If sanctions are too blunt an instrument with which to deal with Iran's nuclear infractions, should Washington concentrate on military reprisals that can be more targeted to regime assets and not the larger population? Such are the complicated trade-offs of statecraft.

Economy
Erik Jones

How the World Ran Out of Everything: Inside the Global Supply Chain
Peter S. Goodman. London and New York: Mariner Books, 2024. £25.00/$30.00. 416 pp.

We may be on the cusp of a new Progressive Era like the one that brought an end to the giant trusts and robber barons of the late nineteenth and early twentieth centuries. In the United States, President Joe Biden's administration is leading the charge with its 'foreign policy for the middle class', while Congress and the courts are also taking action to break monopolies, put an end to price fixing, protect workers and raise wages. The United States is hardly an isolated case; Europe is undertaking similar measures. If this results in the end of globalisation as we have known it over the past four decades, that would only be for the good – not just socially and politically, but also economically.

New York Times business writer Peter S. Goodman makes the economic case for bringing an end to globalisation as we know it through a careful analysis of global supply chains. By focusing on individual firms and sectors, he shows that the logic underpinning the kind of efficiency that advocates of globalisation celebrate leads inexorably to an overreliance on networked industries such as shipping, distribution and retail that feature proliferating choke points including ports, warehouses and processing facilities. The same logic also leads to ever-increasing demand for economies of scale, with a resulting geographic concentration of capacity and expertise.

The problem with this system is that networks and choke points do not work like markets. As manufacturing shifts from producing everything in one place to collecting things from across the globe and bringing them together, the price of manufactured goods depends increasingly on the cost and reliability of shipping, distribution and retail. Treating these services like markets means the emphasis on cost will naturally favour the companies with the most capital and the widest networks. In turn, those companies will give price discounts to their largest customers, raising barriers to entry and killing competition in other sectors. The same is true for the ports, warehouses and processing facilities – particularly when they are owned by the shippers, distributors or retailers.

The concentration of capacity and expertise is disruptive for markets. The problem is not just that large firms can dominate key sectors of manufacturing; the geographic concentration of an activity in one part of the world also creates its own distortions. Chinese manufacturers may compete ferociously with one another, but if China is the only place one can find the expertise and capacity to manufacture plastic toys, then the toy market is no longer global.

Goodman depicts a global economy in which everyone uses the same networks to move the same things produced in the same places through the same choke points at the same time to assemble them somewhere else. Worse, they are doing so with little inventory to use as a buffer in case one or more key pieces of the puzzle fails to show up. The COVID-19 pandemic revealed the fragility of this arrangement, but it was hardly the first such revelation and will not be the last. Goodman does a brilliant job showing that the global economy is inherently, structurally unstable.

How the World Ran Out of Everything ultimately reveals how globalisation has undermined the functioning of the market in both the United States and Europe, especially for working people. The consultants, investment firms and shareholders advocating 'efficiency' are counting on the profits they know they will receive from monopolistic pricing and other uncompetitive and abusive practices. The globally networked economy is not a natural marketplace in which prices emerge from the interaction between supply and demand. Only effective regulation can break monopoly power, end abusive practices and restore market competition. That is what the original Progressive Era taught us. Hopefully we can apply these lessons again.

The Assault on the State: How the Global Attack on Modern Government Endangers Our Future
Stephen E. Hanson and Jeffrey S. Kopstein. Cambridge: Polity, 2024. £20.00. 182 pp.

Much of the debate about the rise of populism and the death of democracy misses a crucial point. Anti-elite politics and procedural irregularities distract from a deeper threat to the functioning of the modern state: the replacement of the 'rule of law' with the 'rule of men' (p. 3). The personalisation of politics and the substitution of loyalty for merit when selecting key personnel jeopardises state institutions' ability to tackle complex problems or even to administer routine public services. Worse, the rot spreads quickly through ever-lower levels of the bureaucracy as each new layer of appointments applies the same principles in selecting the next – alienating or demoralising competent bureaucrats who leave, making space for more sycophants. By implication, the replacement of populists with mainstream politicians or even a broader democratic revival can do little to address the structural damage without a major and painful overhaul of state institutions.

This assault on the state is the central theme in modern politics, according to Stephen Hanson and Jeffrey Kopstein, because it challenges every state based on the rule of law, whether a democracy or not. As additional states succumb to patrimonial leadership, would-be strongmen in more resilient polities find new allies and sources of inspiration in their efforts to undermine the administrative state. This process is not only diminishing state capacity in an increasing number of countries, but also threatening to end the 'experiment of modern statecraft' (p. 136) – and hence our ability to solve problems no state can address on its own.

At least part of the solution, say the authors, is to build a foreign policy around state capacity-building and the promotion of the rule of law. The European Union is one example of what such a policy might look like. Its rules for accession are guidebooks for modern state-building. The results are not perfect – as the cases of Hungary and Poland suggest – but the EU has been more effective with the countries it has embraced than the United States has been in promoting democracy in the Middle East or Afghanistan. Whether the EU will succeed in Ukraine in the aftermath of Russia's full-scale invasion remains to be seen, but the point worth underscoring is that Vladimir Putin, the archetypal patrimonial ruler of Russia, ordered attacks on Ukraine in 2014 and 2022 precisely because he sought to thwart the EU's influence. That his armies got bogged down is evidence of the self-corrosiveness of his regime.

An even more important piece of the solution is to promote and celebrate public service while pushing back against critiques of meritocracy as they emerge both on the right through 'deep state' conspiracy theories and on the left through overly ambitious plans to democratise public administration. Hanson and Kopstein do admit that the administrative state is not perfect, either in terms of its efficiency or in representing diverse societal interests. But they argue that it is probably better than one might think, including in comparison with the private sector.

There is much to like in Hanson and Kopstein's argument. They certainly display impressive knowledge of their key illustrations – one rarely has the chance to read detailed analysis of countries as diverse as Hungary, Israel, Russia and Turkiye in such a slender volume. Where they overreach is in placing Putin's Russia at the centre of the story. Putin's success may have reinforced the trend toward personalised rule, but it was not necessarily catalytic. Indeed, Putin drew inspiration and support from Italy's Silvio Berlusconi. The assault on the American state began at least as far back as Richard Nixon's 1972 re-election campaign. Viktor Orbán's intention to rewrite the Hungarian constitution was clear in 1998, as was his personalistic style of leadership. And, as Hanson and Kopstein admit, Recep Tayyip Erdoğan had good reasons to be paranoid about the 'deep state'; the Turkish tragedy has domestic roots and did not require a Russian example.

**How a Ledger Became a Central Bank: A Monetary History
of the Bank of Amsterdam**
Stephen Quinn and William Roberds. Cambridge: Cambridge
University Press, 2023. £25.99. 400 pp.

The conventional wisdom is that modern central banks emerged from the
Crown's need to have reliable access to credit. In 1694, King William III convinced the Parliament at Westminster to charter the Bank of England as a
limited-liability joint-stock corporation owned and capitalised by the country's
largest investors. The bank did support the Crown's borrowing, but it also
evolved to strengthen instruments of payment, safeguard the financial system,
maintain the value of the pound relative to gold, and transform the City of
London into the financial capital of the world. Having some knowledge of this
history is often seen as important to any understanding of central banks today.

Then again, Stephen Quinn and William Roberds suggest that it may be
even more important to understand the functioning of the Bank of Amsterdam.
Chartered in 1609 and owned by the city of Amsterdam, the bank was tasked
with making sure that the coins in circulation retained the trust of local merchants and international traders alike. Safeguarding the currency may sound
like a more 'blue collar' occupation than bankrolling a monarchy, but it is
fiendishly complicated. Coins made of rare metals are hard to assay and easily
debased. It is virtually impossible to enforce a monopoly on the minting of
such coins when the real value lies in the metal, and incentives for debasement
abound – monarchs like King Frederick II of Prussia found they could counter-
feit and debase silver and gold coins to finance their military campaigns.

Through a forensic examination of the archives and ledgers of the Bank of
Amsterdam over almost two centuries of operation, Quinn and Roberds show
how it succeeded in its mission using two very modern innovations. Firstly, it
created a fiat currency that existed as transferable entries on its balance sheet
and that could be held in accounts available to customers of good standing
and significant means. Secondly, it allowed customers to fill those accounts
by handing over gold and silver coins of a specific type and in standard units
against a transferable receipt that entitled them to reclaim the same kind and
quantity of coins six months later, paying whatever money they originally
received in their accounts (as an accounting entry) plus a fixed fee. That second
innovation worked much like modern-day repurchase agreements, but without
a formal requirement to exercise the option, in which case the coins belonged
to the bank.

Together, these innovations effectively created two different kinds of bank
under the same roof. The fiat-money bank could expand its balance sheet by

writing accounting entries to purchase assets or make loans – primarily to the Dutch East India Company – without facing a run on deposits (since the accounting entries never left the bank). The other bank held on to coins worth at least as much as any receipts outstanding would allow customers to repurchase. This combination not only created a currency as trustworthy as the Bank of Amsterdam's accounting controls, but it also succeeded in disconnecting that currency to a significant degree from the underlying quantity and quality of the coins in the bank's vaults. Merchants worldwide could use bills of exchange to be settled in Amsterdam as payment, and local businesses could exchange these transferable bank entries for physical coins (minted in small denominations) to pay taxes or wages.

Quinn and Roberds do an amazing job of showing how the Bank of Amsterdam worked like a modern-day central bank to stabilise the size of its balance sheet and hence control the money supply. They also show how its practices are likely to have influenced the development of the Bank of England. Finally, they describe the bank's ultimate undoing, which was the result not of a run on deposits, but of a wider loss of confidence that led to its abandonment. These are all powerful lessons both for today's central bankers and for anyone interested in modern finance.

Seven Crashes: The Economic Crises That Shaped Globalization
Harold James. New Haven, CT: Yale University Press, 2023.
$32.50/£20.00. 376 pp.

The creation of a global economy was never inevitable, either in theory or in practice. Yes, developments in transportation, communication and finance have transformed the way we think about distance. The spread of market institutions has created powerful incentives in the form of relative prices. The inclusion of ever-larger numbers of people in activities related to trade and commerce has accelerated the pace of innovation. These are all powerful forces for change, but such change is not always fortuitous. Bad things happen, and when the global economy goes into crisis – usually from some kind of supply shock that propagates across national borders through changes in relative prices – people draw different lessons. Sometimes those lessons point to a more global economy, and sometimes they point to the opposite. Much depends on the economic ideas that are already in circulation and the people who promote them.

Harold James uses this broad framework to introduce us to three interwoven narratives. The first is about how technological change brings the world closer together, often with unintended consequences. The seeds of each successive crisis are often found in the solution to the one just passed. The second narrative concerns the entrepreneurs who recognise and respond to movements of relative prices. Those entrepreneurs create the global economy in a very practical sense, and must deal with the forces they unleash along the way. The third narrative is about the role of the state, and hence the ideas that guide public policy. James is careful to insist that these ideas come from real people – usually economists – who must fight for attention with no guarantee of influence.

The broad pattern for globalisation that James describes is cyclical. The crises of the mid-to-late nineteenth century pointed to a more global economy powered by steam, financed by gold and characterised by the exchange of manufactured goods for foodstuffs. This is the crucible that gave us Karl Marx and Friedrich Engels's *Communist Manifesto* and the intellectual discipline of 'economics' as distinct from philosophy or politics. That period came to an end with the First World War and the Great Depression. It was replaced by economic nationalism, both in crude protectionist terms and, more importantly, in the form of an active monetary policy and a broader framework for Keynesian stabilisation of aggregate demand. What emerged from that experience was a more limited view of globalisation that centred on trade and multilateral financial institutions while constraining international capital flows and the destabilising potential of global finance.

That limited view of globalisation came apart during the inflationary crisis of the 1970s. Policymakers not only had to recalibrate their understanding of what was possible using monetary- and fiscal-policy instruments, but they also had to accept greater cross-border capital flows and the wider involvement of emerging-market economies like China. Changes in shipping and information technologies facilitated the expansion of the global economy, but political and policy choices made the crucial difference. This new form of globalisation peaked just before the global financial crisis of 2008–09. That crisis, along with the pandemic and Russia's full-scale invasion of Ukraine, have pushed in the opposite direction, toward greater emphasis on national policymaking, economic security and the political consequences of income inequality.

There is much to admire in James's ambitious telling of this story, but there are important omissions. Economists matter in the study of ideas and crises, but non-economists like E.H. Carr, Karl Polanyi, Susan Strange, Peter Hall, Sheri Berman, Mark Blyth and Kathleen McNamara have much to offer. The contributions of key women scholars in policymaking could be more prominent as well. This book is long on Ben Bernanke and Larry Summers, but short on Christina Romer and missing Janet Yellen.

The Future of the Factory: How Megatrends Are Changing Industrialization
Jostein Hauge. Oxford and New York: Oxford University Press, 2023. £35.00/$45.00. 240 pp.

Industrial policy does not always work. If the goal is to produce world-competitive or even productive manufacturing, direct government intervention may end in failure. But industrialisation never works without some kind of supportive policy. If governments do not protect investments and property rights, if they do not encourage innovation and protect intellectual property, if they do not provide essential infrastructure, if they do not educate people to be good investors, consumers, workers, researchers and members of the community, then the economy will not grow in terms of output, productivity or welfare. The same principle holds if the goal becomes addressing global warming and the overuse and depletion of natural resources, because industry, investors, consumers, workers, researchers and community members all affect the environment. Environmental policy is industrial policy. It will not always work, but climate action and resource conservation will never be effective without a comprehensive policy framework.

This focus on industrial policy is important because the 'market' is not going to guide individuals to maximise value added, reduce the emission of greenhouse gases and minimise resource use through the price mechanism alone. At best, relative prices will reflect value added. More likely, relative prices will show the influence of a welter of conflicting institutions, policies and priorities from one country to the next, and tend to benefit the largest advanced industrial economies and the transnational corporations headquartered within them. Jostein Hauge argues that this scenario is a good characterisation of the world we live in today. As a result, weaker, poorer countries have little hope of industrialising, global warming remains effectively unaddressed and sustainable resource use has almost completely fallen off the agenda.

This summary is bleak, but Hauge has written a brilliantly hopeful and insightful short book. The solution, he argues, is within our grasp. Firstly, we must accept that we are all affected by industrial policy – properly understood – and so must scrutinise the trade-offs that such policies entail, both within countries and across national boundaries. Secondly, we must recognise that such trade-offs reflect fundamental tensions in the way we operationalise and understand policy goals. Growth, measured as a real change in gross domestic product, will inevitably involve both greater emissions and more resource use. Emission controls that focus on energy supply – shifting from internal-combustion engines to batteries, for example – will do little to affect demand for output and are likely to place even greater strain on natural resources. A reduction in demand for output and resources will necessarily bring down the pace of growth. Thirdly, the political choice between objectives should not be the same the world over. Poorer countries should focus on increasing value added, while richer countries should pay more attention to reducing their emissions and reining in their consumption of resources.

Hauge is not oblivious to how idealistic this sounds. That is precisely his point. The dilemmas we face reflect the balance of power between rich and poor, north and south. Rich countries want to maximise their control over global value chains without sacrificing 'quality of life' as measured in terms of material consumption. They do so by protecting intellectual-property rights while investing in research and innovation – which sounds like a good thing, but which can create a self-reinforcing monopoly in the context of globally distributed manufacturing processes. Hauge offers some simple policy tweaks for rich countries to make the world a better place: regulate marketing to stop creating unnecessary demand; lengthen warranties to extend the life of manufactured products; live communally to reduce travel and transport; share innovation with poorer countries; and eat less beef. The fact that it is hard to imagine these tweaks being made only underscores the importance of this book – because capitalism as we know it will not survive without that kind of sacrifice.

Copyright © 2024 The International Institute for Strategic Studies

Ersatz Intelligence

Michael Nevitt

I

> In the wake of the Michigan shootings, let us come together as a
> community to reaffirm our commitment to caring for one another and
> promoting a culture of inclusivity on our campus. By doing so, we
> can honor the victims of this tragedy and work towards a safer, more
> compassionate future for all.

At first glance, this campus-wide email from Peabody College's Office of
Equity, Diversity and Inclusion at Vanderbilt University was unremark-
able. After yet another mass shooting, the college administrators' words
seemed just one more genuine if generic message of support. Scrolling
to the end of the mass email, however, revealed something unnerving
that distinguished this 'thoughts and prayers' message from previous
ones: '(Paraphrase from OpenAI's ChatGPT AI language model, personal
communication, February 15, 2023).'[1] To comfort their community, the
stewards of the university had copied and pasted text from the generative artificial-intelligence (AI) application ChatGPT rather than crafting an
original message.

Michael Nevitt is a graduate of Johns Hopkins University's School of Advanced International Studies (SAIS–Europe) in Bologna, Italy. Before graduate school, he worked in technology in Silicon Valley and Washington DC.

Survival | vol. 66 no. 5 | October–November 2024 | pp. 231–240 https://doi.org/10.1080/00396338.2024.2403233

Superficially, this embarrassment merely indicates a perfunctory and perhaps lazy way of communicating with students. Yet it is emblematic of a deeper danger in the application of new and disruptive AI technology. The incident is at least a relatively benign warning about how humankind might sleepwalk into allowing artificial intelligence to supplant human deliberation in insidious and mischievous ways.

AI has become prominent in global discourse, yet very little has actually been said. Use of the term quadrupled in 2023, as seemingly everyone developed an opinion.[2] Relatively few demonstrated true understanding. When asked to identify existing applications of AI, only 30% of respondents to a Pew survey could do so.[3] 'Artificial intelligence' is in fact a general label representing many evolving technologies, including widely used everyday applications such as Gmail spam filters and the algorithm that suggests new songs for Spotify users. But it was the debut of ChatGPT, a free consumer-facing interface, that moved public awareness of AI out of science-fiction movies and onto laptops, delivering human-like written responses in seconds and creating a kind of consumer frenzy. Unlike search engines and other apps, generative AI does not just find information but synthesises content that mimics human creation. The use cases of this one application are infinite, capable of explaining complex linear algebra and writing a 2,000-word blog post about British foreign policy.

AI models rely on unsupervised learning

To offer such capacity and versatility, generative-AI models largely rely on unsupervised learning, a method of analysing massive amounts of data to identify patterns in order to determine the next word in a sequence. When a user types a prompt into ChatGPT, the response is a prediction based on billions of words of training data. The tool's tailored outputs result from combining or rephrasing existing knowledge using statistical patterns in previously written content. The phrases produced by ChatGPT may seem as fresh and inventive as text written by humans, but they are simply collections of words most statistically likely to match the user's request. Therefore, while its uses are vast, the one capability that generative AI lacks is true creativity.

Creativity requires originality and surprise, neither of which is possible without the human process. Originality does not imply the absence of influence – academics, artists and other professionals often rely on references in their creative work. What distinguishes influence from simply copying is the human-psychological processes and decision-making that combines and builds on existing ideas.[4] Margaret Boden, who studies the intersection of philosophy, psychology and artificial intelligence, argues that even when combining concepts or working within an existing conceptual space, creativity cannot be completely anticipated.[5] It cannot flow from a predetermined routine. Accordingly, the predictive statistics ChatGPT uses cannot represent an intrinsic creative process. The tool merely acts on the basis of the instructions it was trained to follow. It may produce novel arrangements of words, but it cannot introduce original ideas or information. ChatGPT's written output is only a statistically supported rehashing of already written information.

The training data that enables ChatGPT's predictive outputs is a large corpus of text from across the internet, drawn from academic research papers, social-media comments, news articles, transcribed speeches, novels and more. While relying on some 300bn words to train its models, OpenAI, which invented ChatGPT, has not publicly disclosed the specific sources of this data, noting that they are publicly available and therefore generally within the boundaries of the 'fair use' doctrine.[6] In several ongoing class-action lawsuits, OpenAI has argued that revealing that information could compromise data privacy, threaten proprietary research and facilitate nefarious manipulation of the model by outside actors.[7] Even so, it is widely assumed that ChatGPT is trained on primarily English-language sources, given that more than 60% of internet content is written in English and that eight of the ten most visited global websites are American-owned.[8] With the release of its latest model GPT-4, OpenAI confirmed that most data used is in English and that the safeguards and checks in place to minimise risk are 'US-centric'.[9] Validating this assumption are studies showing that ChatGPT is less accurate and more prone to misinformation when generating content in less common and non-Latin languages.[10] Consequently, the ideas and values ingrained in the data informing ChatGPT are likely rooted in ideologies of the United States and the Global North. Without any cited sources or influences, though, users cannot easily identify the specific theories or authors that may have influenced the output they receive.

It is in a certain sense astonishing that a technology with the potential to transform society and even humanity is being developed by private companies that are completely opaque about what they are building. This essay won't try to address the more apocalyptic scenarios for AI, but it is important to see, and raise concerns about, what is already happening.

II

Over the last year of graduate school, I have seldom attended a class session without spotting ChatGPT on a classmate's laptop screen. Whether drafting an outline for a paper or sourcing a clever question to interject into a lecture, students regularly exploit it for its impressive speed and functionality. This phenomenon has troubled me, because it clashes with another, more noble, aspect of student discourse. Student conversations have revolved around a central theme: frustration with the global status quo and a desire for change. Classmates have formally complained to the administration, arguing that the theories taught in classes fail to acknowledge the perspectives of the Global South. Before US President Joe Biden bowed out of the 2024 presidential race, they lamented the two superannuated options in the American presidential race, fearing a future locked in the worn assumptions of their grandparents. They have protested in the streets of Bologna against the enduring cycle of violence in Israel and the occupied territories. Yet, when given opportunities to propose new ideas to address complicated global issues in their assignments, future leaders are relying on technology that entrenches the predominantly Western thinking they purportedly disdain, embedded in an opaque set of sources. They fail to see the irony in this behaviour.

We've already seen how innovative technology applications – social media – can enforce political and intellectual conformity. At first, as its advocates anticipated, social media played a significant role in revolutions and global social movements. Facebook was an important tool for outreach by the Obama campaign and communication during the Arab Spring. During the Trump administration, however, 'clicktivism' took over. In response to crises, individuals faced intense social pressure to demonstrate their activism and world views through likes, clicks and shares. This came to a head during the protests over the murder of George Floyd and the COVID-19 pandemic. Within my online network, individual social-media use was scrutinised. Those who posted about other topics during the weeks that followed Floyd's murder were accused of insensitivity, prompting questions about their priorities during a national moment of reckoning. Others who posted the infamous black square in an attempt to show solidarity with the black community were branded ignorant. Those who refrained from posting drew passive-aggressive public commentary to the effect that their silence was deafening.

While social media brings attention to important social movements, including Black Lives Matter, it has created unrealistic expectations for each individual to act as an expert across a broad spectrum of topics, from climate change to epidemiology and racial injustice. The war in Gaza has reinforced this social phenomenon. Throughout this conflict, private individuals, many well-intentioned, have reposted information or stories from unverified accounts, creating a cycle of resharing that has made sources impossible to identify. Users have then contributed their own written statements, often resembling curated press releases prepared by public-relations agencies on behalf of non-governmetal organisations or public figures. Navigating these new patterns of social posturing involves considerable time and effort. Pressure to reshare perfectly prefabricated content to appease social-media audiences exhausts individuals' capacity to meaningfully understand an issue. Obsessively conforming to social expectations by publicly sharing and producing the 'correct' content has further hindered Americans' ability to receive and critically analyse new information.

AI seems likely to shape public discourse and everyday life in similar hidden ways. The societal shift towards AI is only beginning. As with other sweeping technological innovations, complacency and overreliance on AI apps seem inevitable without intervention, as everyday use becomes habit-forming. Consider the last time you navigated to a new destination with Google Maps. As you drove, how aware were you of the area beyond the prescribed route? Once safely guided, how likely were you to be able to explain the path you just took? The answer most people would provide, if they were being frank, is not very. Research indicates that the overuse of GPS has harmed spatial memory, stored in the hippocampus, as the technology has replaced the human need to develop this function.[11] In early tests of vehicles that were autonomous to varying degrees, human passengers reported difficulties at driving modes in which the vehicle was largely autonomous but human intervention was required in certain emergency situations. People got too comfortable with the vehicle's capabilities and became unreliable co-pilots for functions the car could not perform unassisted.[12] Humans have a natural tendency to welcome convenient results before meaningfully questioning their broader impacts.

ChatGPT and similar AI technologies, presented as workarounds for creativity, critical thinking and problem-solving, remain poorly understood tools. One potential impact of constant reliance on and indiscriminate adoption of ChatGPT is the homogenisation of ideas. As humans increasingly rely on AI technology to produce content, OpenAI and companies like it may use AI-influenced and -generated works to train future models. The ideas and writing styles recycled by AI and reflected in their output will perforce become more prevalent in the training data. This increases the statistical probability that ChatGPT will recognise them as the 'correct' answer to user prompts and reflect the ideas they generate. As this cycle continues, a convergence of style and ideas seems inevitable. Social-media groupthink and insular academic communities have already narrowed the range of intellectual discourse, as outlined above. AI stands to exacerbate the trend, filtering out unconventional prose and content in languages and dialects that are not widely spoken.

Incentives to game the system for individual advantage are also likely to increase. While this will occur in many realms of human activity – including the strategic domain – academia is an obvious and prominent one. Consider hypothetical AI software for scoring student papers. The algorithm would be trained on past assignments, analysing the characteristics associated with higher grades. If, for instance, historical data indicated that past papers with longer words correlated with better grades, the algorithm could award higher scores to papers with more formal, connotative or colourful language, marginalising consideration of the intellectual quality of the content and the stylistic merit of the prose. Over time, astute (if cynical) students might discern this pattern and prioritise writing with longer words rather than cogent argumentation and sound composition. If this bloviatory writing style continued, future algorithms would only reinforce and perpetuate the practice.

III

Given the high stakes that the advent of AI imposes for the future of creativity and innovation, proactive guidance appears necessary. Historically, technology has prioritised outcomes over transparency. The technology behind many popular apps is deliberately opaque, captivating users with results while stifling their ability to ask what makes it possible. AI companies have limited motivation to educate consumers. OpenAI, as noted, has been unwilling to share details about its training data. The US government is also institutionally disinclined to inform the consumer due to its own incomplete understanding of technologies and a persistent habit of relying on corporate self-regulation in the technology sphere.[13] With so little scope for meaningful intervention from the private sector or government, the task of educating people about digital literacy in light of new technology may be left to schools and universities.

They have been here before. In the early 2000s, Wikipedia – which now seems old-hat – was a disruptive new digital tool. Although the concept of an online encyclopaedia had been introduced, its crowd-sourced content created ethical dilemmas and public debates about its appropriate use. Some universities banned the tool in their research outright, while academic journals explored the risks and applications of this new tech resource.[14] Like any junior-high schooler of the mid-aughts, I remember the introduction of Wikipedia into the classroom. For young students writing their first term papers, an easy-to-use resource that offered up-to-date, free information was practically impossible to resist. As students started to use Wikipedia and accept its entries as unquestionable facts, the librarian instituted a data-literacy training programme centred on Wikipedia. Rather than deterring us from using it altogether, she taught us how to evaluate its information sources, identify its vulnerabilities to bias, and critically determine how Wikipedia could soundly support our research projects.

Everyday use of AI technology seems inevitable. Rather than ignoring or banning it, we need to understand it. While the technology behind ChatGPT may be vastly more complex than Wikipedia, schools and universities can facilitate an understanding of AI apps by developing similar digital-literacy curricula. Despite ChatGPT's ubiquity, such curricula are not the norm. In mid-2023, four months after ChatGPT had reached 100 million users, fewer than 10% of schools and universities had adopted official AI policies, let alone generative-AI training.[15] Academic institutions still have the time and opportunity to cultivate a future with effective and responsible AI use through training programmes that clearly explain how AI technology works, what its risks are, and how to apply it with integrity.

Without proper guidelines, AI could distil writing and idea formulation into a few predicted outcomes and extinguish true creative thought. The history, data and context that AI applications consider are important, but present and future analysts need to formulate their own innovative ideas and perspectives to, among other things, combat climate change, resolve persistent conflict and reduce wealth inequality. No matter how sophisticated or impressive technology becomes, it will not surpass human ingenuity, and we cannot allow it to become an ersatz substitute.

Notes

1   Rachael Perrotta, 'Peabody EDI Office Responds to MSU Shooting with Email Written Using ChatGPT', *Vanderbilt Hustler*, 17 February 2023, https://vanderbilthustler.com/2023/02/17/peabody-edi-office-responds-to-msu-shooting-with-email-written-using-chatgpt/.

2   See Esther Addley, '"AI" Named Most Notable Word of 2023 by Collins Dictionary', *Guardian*, 1 November 2023, https://www.theguardian.com/technology/2023/nov/01/ai-named-most-notable-word-of-2023-by-collins-dictionary.

3   Brian Kennedy, Alec Tyson and Emily Saks, 'Public Awareness of Artificial Intelligence in Everyday Activities', Pew Research Center,

15 February 2023, https://www.
pewresearch.org/science/2023/02/15/
public-awareness-of-artificial-
intelligence-in-everyday-activities/.

4 See 'Creativity', *Stanford Encyclopedia
of Philosophy*, first published 16
February 2023, https://plato.stanford.
edu/entries/creativity/#WhatCrea.

5 See Margaret A. Boden, 'Creativity
and Computers', *Current Science*, vol.
64, no. 6, March 1993, pp. 419–33.

6 See, for example, Robert Freedman,
'OpenAI Seeks to Trim NYT Lawsuit
to Fair Use Question', Legal Dive,
28 February 2024, https://www.
legaldive.com/news/openai-seeks-
trimming-nyt-infringement-lawsuit-
to-fair-use-question-copyright-law-
chatgpt/708805/; and Alex Hughes,
'ChatGPT: Everything You Need to
Know About OpenAI's GPT-4 Tool',
BBC Science Focus, 25 September
2023, https://www.sciencefocus.com/
future-technology/gpt-3.

7 See Ian Krietzberg, 'Here Are All
the Copyright Lawsuits Against
ChatGPT-maker OpenAI',
TheStreet, 29 February 2024, https://
www.thestreet.com/technology/
copyright-lawsuits-against-openai-
microsoft-chatgpt.

8 Amy Chua, 'The Rise of English:
Global Politics and the Power of
Language', *New York Times*, 18
January 2022, https://www.nytimes.
com/2022/01/18/books/review/the-
rise-of-english-rosemary-salomone.
html; and 'Top Websites', Similarweb,
accessed 1 May 2024, https://www.
similarweb.com/top-websites/.

9 OpenAI, 'GPT-4 System Card', 23
March 2023, https://cdn.openai.com/
papers/gpt-4-system-card.pdf.

10 See, for example, Changchang
Fang et al., 'How Does Chatgpt-4
Perform on Non-English National
Medical Licensing Examination? An
Evaluation in Chinese Language',
PLOS Digital Health, 1 December 2023,
https://journals.plos.org/digitalhealth/
article?id=10.1371/journal.
pdig.0000397; and Macrina Wang,
'NewsGuard Exclusive: ChatGPT-3.5
Generates More Disinformation in
Chinese than in English', NewsGuard,
26 April 2023, https://www.
newsguardtech.com/special-reports/
chatgpt-generates-disinformation-
chinese-vs-english/.

11 See Louisa Dahmani and Véronique
D. Bohbot, 'Habitual Use of GPS
Negatively Impacts Spatial Memory
During Self-guided Navigation',
Scientific Reports, no. 10, April 2020,
art. 6310.

12 See Alex Davies, 'The Human Problem
Blocking the Path to Self-driving Cars',
Wired, 1 January 2017, https://www.
wired.com/2017/01/human-problem-
blocking-path-self-driving-cars/.

13 See Melissa Heikkilä, 'AI Companies
Promised to Self-regulate One
Year Ago. What's Changed?', *MIT
Technology Review*, 22 July 2024,
https://www.technologyreview.
com/2024/07/22/1095193/
ai-companies-promised-the-white-
house-to-self-regulate-one-year-ago-
whats-changed/.

14 See Noam Cohen, 'A History
Department Bans Citing Wikipedia
as a Research Source', *New York
Times*, 21 February 2007, https://
www.nytimes.com/2007/02/21/
education/21wikipedia.html; and
Jim Giles, 'Internet Encyclopaedias

Go Head to Head', *Nature*, no. 438, December 2005, pp. 900–1.

[15] UNESCO, 'UNESCO Survey: Less than 10% of Schools and Universities Have Formal Guidance on AI', 1 June 2023 (updated 6 September 2023), https://www.unesco.org/en/articles/unesco-survey-less-10-schools-and-universities-have-formal-guidance-ai.

Copyright © 2024 The International Institute for Strategic Studies

Printed in the United States
by Baker & Taylor Publisher Services

Printed in the United States
by Baker & Taylor Publisher Services